SECOND EDITION

THE 50 BEST

LOW-INVESTMENT, HIGH-PROFIT FRANCHISES

ROBERT L. PERRY

PRENTICE HALL
Englewood Cliffs, New Jersey 07632

Library of Congress Cataloging-in-Publication Data

Perry, Robert L.
   The 50 best low-investment, high-profit franchises / Robert L. Perry.
     p. cm.
   Includes index.
   ISBN 0-13-300393-0
   1. Franchises (Retail trade)—United States.   2. New business enterprises—
United States. I. Title. II. Title: Fifty best low-investment, high-profit franchises.
HF5429.235.U5P47   1994
381'.13'0973—dc20   94-1569
                                                     CIP

Printed in the United States of America

10 9 8 7 6 5 4 3

ISBN 0-13-300393-0

ATTENTION: CORPORATIONS AND SCHOOLS

Prentice Hall books are available at quantity discounts with bulk purchase for educational,
business, or sales promotional use. For information, please write to: Prentice Hall Career &
Personal Development Special Sales, 113 Sylvan Avenue, Englewood Cliffs, NJ 07632. Please
supply: title of book, ISBN number, quantity, how the book will be used, date needed.

PRENTICE HALL
Career & Personal Development
Englewood Cliffs, NJ 07632
A Simon & Schuster Company

On the World Wide Web at http://www.phdirect.com

Prentice-Hall International (UK) Limited, *London*
Prentice-Hall of Australia Pty. Limited, *Sydney*
Prentice-Hall Canada Inc., *Toronto*
Prentice-Hall Hispanoamericana, S.A., *Mexico*
Prentice-Hall of India Private Limited, *New Delhi*
Prentice-Hall of Japan, Inc., *Tokyo*
Simon & Schuster Asia Pte. Ltd., *Singapore*
Editora Prentice-Hall do Brasil, Ltda., *Rio de Janeiro*

To Marilyn, with all my love and gratitude

June 13, 1998

WITH ALL GOD'S
BLESSINGS for your
prosperity,

Robert L
Roy

Acknowledgments

Although I cannot list them all, I wish to thank the more than 70 franchise executives who responded to my often urgent demands for information. I also wish to thank the thousands of hard-working franchisees whose belief in the American dream and dedication to their systems make the success of these 50 excellent companies possible. I also must express special thanks to my editor, Tom Power, who agreed enthusiastically to my proposal to update the first edition of this book. Without Tom's patience, understanding and support, this new edition would not have been possible. Although many people contributed information to this book, I, of course, remain responsible for its content.

Introduction

Since we published the first edition of this book in early 1990, the economy and the franchise industry have experienced a very severe recession which shook both. For the first time in 60 years, American corporations "downsized" middle management and executive ranks, throwing hundreds of thousands of white-collar professionals out of work. These corporate "refugees" found it very difficult to find new corporate positions, so many turned to— and continue to turn to—franchising as a way to own their own businesses with the support of—they hoped—a proven and successful system.

At the same time, the franchise industry saw these intelligent, motivated, well-funded executives as prime candidates for its appeal and courted them assiduously. But some in the franchise industry thought that they could "do business as usual" with vague or exaggerated promises, weak systems, little or no support, and limited communication. To their surprise, these experienced executives demanded far more, and some franchisors had difficulty coping with these new demands.

Furthermore, the trend that created the need for the first edition of this book also created the need for franchises with less than $100,000 start-up costs. And the trend worsened during the early 1990s. With retail store costs of least $150,000 and fast food restaurant costs at least several times that amount, many in the middle class considered giving up their dream of owning their own business. In short, it seemed that the "outplaced, displaced, excessed" middle class would have a very hard time finding a low-cost franchise that they could build into a new career, earn a reasonable salary, grow into a long-term asset, and use to provide for their families and their own retirements.

Or so it seemed. Fortunately for the troubled middle class, despite appearances, they can find not only hope, but plenty of opportunity. Of the some 3,000 franchise companies, many still have total start-up costs below $100,000. And many of these can become very profitable enterprises with which you can meet all of your personal, career, and financial goals. However, the trick is finding the best one for you and your situation.

This book presents the 50 best low-cost franchises that can create this opportunity for you. With low-investment, high-profit franchises, you can earn high returns on your cash investment by working in the franchise and building your own "mini-chain" of stores or your own fleets of service vehicles. The true secret to building significant equity in a franchise is just that: using your profits and cash flow to expand the business, whatever it is, into new territories and to penetrate the potential market in those territories.

Frankly, if you buy a low-cost franchise and do not expand, you can develop an average middle class income in the $25,000 to $50,000 range. But you will be hard-pressed to go beyond that. If you choose that as your "comfort level," you can do well and feel comfortable and satisfied with a low-cost franchise; however, if you are more ambitious and wish to gain more rewards than a corporate career could offer, you must treat your franchise as a means to fulfill this greater potential. Remember that most often, you—and perhaps your family members—will have to contribute your time, your labor, and your resources to build a successful franchise. But almost every successful franchise would assert that the results prove worth it.

The fifty franchises in this book, each excellent in its own way, can help give you a gigantic head start on your quest. I selected them from many sources: 1) my own 16 years' professional experience in the field as an author and consultant; 2) my personal experience with American Leak Detection, Inc.; Dynamark Security Systems, Inc.; Kitchen Tune-Up, Inc.; The Little Gym

International, Inc.; and Molly Maid; 3) the *Income Opportunities* magazine SELECT 200 list (for which I acted as project director); 4) the *Success* magazine Gold 100 list; 5) the *Entrepreneur* magazine Franchise 500 list; and 6) the International Franchise Association's *Franchise Opportunities Handbook.*

All fifty have consistently proven their excellence and leadership in their industries and in franchising. Among these fifty, you will find a preponderance of service businesses—maid services, commercial cleaning, business and professional services, building and house-based services (security systems, home inspection, ceiling cleaning ,and kitchen restoration), vehicle repairs, personal services (fitness, tax returns, real estate, training), and children's services. However, thanks to careful searching, I also present several examples of a fast-disappearing breed—low-cost fast food franchises. In short, you will not find any major fast food franchises or auto aftermarket franchises; they are too expensive for the average franchisee and many now only consider investors.

But this book is not for investors. It is dedicated to those millions of average citizens who want to own and prosper in their own businesses and for whom franchising remains an excellent way to achieve their personal and financial goals.

How to Use This Book

The first three chapters briefly define franchising and all of its "ins and outs" and give a step-by-step method with which you can determine how to buy the best franchise for your situation. The rest of the book consists of five chapters, each based on a range of franchise fees divided like this:

- Franchises with fees up to $8,000 (Chapter 4)
- Fees of $8,001 to $11,499 (Chapter 5)
- Fees of $11,500 to $15,499 (Chapter 6)
- Fees of $16,000 to $20,000 (Chapter 7)
- Fees of above $20,000 (Chapter 8).

The total start-up costs, including all fees, initial investments, and hidden costs, equal *less than* $100,000. A few franchises state that in some rare cases, their total costs will exceed $100,000, but in the vast majority of cases, you can start any of them for less than $100,000 and more than half of them for less than $50,000. So, these costs fall well within the means of the middle class.

Each franchise also has the potential for high profit margins. In terms of annual returns on your *cash* investment, an average person can earn—with any of these 50—at least 50 percent during the first two years in operation, according to published reports and reports from current franchisees.

Within each chapter, a separate section discusses each franchise in significant detail with pertinent comments about its strengths and weaknesses. Each describes the company's basic structure and operation and then analyzes total start-up costs, supported with an easy-to-read chart. Next, it analyzes "what you get" for your fees and payments, that is, the franchisor's package of services, products and support.

Last, but certainly most important, each section discusses specific estimates of how much money you can expect to earn under what circumstances.

I suggest that you read the book like this: Read the first three chapters to make sure you are ready and able to become a franchisee. Then, you can skip from chapter to chapter and section to section to read only those sections that interest you the most. However, I advise that you read all of the sections to make sure that you do not overlook a franchise that might surprise you with its appeal. In sum, use this book as a ready reference tool or as a guide to help you select the best franchise for your goals and your resources.

One caveat: No one can guarantee that you will earn similar returns or make as much money as this book theorizes. Your success depends on how well you manage the business, how hard and smart you work, how well the economy performs, and how good the franchise company continues to be. In fact, under existing law, most franchise companies refuse to make earnings claims. In this book, all estimated earnings come from published reports, reports from current franchisees, and my own financial analyses. I take full responsibility for them.

In short, franchising provides a system of doing business that, if you follow the systems correctly, can provide a significant return. These 50 are proven companies with reliable track records, but no selection system is perfect. Of the 50 franchises in the first edition, one went out of business and two stopped franchising. Dissatisfied with this, I tightened my selection criteria: for this edition, 90 percent of the franchises have been in business at least five years with the average time in business more than 10 years. Only three are less than three years old, and all three were founded by well-known, highly regarded franchise executives who had succeeded with other franchises. In short, I have sought to make the process of choosing a franchise as fool-proof as possible, and I have added warnings about my concerns about franchising in general and individual companies in particular.

However, do not expect to find an infallible "get rich quick" scheme in this book; they do not exist in franchising. Your success depends on your efforts as much as, if not more than, the franchisor's system. Franchising is an excellent way to build your personal wealth with diligent and intelligent effort. Properly managed, these 50 can simply help you achieve your goals faster than most other businesses you could own.

Table of Contents

CHAPTER 3: HOW TO FIND THE BEST FRANCHISE FOR YOU *35*

CHAPTER 4: FRANCHISES WITH FEES OF $8,000 OR LESS *61*

CHAPTER 5: FRANCHISES WITH FEES FROM $8,001 TO $11,499 *123*

CHAPTER 6: FRANCHISES WITH FEES FROM $11,500 TO $15,999 *181*

CHAPTER 7: FRANCHISES WITH FEES FROM $16,000 TO $20,000 *235*

CHAPTER 8 FRANCHISES WITH FEES ABOVE $20,000 *289*

100 MORE OF THE BEST FRANCHISES *355*

INDEX *365*

1

<hr>

Franchising Fundamentals

Visit any highway intersection, strip center, or shopping mall in the United States and Canada, and you will almost certainly find a familiar name: McDonald's, Dunkin' Donuts, Midas Muffler, Domino's Pizza, Baskin & Robbins, or any of 3,000 more. These names represent an old method of doing business that has become the most successful business concept of the second half of the twentieth century. This method, of course, is franchising.

Since the mid-1950s, franchising has become the most successful retailing concept in North America. By mid-1993, more than 650,000 establishments founded through more than 3,000 franchise companies accounted for 35 percent of all U.S. retail sales and a similar percentage of Canadian sales. Despite a difficult recession, the short- and long-term prospects for franchising appear very bright as thousands of "outplaced," "downsized," and "excessed" corporate managers and military officers took their severance pay and bought franchises. They brought with them an attitude of "they'll never do that to me again" as they have learned the hard way that they can only truly trust themselves to protect their own interests. On a more positive note, many Baby Boomers approaching middle age have decided that they are ready to establish their own businesses, choosing franchising because they wished to avoid the extreme and unnecessary risks that starting a business from scratch brings.

Yet, despite the continuing growth of franchise companies through the recession, a negative side appeared.

First, only 55 major companies, such as McDonald's and Burger King, accounted for more than half of all franchise revenues. This market share has remained consistent through the recession and may have even increased. Thus, the remaining 3,000-plus franchises and 90 percent of the total units had significantly lower sales per unit than the giants.

Second, under severe pressure during the recession, some franchises reverted to the same unethical and illegal high-pressure sales tactics that had damaged franchising's reputation during the last severe recession of the 1970s. To combat this situation, the International Franchise Association (IFA) adopted a tougher Code of Ethics; unfortunately, only about 20 percent of all franchises belong to the IFA, and the IFA has limited enforcement power. Thus, it has become more important than ever before for franchise buyers to investigate every franchise very carefully before they buy.

Third, the trend to increasingly expensive franchises has strengthened; it has become very difficult to find a food franchise that costs less than $125,000 to open. Fortunately, in this book, we identify several excellent low-cost food franchises that should yield high profits. But it was tough to find them. Fourth, the trend that concentrates the ownership of the most lucrative franchises in the hands of a very few well-heeled franchisees and even corporate giants has grown stronger. Thus, the proverbial "little guy" may find it more difficult than ever before to grasp a new opportunity and become the next multimillionaire.

Finally, and most important, it has become clear that owning only one franchise or one territory means that you "buy a job." You invest your savings or your "golden parachute" in one franchise, but end up with little more than a job with long hours and relatively low pay. However—and very fortunately—by expanding into multiple territories, you can build your own "chain" of stores or activities and build a substantial net worth. Despite the negative trends, you can reach your ultimate financial goals of security and prosperity for you and your family.

The Simple Concept

As a business concept, franchising is very simple; through it, a parent company—formally called a *franchisor*—licenses or gives the rights to sell the company's products or services and use its systems, trademarks, and so on to an independent businessperson.

As importantly, you need to understand what franchising is *not* as well as understand what it is. Franchising is *not* a dealership, distributorship, or a chain store, although it definitely includes aspects of all three. Like a chain store, a franchise does have unique signage, logos, registered trademarks and service marks, practically identical storefronts, similar interior design schemes, and standard services, products, and procedures. Like a dealership, a franchise normally sells its products and services to the consumer at retail prices. Like a distributor, a franchise that sells goods, but not services, often obtains its products directly from a manufacturer at wholesale prices. But there the similarities end.

Unlike a chain store manager, a franchise operator—formally called the *franchisee*—*owns* his or her business. The franchisee signs an agreement with the franchise company and agrees to follow a detailed set of standards and procedures, but the franchise company does not have any ownership rights in the individual operation. The franchisor does, however, retain ownership of its trademarks, operating manuals, and unique business procedures.

The differences can be difficult to understand, but the basic relationship functions this way: A franchisee, John Donner, buys a license to operate a Super Shoes franchise. He puts up the Super Shoes sign, installs Super Shoes fixtures, follows Super Shoes company policies and procedures, and, most importantly, buys his inventory wholesale from Super Shoes or from its list of approved shoe vendors. After a year or two, John Donner becomes dissatisfied and wants to run his own store. After a lengthy discussion and possibly a legal battle, Super Shoes says, "OK, run your own shoe store, but you can no longer use the Super Shoes logo. You have to move your store because we control the lease. You cannot use a Super Shoes sign. You can no longer use our fixtures, materials, operating manuals, and procedures, and you can no longer get the favorable discounts and terms available from our approved vendors. You are on your own. Good luck."

In a chain store, you would act as an employee manager, and you could be fired, demoted, transferred, disciplined, and so on if you tried to do things your own way. If you did drop out of a franchise system, you could still own your own business (unless a court enforced a noncompete clause in the franchise agreement), but when you canceled the contract, you would have to run your own show without any support from any other entity.

Of course, without the attraction and reputation of the franchise's name, your business may suffer. By the same token, many people who leave franchise systems do succeed on their own. Moreover, despite the myths to the contrary, franchise companies do go out of business, go bankrupt, or suffer serious growing pains and financial difficulties.

During the 1989–91 recession, the failure rate of franchise companies appeared to increase. Although I do not have scientifically valid evidence, I can relate one study I did during 1992. Working on a different research study, I mailed surveys to 100 new franchise companies—those that were three years old or younger. I found out that 15 of that 100, or 15 percent, had apparently gone out of business during the previous two years. In short, during a recession, new franchise companies need more financial support, better management skills, and higher-quality managers. Be sure you investigate these aspects of any start-up franchise before you buy a franchise less than five years old. If you are an unlucky—or unwary—franchisee and this happens, you would be forced to go it alone or fold your own tent.

Even then, on occasion, well-established franchisors do fall into serious trouble. In mid-1993, the parent company of NutriSystem weight loss centers closed several hundred company-owned stores and filed Chapter 11 bankruptcy proceedings to give the company breathing room to reorganize its financial and management functions. However, many of its very angry franchisees filed lawsuits to force the company into Chapter 7 bankruptcy that would force the parent company out of business. The franchisees did this so they could be free of their franchise agreements, stop paying royalties and fees, and run their own operations. By early 1994, this situation had not been resolved.

Unlike a dealer, a franchisee usually buys products or offers services only from suppliers whose products or services meet the company's quality and performance standards. As a dealer, you can buy from any manufacturer or distributor you please and with whom you can reach an agreement. As a franchisee, you are constrained by the franchise agreement and the franchisor's requirements.

Franchisors can require you to buy their unique, patented, trademarked, or copyrighted products, but for most products and supplies, they cannot force you to buy from selected suppliers. However, they can—and do—require you to submit to them for approval any products, supplies, or services that you wish to buy from an outside source. The difference is subtle, but legally, you retain your "freedom of action."

Unlike a distributor—at least in the best franchises—you maintain a very close relationship with the franchisor. You must file sales and financial reports to them frequently, often weekly or monthly. The franchisor's field support representative (often called a district or regional manager or trainer) keeps in close touch with you, visits you at least once or twice a year, and talks with you on the phone both to help you and to make sure you toe the franchisor's line. The best franchisors emphasize the "helping" relationship and two-way communications because they know that a positive relationship helps you improve your business, earn higher profits, and pay more royalties. Under the agreement terms, both you and the franchisor must also live up to many conditions that a manufacturer cannot force a distributor or dealer to meet.

Most important, dealers and distributors usually have the right to offer competing companies' products *under the suppliers' own brand names*, but a franchisee can offer only products and services under the franchise company's name or those brand names approved by the franchisor. For example, an ice cream parlor can sell anything from Polar Bars to Breyer's, but a Baskin & Robbins can only sell Baskin & Robbins–approved ice cream with the Baskin & Robbins label.

GENERAL TYPES OF FRANCHISES

Three general types of franchises exist within this framework, but this book mainly concerns the first one.

Business format. When most people say "franchise," they generally mean this type. According to the International Franchise Association's booklet, *Investigate Before Investing*, it means that a company develops and offers a complete retail operation. Fast-food restaurants, car rental agencies, real estate firms, shoe repair shops, and so on come under this type.

Selected distribution. An older franchising method, it is so well established that most people do not recognize it as a formal franchise. It includes independently owned gasoline stations, appliance stores, tire stores, cosmetic stores, and the like. For example, an independent Amoco station cannot sell Citgo gasoline.

Trademark and brand-name franchises. Although very old and very common, this type, too, is not often recognized as a franchise method. For example, independent soft drink bottlers, including most local Coca-Cola and Pepsi-Cola bottlers, are franchisees. The local bottler buys syrups and products from the company and makes and markets the soft drinks for local or regional distribution.

Although the Coca-Cola and Pepsi companies own some bottling operations, most have been independently owned for many decades.

DOZENS OF BUSINESS FORMAT FRANCHISES

Within the business format context, practically every type of service business has been turned into a franchise concept. From mufflers to mailboxes and from burgers to budgies, you can find a retail or service concept that interests you. Within one of the dozens of categories in the list that follows, you may find a concept that interests you or in which you have enough experience to build a successful business. The following list comes from categories that the International Franchise Association and *Entrepreneur* magazine has used in their guides:

Advertising
Auto and truck rentals
Automotive products and services
Beauty and health aids
Beverages
Bookstores
Business aids and services
Children's services
Clothing, apparel, and shoes
Computer and software stores
Construction: materials, services, and remodeling
Dental clinics
Drugstores
Educational products and services
Electronic stores
Employment services
Exercise and fitness studios
Florist shops
Food: baked goods
Food: donuts/pastry
Food: grocery and specialty stores
Food: ice cream, snacks, and candy
Food: manufacturers and suppliers
Food: recreation and public facilities
Food: restaurants
Food: specialty stores
Gift stores
Hardware
Home furnishings
Insurance
Laundry and dry cleaning

Lawn, garden, and agricultural supplies and services
Liquor, retail
Machinery
Maintenance, cleaning, and sanitation: residential
Maintenance, cleaning, and sanitation: commercial
Medical services
Miscellaneous services
Motels and hotels
Pet shops
Photography and supplies
Printing and photocopying
Printing and publishing: direct mail advertising, advertising publications
Real estate sales and rentals
Recreation: travel, sports, and hobbies
Rentals: equipment and supplies
Retail sales
Sales: individually owned equipment, property, and services
Security systems
Sporting goods
Stained glass and supplies
Storage facilities
Stores: general merchandise
Tools and hardware
Travel agencies
Video stores and services
Water conditioning and services
Weight control

This book does not include a franchise from each category; that is not my purpose. For practical reasons, I limit this book to 50 of the most profitable franchises, not the entire universe of more than 3,000 franchise companies.

THE ELUSIVE STATISTICS OF SUCCESS VERSUS FAILURE

Franchising has several inherent advantages compared to starting a business on your own. Franchise companies like to quote government and industry statistics that maintain that fewer than 6 percent of all franchised businesses fail within the first five years of operation compared to the supposedly terrible failure rate of 65 to 90 percent for regular new businesses.

However, you should be aware that these statistics quoted so often may be—and I would assert *are*—misleading and inaccurate, although the general idea is correct. For example, for this book, I looked for companies with failure/termination rates of less than 3 to 5 percent per *year*. If a company has 100 franchises, no more than 3 to 5 of them should fail or be terminated per year. You also need to understand the difference between failure and termination and to know that the company statistics on these are almost always jumbled and out of date, and sometimes deliberately inaccurate. Although a new regulation makes franchisors report more specific types of terminations and failures, you must read the offering circular very carefully and ask probing questions. You should also call the failed franchisees, whose names, addresses, and phone numbers must be listed in the required disclosure document, called an "offering circular," and discuss with them why they failed.

A franchise "failure" means that the owner did not succeed. For his or her own reasons, the business failed. Many franchises fail for many reasons that have nothing to do with whether the franchisor is "good" or "bad": Partners disagree and split up, spouses divorce, people change their minds and give the business up, people become ill and close the business, owners have too little capital and poor management skills and can't make it, and so forth. Of course, the franchisor can (and most do) try to help the franchisee with problems to stay in business and succeed.

On the other hand, a "termination" means that a franchisee failed to follow the very precise rules outlined in the agreement and the franchisor revoked the franchisee's right to run the business. By far, the most common reasons for termination come from three causes: failure to pay required royalties, failure to meet minimum sales or purchase requirements, or failure to follow quality control standards. Most high-quality franchises bend over backward to work with troubled franchisees who are not paying royalties: they send in management teams to retrain and revamp marketing and operations efforts, they give the franchisee a longer grace period to catch up on overdue payments, and they encourage other franchisees to help the troubled one. In short, they realize that the foundation of their success rests on the success of their franchisees, so they do all they can to keep them afloat.

However, and here is where the trouble begins, some franchisors do not really care about their franchisees and fail to provide adequate up-front training and support. Some franchisors desperately need cash flow, so they sign agreements and take checks from people that they know will probably fail. Some encourage or turn a blind eye to overzealous salespeople (who may be independent sales reps working on commission) when they sell franchises to marginally qualified applicants. Further, the franchise managers may not make adequate background checks or allow salespeople to use high-pressure sales tactics to prospects who cannot succeed with their concept. For example, an engineer who does not like working with the public would do poorly as the "front person" for a women's clothing store. But I know several former engineers who have turned into excellent back office operations managers while their more customer-conscious spouses manage employee and customer relations.

In fact, franchise failure is particularly serious when the franchises are growing very fast. Franchisors find it very difficult to develop competent, well-trained support staff when they grow very fast. For example, several years ago, Environmental Biotech stopped selling franchises so it could increase and train its support staff, expand its facilities, and add new computer systems so it could cope with rapid growth.

Franchise failure also seems more problematic in certain industries, particularly those that rely on blue-collar franchisees who do not have sales and business management backgrounds or inclinations. Commercial cleaning and janitorial services and franchises that rely on part-time work appear to experience relatively high failure rates. Note, however, that this book includes several of these franchise types because of their low start-up cost and high profit margins—if you succeed. The companies in this book provide far-above-average support and are dedicated to their franchisees' success.

Other problems with the often-quoted failure statistics include the following:

- Franchisors will take many steps so they can avoid putting a failure or termination on their books. First, they may help find a buyer for a struggling franchise; this helps the owner and the company, but it hides a failure statistic. Second, most franchise agreements have buy-back clauses that allow the company to take back the license, the location, and so on, and run the location as a company store with a payment to the failed franchisee. However, this never shows up as a failure statistic in many offering circulars. The new regulation should correct this problem.

- Individuals with a greater desire for independence and freedom of action than a franchise will allow may buy a franchise. When they rebel against the agreement's strict rules, they do not follow the system and often fail.

- New franchisees who run into difficulty may find it impossible to turn around their situation if a rapidly growing or financially strapped franchisor is unable or unwilling to give them the support and long-term assistance they need.

- A franchisor may deliberately seek to force out of its system unprofitable or less profitable franchisees rather than work with them to build their revenues and profits. During the recent recession, some franchise companies lost 15 to 20 percent or more of their franchises, yet increased the company's profits or protected them from heavy losses because the poor economy weeded out the poor performers.

Are these failures the franchisor's fault? Not directly, but this survival-of-the-fittest attitude flies in the face of the stated goal of the franchise industry. Most franchise companies—indeed the industry as a whole—base their appeal—and their franchise fees— on this key point: You are more likely to succeed with a franchise than you are on your own. Yet, these unreliable statistics—and the failure rate of franchise companies themselves—mean that you must be very wary and pose serious questions to the franchise companies about the statistics in their offering circulars. I have done so for this book, and I have sought to clarify what each company's statistics mean, but you must do the legwork. I urge you to call the franchisees listed as failures and discuss their situation with them.

Remember, too, that a franchise company does not have to give you your money back. I know of only a handful with money-back guarantees, and at least two are in this book—Video Data Services and K & N Mobile Distribution Systems. Most agreements and disclosure documents clearly state that franchise fees and related charges will not be refunded. You need very strong legal reasons— for example, a violation of the Federal Trade Commission or state regulations—to sue or file for arbitration against a company to get a refund or even a portion of your money back.

In short, when you search for a desirable franchise, consider carefully its failure rate, investigate the reasons, question the failed or terminated franchisees, determine the company's attitude toward those failures, and analyze what actions the company actually took to try to prevent the failure. Of the 50 franchises in this book, practically none has a high failure rate, which we define as more than 5 percent of franchised units per year.

On the other hand, the statistics that describe the high failure rates of independent businesses are also inaccurate and unreliable for many reasons. First, many "new" businesses are legal "shells" and do not really operate at all; their owners set them up for short-term legal reasons and shut them down when those reasons no longer apply. Second, many businesses, particularly in volatile industries such as fashion and cosmetics, are put into bankruptcy by their owners as a tactic to avoid paying creditors. Third, many new businesses that incorporate or file business names never open their doors. Fourth, many independents never file legal paperwork and run part-time jobs out of their homes. Yet, the government statistics do not consider the *intent* of the person who starts an independent business. By the same token, franchise failure rates do not consider the ways that franchise companies prevent a failure from looking like one.

With these considerations in mind, it still remains mostly true that franchisees succeed more often than new independent businesses for several reasons:

- A smart franchise company carefully weeds out bad prospects before they sign franchise agreements. Most franchise companies seek to pick the candidates with the best skills and have the best aptitude for that kind of business. In fact, the franchise companies with the lowest failure rates may be the ones that do the best job at picking candidates; in short, they prevent failure from the beginning. An independent selects himself or herself to start a business, often with no serious thought as to whether he or she would understand the business, could manage it correctly, and would be willing to do the work the business requires. So, a franchise can save itself a lot of trouble with careful selection and prevent you from making a colossal mistake.

- A franchisee must have a strong desire to succeed. Once he or she is culled from the many applicants, a franchise buyer will probably be more strongly motivated and put more effort into succeeding than the average business beginner.

- Franchisees do usually receive far more training and support than most new small-business owners. On the other hand, many independents start a business in industries they know well whereas many franchise buyers know little or nothing about the industry or business they enter, so without the company's training and support, they would have even less chance of success than the knowledgeable independent. Thus, this factor may be a wash.

It would be interesting to study the success-failure rates of independents whose owners gave as much study, preparation, and effort to begin their businesses as franchise companies give their buyers.

- Last, and most important, the business system itself. The franchisee receives—or the promise is that he or she will receive—carefully planned, tested, and proven business systems and procedures. They are supposed to have been tried in the "field of battle," at least as a corporate store or long-running successful enterprise. The company is supposed to have perfected the system before it offers it to buyers. This does not always happen, so I have paid special attention to include franchises with years of experience. The new franchises in this book, such as The Little Gym, were generally founded by or are owned and managed by executives who have built other highly successful franchise companies.

In short, franchisees should succeed at far higher rates than independents because they do not have to reinvent the wheel and they should have a significant corporate staff who carefully selected them and very deliberately support them. Perhaps the real question is why franchise failure rates are as high as they are, not praising how low they seem to be.

SIGNIFICANT FRANCHISE TRENDS—1995 AND BEYOND

The franchising industry had a very difficult three years between 1990 and 1993 because financing from banks practically dried up. It became very difficult for the average person to buy a franchise that costs $100,000 or more. Banks stopped lending money against equipment as collateral, and usually, home equity loans could not cover the total cash requirement. This negative action helped push the industry toward several trends. First, thousands of former corporate middle managers and forcibly retired military officers took their minigolden parachutes, nest eggs, retirement funds, and separation payments and bought franchises. This sharply increased the intelligence, business experience, and sophistication levels of the average franchisee. Franchisors found that even for low-cost franchises, the applicants were corporate refugees and military officers. For example, I attended several national conventions during 1993, and most of the new franchisees were former marketing managers, engineers, officers, sales managers, administrators, and the like. Thus, it has become much more difficult for people in blue-collar occupations to buy a franchise. By the same token, franchise companies have been forced to develop far higher-quality systems, provide more sophisticated support, and be more rigorously ethical in their conduct. They have also had to provide far more and more sophisticated financial justification of why someone should buy their franchise. I strongly believe that this trend has helped make the franchise industry much stronger.

Second, the trend toward master franchises, subfranchisors, area development agreements, area representatives and the like has gained strength. Again, and very unfortunately, the industry does not have standard definitions for these terms. But roughly based on the state of Illinois legal definitions, I define them this way:

- *Subfranchisor*. This person buys the right to sell franchises, sign contracts, receive payments and royalties, train franchisees, help them open the store, and provide services and support to franchisees within their areas. He acts in all ways like the parent franchisor. He accepts the money and sends payments to the franchise company. Many companies call these arrangements "master franchises." He may or may not open and operate his own stores or locations.

- *Area representative*. This person sells franchises within a given territory and provides training, service, and support. He does *not* sign contracts and he does *not* receive payments directly from the franchisee. The franchise company receives the payments and sends his share to the area representative. He, too, may or may not open his own stores. This type is also called a "regional representative" or—helping cause confusion—a "master franchisee."

- *Area developer.* This person acquires the right to open additional stores or locations and/or expand his territory. He does *not* sell franchises to others. He builds his own "minichain" of franchised businesses. He works out a separate area development agreement with the franchise company to open a certain number of stores within a certain number of years. (In fact, all three types usually have strict development schedules through which they must sell or open a specified number of franchises within a set time, or lose the right to the territory.)

So, be sure to find out if you are subject to working through and with any of the first two. The first two routes have advantages and disadvantages. As an advantage for the franchise buyer, you do have more local and immediate support. The subfranchisor would live and work in your area, and her staff should know local conditions better than either you or the corporate staff could. However, some subfranchisors and masters are not as capable or as qualified or as interested in providing support as a corporate manager may be. The theory is that the subfranchisor would be more likely to give you good support because his income depends on your success; the more money you make, the more royalties you pay, so everyone wins, and the subfranchisor gives you good support so you make more money. Usually, it works well, but you need to get to know any area rep or subfranchisor very well because he or she will be your prime contact.

The subfranchisor or area rep approach is used most often by franchisors who want to grow quickly and build regional or national market penetration. Again, you can see the potential danger of fast growth through poorly prepared or uncaring subfranchisors or area reps.

Third, stricter selection guidelines, driven in part by the tight financial situation, and "closed shops" are making it more difficult for outsiders to buy franchises. Some major fast-food franchises only allow current owners or managers to buy new stores. Furthermore, more and more franchises prefer to offer existing and successful franchisees area development agreements, so they can expand their territories rather than sell to newcomers. More and more franchises prefer to attract people who already own different kinds of franchises; the companies reason that they have to provide less training and fewer services to successful franchisees who already understand the basic concept. In addition, more and more franchises are selling to "miniconglomerates" who own numerous individual franchises, often of different types, in the same area. In short, this trend means less and less opportunity for newcomers to franchising.

Further, more and more women are entering franchising. More franchises that appeal to women, especially those who want part-time work or who want to spend time with their families, have been developed. However, more and more sophisticated women from the corporate world are buying franchises, and more and more women are becoming owners, managers, and executives of franchise companies. And the statistics belie women's true role in franchising. They often act as the partner in a franchise that ostensibly belongs to a man, or they act as the key employee and contribute their labor. Often, spouses jointly own franchises in traditionally male industries, such as automotive aftermarket services and water conditioning.

One trend that has reversed since the late 1980s is that toward corporate acquisitions of franchise companies. Although Pepsico stills owns several major fast-food franchises, it sold Burger King, and Avis has become an employee-owned company. I cannot remember the last major corporate acquisition of a franchise. Many changes have occurred in the hotel-motel industry, but those changes consolidated the franchised motels into fewer hands, and Hyatt Corporation has begun franchising. It appears that the corporate acquisitions added layers of corporate bureaucracy to the entrepreneurial process and stifled it. Franchising is very systematic, but it does not tend to flourish under traditional bureaucracy. I hope that this trend away from corporate ownership continues.

An increasingly favorable and key trend for potential franchisees is that toward Franchisee Advisory Councils (FACs). These councils consist of elected or appointed franchisees who advise the franchisor's executives about their problems and concerns. FACs can range from appointed, advisory boards that do little but listen to corporate presentations and rubber-stamp corporate plans to very democratic boards that approve by majority or greater vote all corporate policy decisions. The best situation occurs when franchisees elect FAC board members, and company executives follow their suggestions very closely. One of the key criteria for being included in this book is whether a franchise has an FAC and how that FAC operates. The FAC members discuss support programs, marketing plans, operational changes, product development, and so forth across the gamut. These councils are invaluable tools through which franchisees communicate their issues and problems to franchise executives. You should find out if a company has an FAC, how its members are chosen, what they do, and what authority they have.

Further, in response to some serious problems with some franchise companies, some groups of franchisees have formed franchisee associations. They differ from FACs, an internal, company-approved group; an association is a collective bargaining group outside the company structure that uses joint action to force or persuade an apparently reluctant company to pay attention to its members' issues. Some franchise executives insist that their franchisees form associations, but they are rare. Most franchisors fear associations because their franchisees can take independent legal action or put pressure on the company. In general, an association can be a sign that, at least in the past, the franchise company was not paying careful attention to its franchisees' concerns. And they felt a strong need to protect themselves with collective action. In my opinion, a company faced with an association is a troubled company unless that company welcomes or even encourages the association to form.

Last, and unfortunately, the truly inexpensive franchise continues to become less and less available. Franchise fees often exceed $15,000, even $20,000, and the total initial investment most often exceeds $100,000. This puts most franchises out of the reach of the blue-collar family and makes franchising a white-collar opportunity.

As important, these higher costs mean that franchise buyers often must use more of their own financial resources, including their home equity (which I strongly advise against), or borrow large sums of money through leasing agreements or loans from the franchisors. As you will see in detail, that makes more and more franchises highly leveraged. You must pay the bank for your second mortgage (and run the risk of losing your house), make lease payments each month to the finance company, and pay the franchise royalties and perhaps loan payment, instead of accumulating profits. You could end up working for the lenders and not yourself.

For every negative trend, this book identifies high-quality exceptions and helps point you toward the best available franchises. The next chapter discusses how you can determine whether or not you have the qualities it takes to succeed as a franchisee.

2

Can You Make It on Your Own?

The title of this chapter actually begs the question. Your whole purpose in buying a franchise is to avoid being on your own. You buy a franchise because a franchise gives you—you hope—a complete and proven business system with which you can run a successful operation and make significant profits. But potential franchisees often bring myths with them that need to be dispelled right now. First, a franchise company gives you a system; it does not run the business for you. You are an independent business owner who must manage, operate, and take responsibility for your own success. A franchisor provides the system and can guide you, but you must invest your dollars, brain power, and effort. Second, many franchisors complain to me that some of their franchisees expect to make significant profits within a few months of opening their doors. This is not likely to happen; this book identifies franchises with which you can make significant profits within two or three years—with diligent effort.

In many ways, you function more like a branch manager for a chain store or an operations manager for a highly decentralized corporation. Top management, that is, the franchisor, is mostly concerned about the bottom line, that is, the royalty payments you make to the franchisor. But, just as you would have to follow a chain store's policies and procedures, so must you follow a franchisor's policies, procedures, operations, and quality standards. A franchisor sets you up in business in exchange for your franchise fee, gives you a business format, structures how your business will look and operate, dictates your image, and regulates your products and their quality. Then, the company hands you a "bible," that is, an operations manual, tells you to go forth and multiply, and reminds you to be sure to mail the royalty checks on time each month. Of course, when you have questions or problems, like a good corporate executive, the franchisor will provide answers and support.

The principal difference between a franchise and a chain store is that you own the local business. You simply buy a license from the franchisor, in effect, to borrow his business format and system. Instead of sending all the profits from a chain store to the corporation, you send royalty payments to the franchisor. One hopes that the net profits far exceed the royalty payments. You keep the net profits for yourself, but you also take almost all the risks. If a chain store manager does a poor job, she may be fired, demoted, transferred, or retrained. If you do a poor job, your business fails, and you lose *your* investment. That is most important. You must invest most of the money in your local business. You assume both the financial and the personal risk. Few chain store managers do that; in fact, they receive bonuses when they do well, or the company gives them stock, or they do both.

You receive the profits and build a modicum of equity in your business. You gamble that you can earn a significant return on your investment of time, money, and personal involvement with their system. From the franchisor's viewpoint, franchising is the fastest way for it to grow rapidly with relatively little risk and relatively little capital. It is the only business method in which the managers or operators pay the owners for the privilege of risking their own money and success by selling someone else's products or services. When you buy a franchise, you agree to risk not only your own success, but that of the franchise company. Yet, a franchisor's mismanagement, incompetence, or even fraud may destroy your chance to succeed *and* deprive you or your personal and financial investment. So, this high level of risk makes it absolutely imperative that you thoroughly investigate all aspects of a franchise before you invest.

"Real" Entrepreneurs Need Not Apply

When you buy a franchise, you trade these risks for the advantages of a proven business method. In contrast, unlike enthusiastic franchisees who eagerly follow the established system, real entrepreneurs want to do things their own way. Most honestly believe—and the successful ones are right—that they can do things better than anyone else. They have a unique vision and an overwhelming desire to make that vision come true. In franchising, the true entrepreneurs *found* the companies; the late Ray Kroc who built McDonald's into a colossus, was a true entrepreneur. This type of person tends to do poorly as a franchisee. They chafe under the restrictions and find no comfort running a business the way someone else tells them they must. If you share similar characteristics, if you tend to be a rebel or maverick, it is highly unlikely that you will do well as a franchise owner.

However, if you feel more comfortable with a structured environment, if you work better in an ordered situation, if you respond well to controls from an outside source, you may do well as a franchisee. These reasons may explain why former military officers, former engineers, and former middle managers tend to do well; they come from these structured, orderly environments and tend to feel more comfortable. Yet, these types often run into one key difficulty: They may not have enough experience in rolling up their sleeves and doing the work. They may be too used to issuing orders and expecting someone to carry them out. When they buy a franchise, they issue an order and turn around and find no one to carry it out but themselves!

Furthermore, corporate and military refugees often expect and need more "perks" and support services than their financial resources and a franchise company can provide. They may not be able to cope with the "lean and mean" way a franchisee must function for at least the first few years. They may spend too much money on fancy furniture rather than spend the same amount and more on marketing their services and attracting customers. So, even those comfortable with following established systems must be aware that franchising combines structure with freedom. They must find that delicate balance, that moderate approach that contributes to their success.

Advantages of a Franchise

As you begin to consider buying a franchise, you should consider its advantages and disadvantages and also determine how and whether your personality, attitude, and experience fit in.

Listed as follows, these advantages show why a franchise is preferable to entrepreneurship for the right type of person:

- The strategic and marketing advantages of using a nationally or regionally known trademark and the cumulative positive effect that the trademark will contribute to your growth. In most cases and in most areas, Jazzercise will draw more exercise buffs than will Susie Sweats Swell, and Blimpie will attract more attention than will Sam's Super Subs. Sam's may succeed, but Sam will not have the same power to buy regional TV advertising and regional print media coverage.

- The marketing advantage of having key information about local competition, product demand, customer demographics, and so on.

- The purchasing power of larger discounts and cost savings that you receive by buying raw materials, supplies, and products from national vendors or central warehousing facilities. Most franchisors arrange for suppliers to treat each local franchise like a branch of a national account with far greater discounts than a local store could expect. Many franchisors, of course, manufacture or distribute products to the franchisees and make significant percentages of their profits from these sales. As long as they offer you a better price for the same goods than the competition, you receive the benefit. In many cases, you must buy proprietary products or patented products you cannot find from someone else; conflict often occurs in these situations if franchisors try to take advantage of their virtual monopolies on your essential supplies. If the franchisor charges a fair price for its products, then the situation works to everyone's benefit.

- The additional purchasing advantage of reliable, proven sources of supply and service. For example, the owners of a small Mom and Pop pizza parlor in West Virginia converted to a Fox's Pizza franchise because they could not trust their suppliers to deliver every week or deliver the same quality raw materials every week. With Fox's, a national distributor delivers the same national brands to their door whether they order $100 or $1,000 a week.

- The sales advantage of having customers already familiar with your product. If that is not the case, if you are opening the first franchise in an area, for example, then at least, you can build your local reputation by reference to a regional or national reputation for quality and success.

- Franchising rests on a simple principle: consistent quality regardless of location. When you buy an established franchise, your customers usually feel far more comfortable and come to you much more quickly if they know the name and reputation and feel sure that they will receive the same quality service that everyone else will receive. ServiceMaster, Four Seasons Greenhouses, Management Recruiters, and the like all prove this point. The vast majority of consumers are satisfied with a $1.69 burger that tastes the same everywhere; if you want a gourmet burger, go to a fern bar and pay $6.95 for it.

- The start-up advantage of a structure that reduces guesswork and problems to a minimum, compared to doing it yourself. You do not reinvent the wheel; you put a good wheel to good use in a different location.

- The continuing advantage of a knowledgeable support staff that gives you well-researched advice on finding locations, gathering capital and financing, doing leasehold improvements, negotiating leases, training employees, putting together your store, conducting a grand opening, and so on.

- The ongoing advantage of tested operations procedures spelled out in great detail in operations manuals. Franchisors state over and over that they know franchisees will succeed if they follow the operations manual. They also state that many franchisees don't follow the manual and run into trouble.

- The managerial advantage of established accounting and bookkeeping procedures. For many, this procedure saves hours and days each month. More and more franchises require computer system purchases and provide management and accounting software to help you report your royalties and produce required monthly or quarterly financial reports. Following tight financial controls almost always helps a small business succeed.

- Sometimes, the financial advantages of having financial assistance available, either directly from a franchisor or indirectly by helping you put together a business plan and loan application for your local banker or arranging an equipment lease. Some franchises have subsidiaries that make loans to help you buy their equipment packages; others will allow you to sign promissory notes to make monthly payments for a portion of the franchise fee. Others give significant discounts on purchases of additional territories. Others arrange with leasing companies to help you reduce your up-front cash investment by leasing equipment. Remember, however, that you must have enough working capital or short-term sales to make these payments.

In short, these advantages of a proven system often override the disadvantages. The greatest disadvantage, as we discussed, is that you take most of the risk. If you fail, you will at best receive a small portion of your original investment when you sell to someone else in distress or the franchisor buys equipment back from you at cents on the dollar of the original price.

What It Takes from You

These advantages create an allure for many people who are unsure of whether they can succeed on their own. As noted, people who are middle managers for chain stores or major corporations, people with strong sales and marketing backgrounds, or people with similar backgrounds or who have the same mind-set tend to do best as franchisees. However, farmers have built very successful minichains of commercial cleaning franchises, professionals have opened large territories with fast-food restaurants, and unemployed spouses with young children have become regional directors for exercise franchises. All these people share many or all of certain common characteristics. You need a good combination of these traits and resources to succeed with a franchise.

MONEY

You must have enough cash, borrowing power, or financial assets to get started, with enough working capital to carry you through the first difficult months when you are unlikely to have any significant income from the franchise. This is absolutely essential. Trying to run a franchise on a shoestring, unless it costs very little to begin, will simply not work. And starting a franchise, even an inexpensive one, will cost more than you think. The franchise fee is just the first of a host of expenses. Most of the different expenses that you may have to pay to start a franchise appear in the next list.

Remember that these expenses vary from franchise to franchise and from company to company within an industry. Some franchises pay more up-front expenses to give them a competitive advantage over their competitors; others reduce their franchise fees to relatively low levels, but charge you more royalties or make you pay for services that others include in the fee. Be careful and examine exactly what a franchise includes in the package you receive for paying the fee.

You can expect to pay two types of expenses: The first list includes the most common expenses, whereas the second list includes "hidden" or "extra" costs:

A. *Common Costs of Starting a Franchise*

Franchise fee, paid up-front and usually nonrefundable
   except in unusual circumstances, like failing a training
   course

Royalties and advertising fees (ongoing after you begin)

Equipment purchases or leases

Required product purchases for start-up inventory—often the highest of your costs

Rents/leases and deposits

Leasehold improvement costs

Furniture and fixtures for your office or outlet

Training fee—most often included in the franchise, but not always

Travel and room and board costs at the mandatory training site

Start-up supplies—often included in the fee

Prepaid business expenses, that is, licenses and permits

Insurance—usually at least several types, including personal and product liability, comprehensive, vehicle, inventory, plate glass, key person, and similar coverage

Utility, telephone and security deposits for required lines

Legal, accounting, and professional fees

Operating expenses, including your own salary, employee payroll, loan payments, business supplies, inventory replenishment, and the like—at least three to six months' worth

Grand opening advertising, promotional, and marketing expenses

In many cases, these expenses only begin your start-up costs. Add-ons such as the following can significantly increase your total expenses. Be very careful that you clearly understand exactly what your costs will be.

B. Hidden or Extra Costs

Coupon costs—your revenues may not be as high as you project if you give away coupons or discount your prices to boost grand opening sales.

Construction management fees—often charged by the franchisor if you hire the company to build your location for you.

Memberships in professional, business, or franchise organizations.

Fluctuating loan repayment schedules with variable interest rates—these may lead to higher payments if interest rates rise.

Umbrella or unusual types of insurance.

Site selection and lease negotiation fees paid to the franchisor if he finds a location and negotiates the lease for you.

Option fees if you wish to buy the rights up front to open additional franchises in your territory, that is, sign an area development agreement.

Build-to-suit fees if the franchisor must adapt her architectural plans to fit your location.

Excess advertising and marketing costs for your grand opening—these will vary significantly from place to place because the cost of media varies from market to market.

Utility connection and environmental assessment fees in some states.

Your salary and payroll and benefit costs for managers during construction, training, and grand opening periods.

Legal expenses for incorporation, lease reviews, negotiations, and so on.

Costs of points, fees, and closing costs for second mortgage or home equity loans on your home or real estate if you borrow against them.

Variable costs for rent and lease deposits.

Employment agency fees to hire managers and employees.

Advertising costs to find employees if you do it yourself.

Extra costs for signage if larger than normal.

Fees paid to local planning, zoning and architectural
   review, or sign commissions and boards.
Extra training fees if you take more than the allowed number of people for the initial training class.
Extraordinary visit fees if you request additional help from
   the franchisor during your first few months in operation.
   In many cases, franchisors will not charge these fees
   because they want you to succeed, but many uniform
   offering circulars include these additional fees, and the
   franchisors could charge them if they choose.
If you do not have the financial wherewithal to buy the franchise you want, think again. If you have to scramble for
   cash or get a home equity loan to start a franchise, I
   strongly urge you to reconsider. I advise that you never
   put your home or your retirement nest egg at risk to buy
   any franchise, no matter how good or profitable it sounds.
   Many have done so and succeeded; many have also done
   so and failed and put their homes at risk for months or
   years. And some have even been forced to sell their homes
   at distressed prices and move away. It is highly unlikely
   that a reputable franchise would allow you to buy a
   license if the executives discover that you are stretching
   your resources very thin to buy the franchise. And you
   can only gain—at the very least in worry-free moments—
   if you have adequate funding before you begin. More and
   more franchisees make sure that the family continues to
   have at least one income that covers basic family expenses
   while the other spouse begins the franchise. You may also
   want to make sure that you have few, if any, other debts,
   such as credit card bills, and never live off of credit card
   lines of credit at exorbitant interest rates while you begin a
   franchise. This road leads to serious financial difficulty
   very quickly from which it may take you years to recoup.

PERSONAL COMMITMENT

Even if you buy a part-time franchise, such as Jazzercise, you still must be willing to make the personal commitment of time and energy to succeed. Your success rests on your shoulders, not the franchise company's. In fact, franchise executives tell me that the second most frequent complaint they hear from new franchisees is that they are upset that they are not making more money with less effort.

When you consider a franchise, consider very carefully the demands on your time. A food franchise may be open 12 to 18 hours a day seven days a week. Video Data Services franchisees work most Saturdays videotaping weddings and nights and Sundays editing videotapes. But you protest, "I can hire employees to work weekends and late at night." What do you do, however, at 6 p.m. Saturday evening when your teenaged employee calls and says he's "sick," either in actuality or because he doesn't want to miss the big game or the prom? As owner, you go do the work, and your plans for a nice evening at the movies, a dinner party, or a night out at a fine restaurant go out the window.

You must make many personal sacrifices to own, manage, and succeed with a franchise. If you decide after careful consideration that you are unwilling to make these commitments, do something else or find a franchise that does not make such strenuous demands.

Equally important, you must realize that the franchise may place heavy emotional and financial burdens on your family, at least in the short run. Junior and Jane may not be very thrilled about working in the store on Saturday afternoon when their buddies are at the movies or the beach. Your spouse may not be very happy when you miss dinner—again—or cancel a dinner party or night out at the last minute. Nor may anyone be happy if you do not earn more income than you used to, and they must work harder or take part-time jobs to make ends meet. Any conflicts or disagreements in your family that have been glossed over could come roaring into your face if the franchise puts undue financial and emotional stress on them. To do your best to anticipate the problems, you must sit down and discuss with them these demands and *their and your* expectations before you buy a franchise. Discuss the possible demands on both your and their time, energy, and attention. At first, you may bring home less money than you did from your last job. You should anticipate that you will, so the family budget may be crimped for a few months or even years as you build your business. Is your family willing or able to make that sacrifice, too?

Even if you are primarily an investor or silent partner who hires managers to run the show, you must watch them closely. Ask anyone who runs a cash business, which is essentially what most franchises are, and he or she will tell you that controlling the cash register is the most important thing you must do. That's why large franchises have installed automated cash registers and inventory control systems. In Mom and Pop shops, the owner must literally "count the buns," as the phrase goes, to make sure that your employees are not stealing—too much. You will need to use automated methods and careful inventory procedures to protect yourself. For example, I know a man who was losing at least $25,000 to $50,000 net profit a year in a yogurt franchise because his employees either took money or ate or gave away his products to friends. He owned four stores scattered over a three-state area and only visited the most distant store once a week or once every two weeks. While the cat is away, the mouse will...steal. So, you must thoroughly explore the demands on you and your family before you buy a franchise.

WILLINGNESS

Willingness means an eagerness to cooperate with the franchise company and to follow its system and procedures. It also means a desire to learn, a curiosity about how to improve your operations, and a willingness to share your knowledge and teach your employees how to run the franchise better. Without it and with an uncooperative attitude, you will probably experience problems with your employees and the franchisor. For example, the president of Decorating Den, James Bugg, Sr., told me, "I have never had a franchisee fail who followed our system."

However, after a while, some franchisees begin to believe that they know better than the franchisor how to run the business, so they may lose that willingness and try to do it their way.

Of course, a franchisor should encourage franchisees to share their ways to improve quality and productivity, but the company developed the system. Usually, until it proves otherwise, it deserves the benefit of the doubt that its systems work best.

OBEDIENCE

This means an attitude to do what the franchisor says that you must do, such as meet company deadlines for royalty payments and reports, and follow procedures and restrictions. It also means filing your income and payroll tax forms on time, paying your vendors on time, and so forth. If you have trouble paying your bills and taxes on time, even when you have money in the bank, you can expect that owning a franchise will simply make that problem worse.

OUTGOING PERSONALITY

Few curmudgeons or people with skeptical, cynical attitudes can expect to succeed with a franchise because most franchises rely on good customer service to generate repeat business—the secret to success in any business. You may have a well-known product of good quality backed by a national or international reputation, but if you snarl at or act rudely to the customers, they will not come back. Various studies show that one dissatisfied customer complains to between 9 and 25 other people; a satisfied customer on average tells only four people of your good deeds. In short, you don't have to be a social butterfly, but you often do need a genuine liking for people.

However, many partners or husband-and-wife teams use their complementary personalities. I know of several couples in which one spouse acts as the "front man," working with employees and customers because he or she genuinely likes people and works well with them. The other spouse works in the "back office operations," handling accounting, inventory, and similar tasks, because they best fit his or her reticent personality. If you understand your strengths and weaknesses, find someone—a spouse, partner, or employee—who complements them so your business benefits.

Skills

You don't need to have been a corporate manager or a vice president of marketing or finance to succeed, but you do need good basic organizational skills. Spouses who consistently get their kids off to school on time and the other spouse out to work, who keep a relatively tidy house, and who still have time for part-time work and/or volunteer activities have more than enough organizational skill to manage many franchises successfully.

You also need a modicum of employee relations skills. These skills require no secret formula:

- Treat your employees courteously.
- Praise them when they do well.
- Correct them and train them when they make mistakes.
- Listen to their problems.
- Give them the power to make decisions within their tasks.
- Ask for the help.
- Let them share in the franchise's success.

I have written hundreds of articles about management skills, and all the advice contained in them can be summarized in those seven lines.

Desire

The ambition to succeed can encourage you to learn quickly any skills you do not currently have. The desire to do so can drive you to work smarter, make better decisions, seek more training, seek outside advice, and put forth the effort that success requires. It can help you overcome the handicap of limited financial resources. Bank officers or investors may well be impressed when they sense in you a strong, single-minded desire to succeed. Many people also believe that deeply felt desire frees creative forces within you. Remember, too, that the person, team, or organization that has the drive to win the most almost always defeats the person, team, or organization with less ambition, even if they have more skill and talent.

Persistence

From desire comes persistence, the ability to overcome any obstacle. Persistence enables you to make one more sales call when your previous ten have failed. It motivates you to help a customer try on just one more pair of shoes when you would rather throw the shoes at him or her. It helps you call just one more bank when six have turned down your request for a loan to buy the franchise. It comes from a strong faith in yourself and your goal.

You do not have to be a superperson or possess all these skills and traits in equal measure. In fact, one of the great benefits a franchise offers is that it allows you to take advantage of the cumulative efforts of a group of dedicated, motivated, knowledgeable, willing, and persistent individuals—those whose efforts started the franchise. If you can add your share of these traits to their efforts, you can more than likely succeed as a franchise owner.

3

How to Find the Best
Franchise for You

Finding the right franchise for you means that you should follow a lengthy, detailed process. As Chapter 2 discussed, you must match your personal interests, personality, experience, and financial resources to the available franchises. Understanding your personal "assets" marks only the beginning of your quest: Use them to lead you in the right direction, but only like a weather vane that tells you which way the wind blows, not as the basis for your final choice.

As the title of this book indicates, I have included these 50 franchises here because they offer high returns on your *cash* investment from a relatively low investment. If your goals are primarily financial—that is, you want to run a franchise to maximize your profits and not just to run your own business—then you need to define what the concept of a high return means to you. This chapter explains several ways to define that concept and shows you how to determine the potential return on your investment, even—and especially—when a franchise company cannot or will not give you the detailed information you need to calculate your return. Use these techniques as guideposts to help you identify the best available franchise that meets your other criteria.

In this book I prefer to define the concept of "return" this way: Your return on investment—called ROI by financial experts—is determined by comparing your potential pretax *net income* to your total up-front *cash outlay*. For example, if you invest $100,000 in cash, and if your first year's net income is $10,000 (after you subtract all expenses from your gross income), then your return on investment (*ROI*) equals 10 percent. The formula is simple: Divide your net income (*NI*) by your cash outlay (*CO*) to obtain a percentage, or *NI/CO = ROI.*

As defined, net income is the amount left after you subtract all your expenses. Total cash outlay is the amount of actual money that you pay to start your franchise *before* you receive any income. It does *not* include any expenses you pay after you open your doors and start earning an income. I also use the term *pretax net income.* Since your income tax bill is influenced by many factors, such as depreciation on equipment, tax credits, loss carryforwards, and the like that are not related to your income, this book considers neither your after-tax income or an ROI from your ongoing operations. I consider only your ROI on your *original* investment. The terms *net income* and *net profits* are used interchangeably because most franchisees own 100 percent of their businesses, have partners, or have incorporated in Chapter S corporations that pass the income through to the shareholders' personal income tax returns.

My definition of ROI differs from the classic accounting definition; it usually includes all the money you borrow and the value of assets, such as equipment and furnishings, that you give to the business. Suppose you borrow $25,000 from the bank to get started, and you give to the business a personal computer and some office furniture valued at $5,000. Using our $100,000 example here, your total investment would now equal $130,000, and your ROI would be $10,000 net profit divided by $130,000 or just 7.7 percent.

I do not include borrowed money or other assets for one simple reason: You are going to pay the loans back out of cash flow your business earns and you are easily "loaning" the furniture to the business. Measuring your loans and loan payments would mean that you would have to analyze your net profits, and the interest you pay the bank would have to be considered part of your operating expenses.

I also do not include many of the more elaborate accounting concepts, such as depreciation, loan principal payback, and the like because I want to keep it simple. Most people want to know the bottom line: how much money can you expect to make on the money you put into the business. The simple ratio of cash investment compared to net income gives a clear, concise picture of what you can expect your bottom line to equal.

You can measure your ROI in other meaningful ways. You can include the amount you borrow and add your cash outlays to determine your *return on capital*. In my example, that ROI would equal 8.25 percent.

You can examine your *net margin*, that is, your net income compared to your gross income. You may think that if you receive a gross income of $200,000, you have doubled your original $100,000 investment. That would be wrong because you forgot to subtract all your expenses, including loan payments and interest. If your net income was just $10,000, then your net margin would be just 5 percent. Heck, you could buy a long-term certificate of deposit and make that much, so why bother buying a franchise and working so hard!

You can also look at your ROI by comparing your cash investment to your net profit *plus* your salary. If you took a salary of $25,000 and earned a net profit of $10,000, your ROI would be 35 percent ($35,000 divided by $100,000). However, this method has a serious drawback: It does not give you credit for all the hours you worked during the year.

For example, if you worked 50 hours a week for 50 weeks and took a salary of $25,000, you would earn a wage of $10 per hour ($25,000 salary divided by 2,500 hours = $10 per hour).

Again, many new franchisees think, "Wow, I earned $35,000 this year, so my ROI is 35 percent. I'm doing really well." But you need to determine whether you have paid yourself a salary or taken a draw against your business' income before you calculate your ROI.

Then, you need to consider whether the franchise you want to buy will be worth your time, effort, and most important, your cash investment.

If you do not pay yourself a salary, then you need to determine whether your ROI makes sense. To do this, find out what an average salary for your position would be in industry. For example, if you own a fast-food restaurant and manage it, you should credit yourself with a salary ranging from $30,000 to $50,000, depending on region, type of restaurant, type of food, bonus structure, and the like. Then, you need to subtract that salary—or the total amount of draws you make from the business—from your net income before you consider your net income and ROI.

You must consider these concepts to get a fairly accurate idea of your potential ROI when you begin your search for a low-investment, high-profit franchise. Use these formulas and concepts to determine how much net income or net profit you can realistically expect from each franchise you examine.

INVESTIGATE, INVESTIGATE, INVESTIGATE

Finding out the financial details you need to determine a franchise's potential ROI will be difficult. Although the federal government has eased its restrictions on earnings projections, most franchisors refuse to make earnings claims or publish their franchisees' actual results. Some of the franchises in this book do so, while others publish results from corporate stores or show a range of possible results.

In fact, disputes over projected earnings are among the most important causes of lawsuits and disputes between franchisors and franchisees.

If a company publishes a statement that you could earn $50,000 a year, yet you bought the franchise and earned only $15,000, you would be tempted to sue the franchise for false and misleading statements. Federal Trade Commission (FTC) regulations have made this type of lawsuit more difficult, but most franchisors do not want to risk the expense, trouble, and damaged reputation such squabbles inevitably cause, so most will not give you any earnings claims.

This law and the franchisors' position are ludicrous because unregulated dealers and distributors can make any outrageous earnings claim they want: Earn $1 million stuffing envelopes! We've all seen these outrageously misleading advertisements, but these are not illegal. Yet a franchisor finds it difficult to publish even actual results for fear that a disgruntled franchisee will sue if he or she does not match those results.

The FTC regulations and similar state legislators have created an impenetrable fog that now does more to protect the franchise company than it does to carry out its original intent to protect you from misleading earnings claims. Now, many franchisors hide behind the rule when, with some effort, they could publish acceptable and legal earnings results.

Since 1988, franchisors can *choose* to report average franchise earnings, publish the results of all franchise operations, discuss potential earnings ranges, and take similar steps. But most companies do not because the FTC left open the door for complaints.

However, many franchisors argue that they cannot prepare accurate earnings claims for many legitimate reasons, including 1) franchisees may not report accurate results; 2) too many conflicting criteria prevent them from a uniform approach; and 3) different industries use different accounting methods.

In the meantime, what do you do to find out how much money you can make? You simply have to do the legwork. This and much more investigation are absolutely necessary. I repeat what many experts have said: The single most important statement you can make about choosing a franchise is this: *Investigate, investigate, investigate—and investigate some more.*

Franchise buyers make this mistake more often than any other: They do not investigate thoroughly before they sign an agreement.

Usually, people become emotionally involved in a fad or a field that becomes "hot," much as video stores and yogurt stores did during the mid- and late 1980s. Recently, many have rushed into home delivery franchises without thoroughly analyzing the true market size, the difficulty of the operation, the financial backing behind the company, and on and on. As many yogurt store buyers did, these overeager buyers leverage their assets to the hilt, and when the market growth slows—as it inevitably must in any market—or the franchise company cannot provide the promised support because it grew too fast, they find that their stores fail, and they lose their investments.

I know of one owner of a local minichain of yogurt stores who closed 5 of 9 stores during the 1990–92 recession. I know of a fast-food home delivery franchise that failed in its first three months because the starry-eyed owner overestimated the demand in his territory for a particular kind of ethnic food. And he allowed a competing home delivery franchise with a very popular product to open a store directly beneath his own hard-to-access location! I know of a large 19-store chain of yogurt stores that went out of business because the parent franchisor failed to develop new, more competitive products and got into serious conflict with its franchisees that crippled the company for two years.

So, although in general franchises do succeed more often than independent businesses, just because a company says "franchise" does not guarantee you instant success, high profits, or a free ride. In most cases, a good franchise system will survive a recession, but in all cases, if you do not carefully and completely investigate before you buy, you can easily catch yourself in the "glow" and glamour of an alluring sales pitch and buy a franchise that does not fit your personality, financial resources, talents, skills, or experience.

At the end of this chapter, you will find several checklists you can use to find out the details you need to consider the nonfinancial aspects of the franchises you investigate. Chapter 2 discussed some of these ideas as well. These questions and the discussions in the sections that follow serve as "trail markers" to help you avoid getting lost in the "jungle" of franchise investigation.

WATCH FOR THESE WARNING SIGNALS

Beyond the financial warning signals, you should be wary of franchises for which you develop healthy profit projections, but which also show the following problems:

Question Rapid Growth

Franchises growing very fast may simply not be able to provide you with the support you need to succeed. If your income projections are based on those of early franchises, they may not be as accurate for you and other latecomers. The early bird gets the worm, and in franchising, the most support because the franchise company needs you to succeed so it builds an impressive track record that it can use to convince other buyers of the system's soundness and growth potential. Your royalty payments will also make sure the franchise survives.

Franchisees 1 through 20 may have had the help of the company's founders or top executives who developed the system. If you are going to be franchisee 500, you need to know how the company plans to give you the same quality support that the first few received. In short, thoroughly study the training and local support programs. Get to know the local, state, or regional support representatives and the corporate training staff. Make sure that they have the knowledge, background, and skill that can help you succeed.

Furthermore, talk with new franchisees that have just opened their doors and ask them in-depth questions about the kind and quality of support they received *compared* to the support they were promised.

I know of one fast-growing franchise that seems to illustrate the best one can offer. The Little Gym had 17 years of operational experience before the founder of Sylvan Learning Centers, W. Berry Fowler, bought a controlling interest in the operation. Berry had built Sylvan Learning to 400 franchises before he sold out. Then, Fowler brought on board half a dozen former Sylvan top executives and within the first year had built a staff of 30 people while they sold 50 franchises during the same year. That staff of 30 is adequate to manage growth to between 200 and 300 franchises or more. So Fowler put his support system in place *before* he let The Little Gym hit its growth curve. Of course, he had the experience and financial resources to do so, but in most cases, new high-growth franchises require similar efforts to prepare a foundation for long-term success.

Study System Organization

Furthermore, you need to investigate the company's organization. If the company does not want you to meet key employees or resists your unplanned visit to headquarters, be very wary. They may stage a good performance when they know you are coming, but actually reflect confusion and disorganization when you are not there.

During any visit, meet with managers, executives, and support staff and discuss with them how they manage essential functions: training, operations, new product development, field service, customer-franchisee support over the telephone, response times to inquiries, marketing campaign development, management, and grand opening assistance. If a franchisor seems weak in a vital area, such as grand opening assistance or marketing, compare that weakness to its strengths to consider whether your own expertise can compensate for that weakness. If you decide that you cannot, choose another franchise.

Beware of Verbal Projections

Clearly, most franchisors will not give you the financial projections you need—in writing. So be extremely wary of anyone, especially a zealous salesperson or broker, who makes *verbal* projections or vague promises of great returns. If no one else will back up his or her projections in writing, watch out. Go elsewhere! This is an absolute rule with no exceptions. And that person who has given you those unsubstantiated figures has broken federal regulations and perhaps the laws of some states.

How to Dig Up the Numbers You Need

Face it. You are going to have to dig up the information you urgently need to calculate your potential return on investment. You can use several methods—each of which requires extensive legwork—to get enough information to make an educated guess. None of these ways is foolproof, but you should be able to get enough ballpark figures to do your simple ROI calculations and investment ratios.

First, where I could obtain them, I publish actual results from franchisors. I also give my "best-guess" estimates of how franchisees earn income and extrapolate conservative income estimates.

Second, before you begin your in-depth investigation, consider magazine articles and surveys as a way to obtain general figures. *Entrepreneur, Income Opportunities,* and similar magazines publish these on occasion, but they are often based on interviews with or data received from the company or only a few franchisees, so the figures may not be as accurate or as revealing as you need.

Third, you should ask a variety of existing franchisees—old and new, near and far from your area—about their actual results. In private, many franchisees are willing to discuss, at least in general terms, their gross incomes, net margins, ROIs, and the like. Emphasize the newer and older franchisees in your area because you should experience similar results, start-up costs, and expenses. If you are the first in your area, find franchisees in similar geographic or demographic regions.

Existing franchisees will also serve as fonts of information about the quality of the franchise's support, training, hidden start-up costs, continuing problems with both their operations and the franchisor, and so forth.

However, do not talk *only* to those franchisees that the franchisor recommends. Unfortunately, but quite naturally, many franchisors are unlikely to suggest that you talk with a disgruntled franchisee. FTC disclosure rules require a franchisor to give you a current list of all franchisees; some franchisors will give you only franchisees in the same state, so insist that you get the complete list. Then, pick and choose at random from the list and contact them. And ask the first franchisees you call for references to successful and not-so-successful franchisees so you can find out what problems to expect.

Using the Company's Own Numbers

An easy way to use the company's numbers to determine a rough estimate of potential gross income is to ask the franchisor for non-company *systemwide* revenues, that is, total revenues that the franchisees have earned. Then, simply divide that figure by the number of franchises, and that gives you an average gross income. For example, if systemwide revenues equaled $10 million and the company had 50 franchises, then the average gross sales would equal $200,000.

You could find out the industry average net profit margins from trade publications and associations and calculate a rough net profit estimate. For example, in the pizza industry, the average net profit ranges around 30 percent (yes, it is amazingly profitable!). So, continuing the example, you would multiply $200,000 by 30 percent for an estimated net profit of $60,000. If you invested $150,000, to open a pizza shop, your ROI would be $60,000 divided by $150,000, or 40 percent. Not bad, but not great.

The danger of using systemwide revenues and industry margins, of course, is that the franchisees in that system may be doing better or worse than these averages. Furthermore, systemwide revenues estimates may be deliberately or inadvertently inaccurate. And they may include a host of new franchisees with little or no income during that year.

So, look for franchisor reports that give you systemwide revenues for franchises two years or older for more accurate numbers on which to base your estimates.

That's the easy way. Here is another way if the franchisor does not report or will not provide its systemwide revenues.

You calculate a rough rate of return and anticipated gross income from the information in the franchisor's financial statements. Since this information tends to be at least a year or two old, you can also use it to request more up-to-date information, recent quarterly estimates, or even actual results that will give you a more accurate picture of what gross income you can expect to earn over time. This will take some digging, but it will be worth the effort. Here's the process:

Franchise companies must include in their offering circulars and disclosure documents financial statements (audited and certified by independent accountants) for the past two or three years. I often find that the most recent statement is from the previous year or even the year before, so again, ask for more recent data.

Then, to calculate a rough rate of return and rough potential gross income numbers, follow these steps:

1. In the income or revenue portion of the statement, look for the amount earned from *royalties*. Usually, the income or revenue portion is divided into franchise fees, royalties, product sales, advertising fees, interest, and miscellaneous categories. If the income portion is not subdivided, ask the franchisor for a breakdown; if he is reluctant or refuses to give it, be wary about any earnings claims. For example, a company may have a total income of $25 million, of which $10 million comes from royalties.
2. Multiply the franchise's royalty percentage by 100 to produce a multiplication factor. If a franchise has a royalty rate of 5 percent, then the factor will equal 20: 5 percent multiplied by 100 equals 20.
3. Multiply the royalty income by the multiplication factor. In the example, multiply $10 million by 20 for systemwide revenues of $200 million. This should approximate the gross revenues of all franchisees.

   Remember to account for advertising fees. If the fees are included in the total royalty category, add that percentage to the royalty percentage. However, most franchisors publish them as separate numbers because they put the ad fees into separate funds and bank accounts. If the ad fee in this example were 2 percent, then the total would be 7 percent and the multiplication factor would be roughly 14.3. However, I assume that the ad fee is listed as a separate category because most companies in this book do so.

4. Take the total number of franchises *in operation* during that year. You will find this number in the disclosure documents. For this example, let's assume 500 franchises.
5. Divide the gross income of all franchises by the total number. Here, divide $200,000,000 by 500, which gives you an average gross income per franchise of $400,000 per year.

6. Estimate your *desired* net income. If you want to earn a net margin of 20 percent, then you figure your anticipated net income by multiplying your gross income by 20 percent. In this example, $400,000 times 20 percent equals $80,000.

Then, ask yourself if this is realistic according to what you have heard from franchisees, read in this book or from other printed sources, or have heard about industry averages. If the answer is yes, then calculate your ROI. If no, then go back and do more follow-up questioning of franchisees and the franchisors about what you can expect to net within two to three years.

7. Calculate your ROI with the same formula given earlier: net income divided by cash outlay. In this example, suppose you spent $500,000 and your net income is $80,000: Your ROI would be only 16 percent, not very profitable.
8. Use different percentages to repeat steps 6 and 7 to analyze various net income and ROI scenarios. Use "what if" estimates to analyze best and worst case examples to consider whether the potential return is adequate for the required investment.

Use Helpful Breakeven Analysis Tool

Another way to determine whether a franchise is worth the investment and the effort is to do a "breakeven analysis." This common accounting technique tells you a very, very important number: *the minimum amount of gross income you must have just to break even.* It does *not* discuss profit at all because if you cannot, at the minimum, break even on your projected income within two to three years, you cannot make a profit, and your business will either fail or you will have to prop it up with loans, trade credit, or other sources—steps that I would never advise a franchisee to take. Further, without a profit, you are losing money on your investment, much less earning a return on it.

As a financial tool, breakeven analysis will quickly show you whether the operation will be feasible as it continues. To get these results, though, you first need to find out the actual costs of *running* the franchise, *not* the start-up costs.

Ask the franchisor for a sample monthly operating budget, an operating statement (quarterly or annual), an estimated profit and loss statement from an average franchise, or any related financial document that shows you the real expenses you will incur during your day-to-day operations. If a franchisor will not give you this information, ask franchisees for these figures. You might borrow the information, at least the categories, from the franchisor's accounting manual, or an accountant who works with franchisees.

Then, follow this simple exercise:

1. Set up an estimated operating budget divided into two types of costs: fixed and variable.

   Fixed costs are those that you must pay every month or quarter: rent, insurance, depreciation, property taxes, salaries, fixed utilities, and so on. Variable costs fluctuate according to your sales: inventory, employee payroll, raw materials, and the like.

   Of course, many costs are "semifixed" and "semivariable," that is, the amount changes. These include part-time employee payroll, professional fees, supplies, shipping costs, advertising, telephone, a portion of utility bills, payroll taxes, equipment maintenance, training, and so on. These concepts are essential in determining your breakeven point.

   A sample annual operating budget for an imaginary Go-Go Pizza franchise follows. The first column lists specific expense categories. The second and third columns list fixed and variable costs, respectively. The far right column gives the percentage of variable costs compared to *total sales*.

GO-GO PIZZA FRANCHISE BUDGET: TOTAL SALES = $400,000

Expense Category	Fixed Cost	Variable Cost	Percent
Inventory	—	$150,000	37.5%
Part-time employees	—	80,000	20.0
Full-time employees	$50,000	15,000	3.8
Rent	12,500	0	0
Advertising	10,000	10,000	2.5
Utilities	10,000	2,000	0.5
Payroll taxes	6,000	12,000	3.0
Depreciation	5,000	0	0
Insurance	5,000	0	0
Miscellaneous	5,000	5,000	1.3
Supplies	4,000	1,000	0.3
Maintenance	2,000	1,000	0.3
Professional fees	1,500	2,000	0.5
Telephone	500	1,000	0.3
Totals	$111,500	$279,000	70.0% (a)

a. Rounded to nearest 1 percent.

The variable costs of the Go-Go Pizza franchise totaled $279,000 and make up 70 percent of the total budget.

2. To calculate the breakeven point, use this formula:

The breakeven point equals the dividend of the total fixed cost (*FC*) divided by the difference between 100 percent and the percentage of variable costs (*VC*) of total sales. In this example, the breakeven (*BE*) equals

$$BE = FC/(100\% - VC\%)$$

or

$$BE = \$111,500/30\% = \$371,667$$

Thus, your pizza shop would break even with a gross annual income of $371,667 with that budget, but this leaves you with a net income of just $28,333.

3. To figure out your net profit margin, divide your net income of $28,333 by your gross income of $400,000. That gives you a net profit of just 7.1 percent, very low by industry standards.

4. To figure out your potential ROI, divide your net income of $28,333 by your total cash investment. If your total cash investment is $250,000, then your projected ROI would equal 11.3 percent, not very good either. If your investment totaled $125,000, then your ROI would double to 22.6 percent, a much healthier figure and one more in line with pizza industry expectations.

You should do a similar breakeven analysis for *every* franchise you investigate. It may seem tedious, but you need this very valuable and revealing way to find out exactly what you can expect.

To develop a similar estimated budget, obtain many of the categories and numbers from the start-up budgets that the companies must list in their UFOCs or disclosure documents. For expenses that they do not list, again, you must dig them up from the franchisor, current franchisees, industry sources, or an accountant. You can obtain insurance costs from your own agent. Estimate your needed salary level and those of any full-time employees you plan to hire. Call utility companies and ask them for average monthly or annual bills for similar businesses. Call commercial real estate brokers for estimated rents. Call vendors and supply companies for estimated costs of inventory and supplies. Ask your accountant and attorney for their estimated annual fees.

And be sure to use estimates from the high end. People tend to "low ball" their estimates because they falsely believe that they will "control" their expenses. Remember the variations on Murphy's law: Something always costs more than it first appears it will cost! Further, testing these formulas with artificially low expense estimates will artificially inflate your net profit margins and ROIs. In turn, you will mislead yourself about the potential ROI for a franchise. High estimated expenses will tend to reflect more realistically what may happen. The original Murphy's law tends to hold true during business start-ups: Whatever can go wrong will go wrong at the worst possible moment. So, you will want to add a contingency category to your budgets of at least 10 to 20 percent.

If your estimates turn out to be too high, that is all to the good because your actual ROI will be that much higher, and you will benefit all the more. If a high estimate shows that a franchise is a good buy, then low actual expenses will make it an excellent one.

After you have used several breakeven analyses to test your choices of franchise, you can more easily decide which one may create the best potential ROI.

DEVELOP A BUSINESS PLAN

If you consider that laying the groundwork in buying a franchise seems like an obstacle course or a steeplechase that you must win before you get the "prize," you would be correct. If you are willing to put forth significant amounts of time and effort to make a wise decision, you will sharply increase the chances that you will make a wise and successful investment. You must be willing to do relatively simple things yourself, such as conducting a local site search or survey, or you may find that you lack the desire and drive to make a franchise a success. To pick the right franchise, you really do have to "wear out shoe leather" to gather information, visit existing franchisees, talk to helpful professionals, and so on.

In addition to the ROI and breakeven analyses, you also need to develop a thorough business plan. Many franchisors will give you a prepared one or a fill-in-the-blank plan that you can take to the bank for a loan, but I do not mean this type of plan. I mean that before you sign an agreement, you should draft a business plan for yourself and your franchise. Doing so will give you a complete understanding of exactly what you face and the steps you must take when you buy and start that franchise.

The business plan outline presented here incorporates information that you gather as you follow the steps outlined in this chapter. You can obtain much of the information from the UFOC or franchisor brochures and industry publications.

However, the key idea is this: Writing a business plan clarifies for you each specific aspect of the franchise operation. It gives you the actions you must take both before and after you buy and open your franchise outlet.

Business Plan Outline

A. Executive Summary

List key features and describe the franchise opportunity.

B. The Franchise

1. Define what the franchise is and describe its products and services and its customer base and potential markets.
2. Discuss how and why you became interested in this franchise.
3. Discuss the industry in which the franchise operates and the business background of the franchise company and its management.

C. Products and Services

Describe each type you will offer.

D. The Market

1. Describe your potential customers and where, how and why you are likely to find them.
2. Discuss how large the potential market can grow in your area, and consider how large a share of that local market you can expect to gain.

E. The Competition

Discuss the actual and potential competitors, their sales and market share, and their likely response to your entry into the existing market.

F. The Marketing Plan

1. Define your quarterly and annual sales goals for the first two or three years.
2. Explain your selling, customer service, advertising, public relations, and promotion methods and strategies.
3. Discuss your marketing plan, that is, your organized and orderly strategies and tactics to reach your potential customers, for the first two to three years.
4. Define how much you plan to charge for your products and services, and compare and contrast your pricing structure to your competitors'.
5. Discuss your sales methods and service policies and procedures.

G. Operations

1. Examine your proposed location and why you plan to put your franchise there (or alternative areas).
2. Discuss the equipment you must buy or lease, how much it will cost, and from whom you must obtain it.
3. Describe your product production procedures or service delivery methods.
4. List your potential sources of supply.
5. Describe how many employees you may need, from what groups you plan to hire them, what type of help (full- or part-time, sales reps, technicians, and so on) you need, and the training and/or experience you or the task requires.

H. Management

1. Discuss who will act as managers, how you will find them, and how you and they will work during daily operations,

that is, their duties and responsibilities.

2. Explain management salary and bonus structure.
3. Describe any required or needed management training.
4. List your outside professional support team (accountant, attorney, insurance agent, ad agency, public relations practitioner, banker, financial advisor, and so on).

I. Grand Opening Schedule

1. List the steps you must take to open your store or service.
2. Give deadlines and projected completion dates for each step.

J. Anticipated Problems

Discuss the likely situations that could delay or affect your planned grand opening date and your progress toward it.

K. Financial Outlook

1. Discuss your accounting procedures.
2. Include an estimated profit and loss statement for the first three years.
3. Provide a cash flow forecast for the first two years.
4. Do balance sheets of potential assets and liabilities.

L. Projected Financing

1. Review your total estimated start-up and operating costs.
2. Discuss your total financial requirements.
3. Discuss the sources from which you plan to obtain this amount: your own cash assets, friends and family, private investors, and so on.
4. Discuss how you will use any financing: cash, bank loans, donated assets, and so on.

Doing this thorough business plan will help you protect you from yourself, that is, the tendency to get caught up in the "glow" of buying a franchise or falling under the mesmerizing spell of a sharp salesperson or charismatic franchise founder. It will bring you back down to earth and allow you to make the wisest possible choice.

Two Final Rules of Thumb

Now that you know how to calculate a ROI, net profit margins, and similar essential financial facts, you need to know how to determine when you should go ahead with a purchase. Follow these two simple rules of thumb:

1. If the ROI on your cash outlays will be three to five times greater than that you can earn with a "passive" investment (bank certificate of deposit, Treasury bill, municipal bonds, common stocks, mutual funds, and so on), then you can feel fairly confident about investing in a franchise.

For example, long-term Treasury bills in late 1993 were paying about 6 percent, far lower than they had been in many years. For a franchise to be really worthwhile, you need an ROI equal to between 18 and 30 percent, depending on the industry and risk factors. If you can expect an ROI of only 10 percent or so, why bother to buy a franchise and go through all the effort to begin one and risk failure when T-bills are practically risk free? You could invest your cash and sleep well at night and collect interest payments for 10 to 30 years. You could work for someone else and let the boss have all the worries.

Of course, if you truly want to own your own business and you can willingly accept a lower ROI at first, then you may be willing to make the trade. This may be even more true if you plan to build a chain of franchises in your area. If your analysis shows strong potential for such growth, your future gain should far exceed what passive investments should bring.

Or, you can anticipate the personal, business, and tax benefits of working for yourself and owning a cash business. Some people prefer to earn a salary from their own businesses and do not concern themselves too much with the ROI.

However, I caution potential franchise buyers about this negative aspect: In many cases, you are paying someone else to give you a job. Many franchises do not build much long-term equity or resale value. You can earn a good, steady income as you would from any job, but you may not be able to sell for much more than you put into it. Thus, in the long term you will lose money because inflation will erode the value of your original investment. Low-cost franchises do not lend themselves to building equity; to do so, you need hard assets, such as established accounts, ongoing cash flow, long-term leases, inventory, a growing market in an established industry, and so on.

The solution is to grow your own minichain of franchise territories: Own several fast-food shops, expand to a metropolitan area, or increase the number of vans you have on the road carrying out janitorial and commercial cleaning services, and so on. Or become a master franchise, area representative or subfranchisor, each of which allows you to sell and service franchisees of your own. You receive a big share, usually half of all franchise fees and royalties. In short, you become affluent or even wealthy in franchising by growing the business and taking advantage of opportunities to expand your territory.

During recent years, in a strong new trend, established franchisees with one or two stores in one industry are buying other franchises in similar or different industries. Many fast-food operators now own a burger shop, a taco stand, a pizza parlor, and so on. In fact, I know a yogurt and salad shop franchisee who deliberately set out to buy at least three different food franchises in the same food court of a major shopping mall. He wanted to spread his risk and dominate the revenues from that food court.

He also wanted to buy a food delivery franchise that he could locate near the mall so he could deliver food to the thousands of white-collar workers in office towers within minutes of the regional shopping mall—a shrewd, long-term strategy that could build him close to $500,000 or more in equity when he wanted to sell the entire operation.

All these considerations raise legitimate issues. If your primary concern is your return on investment, then you should follow the rules of thumb given earlier. In fact, the best franchises usually produce ROIs of between 35 and 50 percent a year after several years in business. The 50 franchises that this book describes have shown consistently that you can earn similar or better ROIs with them.

However, I also strongly urge you to consider one more rule of thumb, one that may be most important of all: Do you truly enjoy doing what the franchise requires you to do? If you only buy a franchise for the money, you will find it very difficult to succeed. I strongly urge you to consider your personal and emotional likes and dislikes, and what you *love* to do, before you make your final decision. If you are an outgoing "people person" who enjoys contact with other people, sitting behind a desk making phone calls may drive you to distraction. You may be very happy running a retail store, working with customers, supervising and training employees, meeting salespeople, working with vendors, and so on. If you like to get your hands dirty, you may be very happy with an owner-operator cleaning service. For example, I know a former electrical engineer who had also studied film production. His interests combined the technical and the creative, so he is happily managing a Video Data Services franchise producing videos for businesses. He hopes to develop documentaries *à la* Bill Moyers on important local and regional issues.

In short, do what you love and love what you do. All the money in the world cannot replace the day-to-day joy you will feel. Of course, making a 50 percent ROI at the same time adds even more pleasure to the effort.

The checklist that follows contains dozens of key questions you should ask each franchise before you buy. You may also refer to booklets published by the International Franchise Association, 1350 New York Avenue, Suite 900, Washington, DC 20005, for additional questions.

CHECKLIST: KEY QUESTIONS FOR CAREFUL CONSIDERATION

Investment

1. What is the franchise fee and what products, services, territory, and so on do I receive in exchange for my fee?

2. What other costs does the franchisor *require* me to make for equipment, supplies, start-up inventory, training, signage, leasehold improvements, and so on?
3. What outside costs, such as lease deposits and professional fees, must I pay to open my franchise?
4. What are the "hidden" costs not listed in the offering circular?
5. How am I restricted in my choice of suppliers, and how do these restrictions affect (increase or decrease) my costs?

Operating Costs

1. What are my monthly operating expenses?
2. What are the franchise's ongoing royalty rates and advertising fees and when do I have to pay them?
3. Are there additional fees for extra training for new or additional managers/employees, for extra management visits, for extra field visits, and so on?
4. What are the likely total costs per month of bank loans, franchisor financing, lease payments, paybacks to investors, and the like?
5. What occasional or unanticipated expenses are likely to occur?

Site Selection

1. How is my territory defined (e.g., radius, geographic area, demographics, number of potential customers, and so on)?
2. What are the actual boundaries of my territory?
3. What protection against encroachment (putting other franchises in or near my territory) does the franchisor offer and what does that protection mean under the law?
4. Am I confined to operating, offering my service, or selling my product to my territory?
5. Does the franchisor help me find a location? If so, what form does this assistance take, for example, on-site visits, zip code maps, general advice, and so on? Do I have to pay for this assistance?

6. Who is directly responsible for finding a site and by what deadlines?
7. Who is directly responsible for negotiating a lease or site purchase?
8. How does the franchisor help me negotiate a lease, for example, actual review, actual negotiation with landlord, after-the-fact approval?
9. Does my right to the franchise license depend upon a particular location or lease terms?
10. Does the franchisor provide construction management services, and if so, what kinds and what do they cost me?
11. Does the franchisor provide prepared architectural drawings and blueprints for construction? Do I have to pay more for changes unique to my location?

Restrictions and Controls

1. What specific quality control standards must I fulfill?
2. What approval procedures does the franchisor require to review alternate sources of supply or vendors that I may want to use?
3. How long can the franchisor delay a decision on my choice of alternate vendors?
4. Does the franchise agreement require that I use only the franchisor's products or vendors that the franchisor specifies?
5. What restrictions does the operating manual place on my day-to-day operation?
6. What kinds of equipment, fixtures, leasehold improvements, and so on must I install and according to what specifications?
7. Must I operate the business myself or may I hire managers? What restrictions are placed on managers' activities?
8. What are the required bookkeeping systems and accounting reports I must follow?
9. Who furnishes and pays for copies of these reports and forms?
10. Does the franchisor derive income from the sale, lease, or supply of equipment, supplies, raw materials, and products?

11. Does the franchise agreement guarantee me the benefits of any discounts or quantity purchase agreements?
12. To what types and styles of products and services am I limited?
13. In what required advertising, marketing, and promotional programs must I participate?
14. What kind of national and regional advertising programs does the franchisor provide? Are they aimed at increasing my sales or selling more franchises?
15. What continuing management/field support do I receive, what does that support include in detail, and what do I have to pay for it?

Cancellation/Termination

1. Under what circumstances can I (the franchisee) terminate the contract?
2. Under what circumstances can the franchisor terminate the contract?
3. Do I have the right to "cure" or correct any problems or "deficiencies" before a franchisor has the right to terminate my agreement?
4. How long does the franchise license last, and what are the terms for renewal?
5. What new fees must I pay and new restrictions must I follow when I renew the agreement?
6. What actual practices does the franchisor follow when it terminates agreements?
7. How many franchises have been terminated and for what reasons? How many terminations did the *franchisor* initiate and for what reasons? How many franchisees failed and for what reasons?
8. What kinds of litigation (lawsuits) and arbitration have taken place between the franchisor and its franchisees during the past five years (the offering circular only requires them to list the past several years)?
9. Does my family or spouse inherit the business upon my death and how?

10. If a family member cannot inherit, how does the franchisor manage the sale or transfer of my franchise after my death?
11. Can I sell or transfer the license to someone else? What conditions and restrictions does the franchisor place on my right to sell or transfer the license?

Add these questions to those discussed in Chapter 2 about the franchisor's management team's background and experience in the industry to develop a complete and clear picture of how the franchise works.

4

Franchises with Fees of $8,000 or Less

PERMA CERAM ENTERPRISES, INC.

Joseph Tumolo, President
Perma Ceram Enterprises, Inc.
65 Smithtown Boulevard
Smithtown, NY 11788-9820
(800) 645-5039
(516) 724-1205

With 157 operating franchises by the end of 1993, Perma Ceram is one of the nation's largest bathtub, sink, and wall tile resurfacing franchises. This growth shows a steady increase of about 13 percent since 1989. Perma Ceram offers a unique spray-on "porcelaincote" resurfacing process that provides the same strength and durability as an original porcelain finish.

Its marketing advantage is that refinishing or resurfacing a tub costs less than half the cost of a new tub and one-tenth (10 percent) the cost of installing a new tub. The cost of resurfacing—and changing the color—of the bathtub, sink, and wall tile amounts to about $600 compared to a cost of $2,500 to $5,000 to completely remodel a bathroom. About 40 percent of your market will consist of cost-conscious consumers, but your best repeat customers—and your highest volume and net profit dollars—will come from hotel-motel chains, apartment management firms, home improvement contractors, plumbers, insurance adjustors, and bathroom remodeling contractors.

Since the first edition of this book, Perma Ceram has weathered the recession very well. Company executives say that although franchise sales slowed, its existing franchisees showed a significant increase in business. They noted that this recession-resistant industry provides a very affordable service not tied to new construction. In fact, the industry benefits because during a recession, more people are willing to repair rather than to replace their bathroom fixtures. There are few if any slack times in this business; the combination of commercial and residential customers makes this a relatively steady industry.

Perma Ceram is an interesting franchise because you can work part or full time. You can work from home, you can use your own vehicle, and you can hire small crews to do the hard labor while you concentrate on marketing and selling your service to high-volume, repeat commercial accounts. For example, 85 to 90 percent of all new franchisees start this business part time and do the work on weekends until they reach a comfortable income level. Then they change to full time and hire crews to do the work. Two men—usually independent subcontractors—can easily do between 15 and 30 jobs a week, even more if you have a commercial contract where they can remain in one place and avoid constant travel from one job to the next.

How Much It Costs

Perma Ceram still has *no* franchise fee and you pay no royalties or ad fees. The company charges you a flat fee of $24,500 for all equipment and supplies; five days of training; transportation to and from an established location for that training; business and advertising materials; and operating, technical, and business manuals.

The company makes its profits by selling you the equipment, products, and services, including its proprietary "porcelaincote" materials that you must have to carry out its resurfacing process.

Perma Ceram is the only source for these materials, and it charges a normal markup.

What You Get

For the total $24,500 payment, you receive the following:

- Five days of training, including, especially important, on-the-job work with an existing franchise.
- A nonexclusive territory determined by potential market size. Company executives added that in a small area, such as Albuquerque, New Mexico, you could arrange an exclusive territory. But in a major metropolitan area, such as Washington, DC, the company might place several franchisees to cover the huge 3 million population market.
- Payment for your transportation to and from the nearest training location and four days' room and board for one person. You must pay for additional trainees, but this remains one of the more generous offerings that this book discusses.
- Marketing, advertising, and business management manuals that you learn how to use during the training period.
- Enough "porcelaincote" and other materials to refinish about 75 bathrooms. The equipment and materials should allow you to earn between $15,000 and $20,000, depending on how much you charge per job and how efficiently and effectively you apply the materials.
- Ongoing assistance from the company's technical support group.

Start-up and Operating Expenses

Your $24,500 payment does *not* include a range of ordinary start-up and operating expenses. You'll need transportation unless you own an appropriate truck, minivan, cargo van, or station wagon. You can use your own vehicle.

Other expenses include business telephone deposit, Yellow Pages or other advertising costs, an answering or paging service, and—especially—working capital. This must include your living expenses until you establish your business as a going concern.

Company executives agreed that the $5,000 to $10,000 additional start-up cost estimate is reasonable at the high end. They noted that many new franchisees do not buy Yellow Pages ads during their first year in business, but add that during the second year. They suggest including $2,000 for initial newspaper advertising to bring in your first wave of consumer customers.

To obtain a total start-up cost estimate, add that $5,000 to $10,000 to the $24,500 payment for a total that ranges between $29,500 and $34,500.

The Market for Your Services

The market for this service continues to grow steadily, even with some limited competition in the industry. Rising prices for bathroom renovations and the consumers' and property managers' strong need to reduce costs make Perma Ceram a very attractive service to commercial customers.

Although limited, old house restoration also makes up a good market because people who restore old homes prefer to preserve the old, claw-footed porcelain tubs. You might offer your services to or through antique stores or yards that specialize in restoration materials.

You reach your markets by direct sales—cold calling, visiting contractors, and so on—by direct mail to residences through discount coupon mailing, with weekly shopper and daily newspaper advertising, and by Yellow Pages advertising under plumbing or bathroom furnishing listings. Most of your business will come from referrals and word of mouth, but you need to establish repeat business through commercial accounts as quickly as you can to reduce your selling time and your expenses.

Start-up Strategy

You can approach this franchise in one of several ways. First, like the vast majority, you can start part time, working on nights and weekends, until you establish the commercial business. You might involve a spouse at home as a telemarketing salesperson or office support staff to answer the phone, manage weekday job schedules for your contractors, and so on. Second, you could reverse the roles and go it alone full time while your spouse works full or part time to pay the household living expenses. Third, with enough cash on hand, you could go full time and hire contractors to do the work while you market your service to commercial accounts.

What people actually do depends on their comfort levels. Some prefer working as a manager, so they manage crews and market. Some prefer the hands-on approach and leave the sales calls to a spouse or salesperson. Much depends on how much money you have and the size of your financial cushion.

How Much Can You Make?

The dollars and cents of Perma Ceram are attractive if you play the right strategies. Simply put, aim for repeat customers and volume business, and hire independent contractors to offer all the services you can at prices half the cost of buying new bathroom fixtures or less. During 1993, existing Perma Ceram franchises were charging between $250 and $300 for a standard bathtub reglazing and $5 per square foot for regrouting, resealing, and resurfacing ceramic tile. An average bathroom has 80 square feet of tile for a cost of $400, and a total income equal to $650 to $700 per job. After your materials costs, payment to technicians, and overhead expenses, you should earn a net profit of between $250 and $300 per job.

Note that these prices have not changed since 1989, a significant effect of the recession and a significant damper on your gross income.

To earn a net income in the first year to equal your cash investment of about $34,500, you would need to do between 115 and 140 jobs, between 2 and 3 per week. If a two-person crew or an independent contractor and you can do 15 to 30 tubs per week, you can see how quickly your net profits could rise.

You obtain high-volume commercial accounts through a bidding process. Your prices would fall according to the number of tubs you had to resurface, but the volume work would double or triple your net profits. Thus, recouping your investment in the first year is practical, even if you work part time. If you follow the normal course and work part time during the first year and go full time during the second year, you should recoup your initial investment in 18 months and turn 100 percent or greater returns on investment (ROIs) as your business expands. After you establish numerous commercial accounts, you may increase your expenses somewhat by renting inexpensive office space and hiring part-time help. But your business cannot continue to expand unless you get the help you need to make your services available to more customers in all your markets.

Low Failure Rate

Perma Ceram also reports a modest failure rate of 5 to 6 percent per year, a relatively low rate in a blue-collar field. Company executives noted that the company has retained a solid core of franchisees, some for 15 years. Further, many franchises have sold to others while the owners have retired or moved on to new ventures. For example, company executives stated that one ten-year franchisee in New Jersey sold his substantial Perma Ceram business for $110,000, three to four times his original investment, to an existing customer. In sum, Perma Ceram represents an excellent opportunity to explore in the steadily growing and steadily profitable bathroom remodeling industry.

JAZZERCISE, INC.

Jazzercise, Inc.
2008 Roosevelt Street
Carlsbad, CA 92008
1-800-FIT-ISIT (348-4748)
(619) 434-2101

Jazzercise, Inc., continues to offer the single best opportunity to invest in a low-cost, high-return franchise. For total start-up costs of less than $2,500, you can earn net profit margins of 30 percent or more and an annual return on your investment of hundreds of percent, but you literally have to sweat for it as a Jazzercise dance and fitness instructor.

With 4,972 franchisees worldwide by late 1993, Jazzercise, Inc., is the leading dance fitness and exercise franchise by far. Since it began franchising in 1982, Jazzercise has been among the fastest growing, yet it has also maintained a quality reputation among its instructors-franchisees.

Simply put, franchisees offer exercise classes to anyone who wants to attend, but as an average franchisee, you do not establish storefront health clubs, spas, or fitness centers. Rather, you give hour-long "dance exercise" classes at community centers, church halls, school gymnasiums, or similar facilities that you rent at low cost per use or lease for small sums.

Jazzercise classes are aimed at a predominantly (95 percent or more) female audience who want to do aerobic/muscle-strengthening and toning workouts in the mornings, after work, or on weekends to keep their bodies trim and in shape. Jazzercise specifically avoids the heavy-duty workouts that other companies favor, although it has added to its offerings a wider variety of classes. They now range from light aerobics to "power" workouts (circuit and step) to lighter workouts for those unaccustomed to exercise and senior citizens. Regular Jazzercise classes tend to attract a broad group of people, ranging in age from their late teens to their sixties, with most "students," as they are called, in their late thirties and early forties.

You make money in two basic ways: You charge a per-class fee with a variety of discounts and special promotions, and you can earn income on the sale of Jazzercise items and clothing. You can also earn money with a third option: the "Know More Diet" weight management program.

How Much It Costs

Jazzercise continues to have among the lowest of all franchise fees: $650. Jazzercise encourages former instructors who dropped out to return by offering a very low $75 reinstatement fee to dropouts who return within 12 months and a half-price ($325) fee to those who return after more than one year. The company also refunds all of your fees if you fail the training process.

Your total start-up costs are minimal compared to most franchises, but you can expect to pay for the following:

- *Audiocassette player and microphone.* Jazzercise recommends vendors who sell audio equipment that meets its specifications. The company does not sell the equipment. It should range in cost from $1,000 to $1,300.
- *Videotape player.* To learn the choreography and dance routines, you must also have a VHS videocassette player, but you can use the one you already own. Buying a new videotape player ranges from $200 to $500 for appropriate models.
- *Routine packet.* You receive a free start-up package of videotapes and printed choreography sheets of exercise routines. Then, every two months, you must buy a new set of audiotapes to go with the free training videotape of new routines. You can expect these to cost $400 to $600 per year.
- *Apparel.* You should add $100 to $150 for athletic shoes, leotards, and exercise apparel. Again, you don't have to buy Jazzercise clothes, but the company's discounts probably mean better prices than those you could find elsewhere. And your clothes advertise your classes, so you would want to wear them during your classes and in informal situations.
- *Rental.* Jazzercise estimates that rent or lease of facilities from schools or community groups will average 25 to 30 percent of your total gross income, with the actual costs ranging from nothing (free space use) to 50 percent, or an average of $0 to $50 per class. The $100 to $500 estimate in the table that follows should cover one month's operating costs, but you will probably pay for this from your operating cash flow.
- *Business stationery.* You need to add $25 to $75 for business cards, stationery, accounting forms, and so on.
- *Training travel.* You need to add the costs of traveling to a weekend-long training workshop in your area. Jazzercise has salaried district managers in most states who give these training classes periodically. Most new instructors can travel to and from home to these classes, but if you must stay overnight, you have to pay all costs. Add $200 to $500 for a weekend stay.
- *Insurance.* You must buy liability insurance for minimum required coverage of $1 million for various types of personal,

employer, and professional liability insurance. This ranges in cost from $115 to $350 per year, depending on the insurance carrier. Jazzercise offers a low-cost insurance plan.

- *Raised platform.* If the facility you rent does not have a raised platform or stage, you will need to build or buy one. You, your spouse, or a friend may be able to build one for $50 in materials, or you may pay a carpenter to build one.
- *Performance royalties.* The performing artists' guilds (ASCAP and BMI) require you to pay annual royalties that range from $60 to $240 depending on the number of students you teach.
- *Facility build-out.* During the past three years, more than 300 Jazzercise centers have opened as full-fledged workout clubs with classes during most day and evening hours. If you wish to open a full-time workout center, you will need to lease space in a shopping center or light industrial-office area, pay for leasehold improvements, and add furnishings and fixtures appropriate for a workout facility. This ambitious step, of course, may add $10,000 to $30,000 to your costs.

Most new franchisees do not take this step, but those who want to build full-time businesses gradually work their way into a center, and use their profits and loans to open it.

Total start-up costs equal the amount shown in the table that follows:

	Minimum	Maximum
Franchise fee	$ 650	$ 650
Equipment	1,000	1,300
VCR	0	500
Routine tapes	80	100
Apparel	50	150
Rentals	100	500
Insurance	100	350
Travel	0	500
Business stationery	25	75
Platform	0	100
Total	$2,005	$4,225

Ongoing Fees and Expenses

Your ongoing expenses will be relatively low, too, and will include the following items:

- A royalty of 20 percent of all enrollment fees received from adult students and 10 percent of all enrollment fees received from children's programs and "Know More Diet" classes. Jazzercise has also instituted a new minimum continuing fee of $100 per month.
- As noted earlier, you also must pay $65 to $100 about every two months for new audiotapes and $60 to $240 per year for performance royalties for the right to use the songs.
- You can also expect to pay about $1,000 to $2,000 per year for advertising and promotional materials, including flyers, brochures, handouts, and so on to help you build traffic.
- Optional exercise apparel, books, and so on that you buy at a discount from the company.
- Auto and gas expenses to commute to and from your class facilities.
- A fee of $175 to become certified to teach the optional "Know More Diet" weight management program. By late 1993, some 600 Jazzercise instructors had trained to offer the "Know More Diet" program and materials to their students.

Changes in Jazzercise

Since the first edition was published in 1990, Jazzercise has made few significant changes. The company began the "Know More Diet" weight management program, emphasized classes for senior citizens and children, developed alternate class formats, such as step and circuit, and expanded very rapidly throughout the world. By late 1993, Jazzercise had more than 600 international franchisees, most often women either in the military or married to members of the Armed Forces who had been transferred from the United States to foreign posts.

The Know More Diet program can add significant profits because the price of the books and training to the student can range from as low as $25 to as high as $100 with profit margins greater than 50 percent.

More importantly, Jazzercise changed its district manager structure. In the past, they were active franchisees who bought a large territory to oversee on Jazzercise's behalf. Now, however, all district managers and regional administrators are salaried company employees more directly accountable to the corporate executives. The district managers train new franchisees, maintain quality control, help set up and manage special events, and arrange district advertising and promotions.

Among the franchisees themselves, the most significant change has been the growth of full-time centers with serious owners who may gross $100,000 or more per year. By the end of 1993, some 20 percent of all instructors were working full time whether they had established centers or not. Jazzercise executives, however, noted the company does not push its franchisees in either direction; you can do a few classes per week to earn a part-time income or you can build a center with classes of 100 people per hour all day long.

Terminations and Litigation

Considering its size and the volatility of part-time franchisees, Jazzercise reported a very low failure/termination rate of 2.4 percent per year. During 1992, for example, Jazzercise had 797 new or reinstated franchisees, 120 terminations, and 359 resignations, for net growth of 318 franchisees, or 7 percent more than the previous year.

Company executives reported that the 120 terminations occurred for nonpayment of royalties and fees, failure to purchase required insurance coverage, and failure to meet quality standards. Of the 359 resignations, 58 percent occurred for personal reasons (work, school, and relocations), 19 percent for unspecified financial reasons, 9 percent for medical reasons, 3 percent for "burnout," and 11 percent for unknown reasons.

In terms of lawsuits, the Jazzercise UFOC reported only three lawsuits since 1990, a very small number for a company with almost 5,000 franchisees.

How Much Can You Make

Now the good news. On his or her initial investment, a Jazzercise franchisee can earn a net return of 800 percent during the first year. Here's how it works. You charge a per-class fee to each student, which ranges from $1 to $5 per class, with a $3 median. You also offer special discounts, such as $50 to $60 for two months of unlimited classes. These discounts reduce your per-student average gross income, but they sharply improve your cash flow and increase your class size. And the larger the class, the more attractive people find it.

The average class size equals about 30; it can range from a handful to 100 or more, depending on your facility size. On average, that means each class brings in $90. Of this, you pay Jazzercise $18, and the rent should cost about $30. This leaves you with a gross profit of $42. Your pretax net profit margin after all expenses should be 80 percent of your gross profit, or $33.60 for one hour's work!

If you hold 10 classes a week, or 2 one-hour classes five days a week, you can earn a net profit of $336 per week, or $16,800 for a 50-week year with a week off around Christmas and another week during the summer.

Even better, you can arrange your Jazzercise schedule to fit your life-style and to match the income level you want to earn. You can offer more discounts, offer more classes, charge higher prices, do promotions, participate in special events, and so on to help boost your visibility, increase your class size, and add to your income.

In short, if you are an intelligent, fitness-minded person, and if you want to build a superior part-time or, in some cases, full-time business and earn what may be the highest net ROI in franchising, you should seriously consider becoming a Jazzercise instructor.

WorkEnders

WorkEnders
P.O. Box 810455
Boca Raton, FL 33481-0455
(800) 634-1717

WorkEnders is a very rapidly growing new franchise that has combined the talents of a nationally known owner of and writer about cleaning services and the founder of the very successful Tidy Car franchise that Ziebart (Tidy Car) bought in the late 1980s. Operations Vice President Jeff Campbell has written three very popular books about house cleaning that have sold more than 1 million copies. And for more than 15 years, he has owned a cleaning service in San Francisco that now does 15,000 house cleanings a year. President and CEO Gary Goranson is the very-well-known and respected founder of Tidy Car; he grew Tidy Car to almost 1,000 franchises in eight years. Goranson and Campbell founded WorkEnders in 1991 and, by the end of 1993, had sold more than 80 franchises in three countries with very ambitious plans to sell 2,000 by the year 2000.

In fact, they could reach their goal because WorkEnders is a very-low-cost franchise with a basic franchise fee of $1,500 and a territory fee that brings the total fee to between $3,000 and $9,000, much lower than any similar home cleaning franchise.

WorkEnders "works" through what it calls its FasTrack System based on three-person cleaning teams and a method that trains the team to clean the average three-bedroom house in under an hour and a small apartment in 20 minutes. Thus, in a six-hour day—and earning wages through an incentive commission plan—the team should clean five to six houses a day at an average price of $62 each, somewhat higher than the national average for all franchised cleaning services. The FasTrack system also emphasizes recruiting and retaining quality cleaning people, managing your own goals and your business, and depending on the company's support team.

WorkEnders functions in principle like every other cleaning franchise. You market your service, recruit and train cleaning teams, keep your overhead low, manage the business, and expand the number of teams you put in the field. You seek your customers among dual-income and single-parent households with adults between 25 and 55 years old with household incomes above $35,000. But it has significant differences that relate to its franchise fee and total cash investment.

How Much It Costs

The base franchise fee equals $1,500, but you must pay 30 cents for each "qualified household," defined as a residential domain, including apartments and condos, with household incomes above $35,000. Each territory must consist of one or more zip codes, and the company assigns only complete zip codes or multiple zip codes, not partial areas of any kind. So, the franchise fee may vary from $3,000 to $9,000, depending on the number of qualified households in each zip code.

The company noted in its UFOC that you need at least 2,500 qualified households to make a profit from one team, so you should plan to license a territory with at least 10,000 households so you can grow into it; most territories range from 7,000 to 15,000 households.

You must also buy an initial equipment and supply package; WorkEnders gives you three choices, two of which you can partially finance: (1) $993 base package, (2) $2,399, and (3) $4,388. You can finance $1,000 of the second package and $2,000 of the third at 12 percent interest for 12 months.

You also pay a low 4 percent weekly royalty and a 2 percent weekly marketing fee, the latter for a national advertising campaign, probably beginning in late 1994, to directly benefit the franchisees; if your weekly sales fall below $500, you have to pay a minimum $20-per-week royalty. The marketing fee is controlled by the company. The table estimates total start-up costs:

Category	Low End	High End
Franchise fee	$ 1,500	$ 1,500
Territory fee	1,500	7,500
Equipment package	993	4,388
Training travel	0	500
Insurance (a)	500	3,000
Initial advertising (b)	1,500	5,000
Business phone deposit	200	400
Office supplies (c)	325	550
Professional fees/licenses	150	600
Working capital (90 days)(d)	1,500	4,000
Total	$ 8,168	$27,438

a. Business liability insurance, required honesty bonding, workers' compensation, and so on.

b. Doorhangers, coupon advertisements, direct mail, pennysavers, and so on to generate your first wave of customers.

c. Stationery, business cards, any office equipment, and supplies.

d. Three months' of business operating expenses. This assumes that a spouse or partner brings in enough income to pay for living expenses.

Goranson explained that most franchisees spend $15,000 or less to begin and that most begin part time on weekends and evenings, so they do not need to include living expenses in their start-up cost estimate.

What You Get

- *Exclusive territory.* As noted, you receive complete zip codes with as many qualified households for which you want to pay 30 cents each up to 25,000 or so.
- *Training.* WorkEnders does *not* require any training, but it does offer free two-day, weekend training programs, called the FasTrack Weekend, for those who want to take the course. Goranson said that the most successful franchisee, one in Alaska who can charge $82 per cleaning, one-third more than average, never attended the course, so you can make it without the training. But the company does encourage you to attend either that weekend or regional training seminars.

WorkEnders does provide training videos and manuals that teach you how to clean houses, recruit employees, and manage and market the business. The company holds its FasTrack Weekend training programs on a bimonthly basis.

- *Staff support*. Without much formal training, you may need more staff support. Goranson noted that the director of member services is a former cleaning service franchisee and the director stays in constant phone contact with WorkEnders franchisees. The company also publishes a very upbeat monthly newsletter that discusses key business-building topics and promotes a "positive mental attitude" among franchisees.

- *Communication*. In addition to the support newsletter, the company uses formal questionnaires to improve its program and materials. Goranson also encourages franchisees to network and to give feedback to him and other executives. The company formed a duly elected advisory council at its first annual convention in November 1993. It consists of a president, vice president, secretary, and two at-large members.

Perhaps more important is the very positive, motivational tone that everyone in the company expresses. WorkEnders' literature seeks to motivate the franchisees and prospects to believe not only in the system, but also in themselves and their ability to succeed. Its executives say that they strongly believe that their inexpensive approach to the cleaning service industry broadens the opportunity for thousands of people who otherwise could not afford to risk this venture. In short, they preach the gospel according to WorkEnders and encourage their franchisees to follow it on their roads to success.

While this persuasive approach does keep franchisees "pumped up" about the system, it seems that the low-cost approach with little formal training could encourage too many unqualified and unprepared prospects to license this system. In my view, WorkEnders has a responsibility to screen prospects carefully so the "dreamers" with little chance of success do not enter the system and fail. I do believe that Goranson is doing this and that WorkEnders has the resources to support its rapidly growing franchisee family.

Managing that growth well also forms an essential concern for this and any other rapidly growing franchise. Goranson has done it before, but after Ziebart bought Tidy Car, originally a low-cost franchise, the vast majority of Tidy Car franchisees dropped out of the system. Ziebart turned from a low-cost approach to an expensive approach that combined Tidy Car auto detailing with its far different auto protection services, such as rustproofing, security alarms, and so on. If Goranson is building WorkEnders for the long haul, I believe that his franchisees will do well; I am concerned that Goranson will build WorkEnders to 1,000 or more franchisees and sell the company. That has happened before, too. Goranson insists that indeed he is building WorkEnders for a long-term success, but prospects should question Goranson on his commitment.

How Much Can You Make?

With WorkEnders, how much you make truly depends on your commitment to the effort. Workenders discourages part-time owners and requires absentee owners to have enough capital so they can afford to hire a qualified manager, preferably a "partner," as Goranson put it, to manage the business. Working full time, you can grow rapidly, adding teams to a relatively large territory, and make an upper five-figure net income in two or three years.

Goranson suggested that you start as the team leader for your own three-person team to learn how the business works. You could also work with a spouse or relatives to keep recruiting costs down and develop the territory. Although the mix of weekly and biweekly clients varies from franchisee to franchisee, you need 40 to 70 clients for any given team to fill its weekly work schedule.

Goranson said that you generate this first batch of clients with inexpensive doorhangers that you hand out on weekends or afternoons, use direct mail advertising, and give incentives (a small finder's fee) to team members to hand out brochures in the neighborhoods where they clean their first set of houses.

When you advertise at first, you can expect your initial "client acquisition cost" to range from $50 to $100 each, or a total of $2,500 to $5,000 for your first team to build its client base to maturity.

To increase your profits, you keep your overhead low by working from home. Goranson noted that you do not need uniforms, rented office space, or specially painted cars to build this business; you merely need to offer high-quality service to satisfied customers. Then, the power of word-of-mouth advertising and referrals begins to attract new customers.

You must pay slightly higher wages to attract and keep quality cleaners (note that WorkEnders does *not* use the term "maids)," so you spend more than average—about 50 percent of gross revenues for all payroll costs, including workers' compensation, social security, and state and federal unemployment taxes. But you contain other costs.

So, within 6 to 12 months, you should have about 60 regular customers paying on average $62 per cleaning. Depending on whether the franchisee uses a two- or three-person team and depending on how well the teams have been trained in efficient cleaning methods, one team can earn gross revenues between $1,000 and $2,000 per week. If half your clients use your service every week and half every other week, then your gross income would total about $5,580 per month, or about $66,000 per year. After expenses, labor, and overhead, you could expect to net about $15,000 to $25,000, perhaps somewhat more if you work on the team full time.

Goranson noted that the length of time it will take you to develop a given team to "client maturity" depends on the amount of advertising that the franchisee is willing (or able) to invest in a given time. For example, he added, if it costs $4,000 to develop enough clients to fill one team's schedule, then the time required to build that team's client base depends on the time during which you invest the money in ads. If you stretch it out over a year, you might take up to a year to develop one team's client base; however, if you invest during the first 90 days, that team should reach maturity within three months.

In an example of rapid growth, the Gulfport, Mississippi, franchisee built three teams and more than 150 customers in just three months—before he attended the FasTrack training session.

You can see the virtue of adding new teams and investing early profits back into the business because each team should return to you $20,000 or more net profit each year after the first two to three years.

But adding new teams and territory costs money—about $900 to $1,500 for equipment and supplies and $2,500 to $5,000 more to advertise and market to your prospective customers and recruit new team members. Goranson added that marketing becomes easier when Yellow Pages ads are published and referrals begin.

Over and above your income from cleaning regular clients' homes, you can generate additional revenues from first-time cleanings, spring cleanings, window cleaning, and assignments such as cleaning ovens, refrigerators, patios, and other special requests.

Goranson said that if you follow the guidelines, build an efficient team, stabilize your employees, and keep your overhead low, you will begin to turn a profit on your initial investment in 6 to 12 months. From the average initial investment of $10,000 to $15,000, you could realize ROIs in the hundreds of percent per year within three years.

So far, the success rate of WorkEnders' first wave of franchisees has remained high. Goranson said that only 5 of the first 80 franchisees—the latest numbers from late 1993—had used the mutual termination clause. He insisted that he was not in this industry to "churn" territories to bring in franchise fees. He asserted that his commitment is to help people with relatively few resources own their own business and achieve the success that they want. Given his background, Goranson is certainly capable of doing just that.

HEEL QUIK! INC.

Heel Quik! Inc.
6425 Powers Ferry Road
Suite 250
Atlanta, GA 30339
(800) 255-8145
(404) 951-9440

Heel Quik! and its sister franchise, Heel/Sew Quik!, offer six types of shoe repair and accessories franchises with franchise fees ranging from as low as $2,500 to $17,500. The standard Heel Quik! shoe repair and accessory store in a regional mall has a franchise fee equal to $15,500, so the company is included in this chapter. Here are capsule summaries of each type:

Franchise Type	Franchise Fee	Start-up Costs
Pick-up route	$ 2,500	$10,000–19,000
Conversion	$2,500–$5,000	6,000–10,000
Mini walk-by	12,500	32,000–46,500
Strip center store	15,500	63,500–84,500
Standard mall store	15,500	73,500–103,500
Heel/Sew Quik! store	17,500	71,500–127,500

- *Pick-up route* In this very-low-cost effort, you use a van to pick up and deliver dry cleaning, shoes to be repaired, and clothing for alteration. It could become the basis for a part- time or very low-cost start-up.
- *Heel Quik! conversion.* This allows existing shoe repair store owners to convert their shops to a more professional brand name. The start-up costs pay mostly for signage and inventory. The company also offers a $5,000 conversion fee for dry cleaners.
- *Heel Quik! minifranchise.* You place this small, walk-by location near the entrance to a major supermarket, a discount department store, or a mall for quick drop-off and pick-up service, and you only offer shoe repairs and accessories.
- *Strip center.* This is a complete store in a shopping center.
- *Standard mall location.* This location offers shoe repair, shoe shines, accessories, umbrellas, and similar products.
- *Heel/Sew Quik!* This high-end franchise offers monogramming, gift wrapping, key making, and other low-cost, high-profit services that people traditionally associate with shoe repairs.

I chose Heel Quik! because it was an international success before it ever arrived in the United States. By the end of 1993, it had 134 U.S. franchisees with a total of 336 open franchised or affiliated stores in the United Kingdom, Japan, Argentina, and Brazil with commitments to open 600 more stores during the next three years. It was opening 5 to 10 new stores a month in the United States in early 1994 and planned to increase that pace as the economy improved.

President Ray Margiano said that his growth goals include up to 1,600 stores in the United States, 400 in the United Kingdom, 600 in Japan, 200 in Argentina, and 300 in Brazil within five years. With the global recession, a ten-year buildup may be more reasonable.

With these aggressive growth plans, Heel Quik! offers another significant advantage: It has the exclusive right to distribute the repair machinery, so it can sell the equipment to its franchisees $15,000 cheaper than any other competitive line you can buy. You save up to 30 percent of the costs of a different shoe repair franchise.

Even more significantly, two out of three new franchisees open a second store within their first year, so you can grow and build your ROI rapidly.

Furthermore, the market for shoe repairs continues to consolidate in favor of chains and franchises. From a high of some 65,000 shoe repair shops during the 1950s, the number has dropped to between 12,000 and 16,000. As the Mom and Pop shops die out, the market is turning to more professional shops either in regional shopping malls or major strip centers. Some portion is also going to drop-off services in dry cleaning stores.

Finally, the company has been highly rated by leading magazines, including the best in its category since 1986 in one major list, two years among the top 100 franchises in a different rating, and a listing in a women's business magazine as the top service for women.

How Much It Costs

I will not divide the start-up costs for each franchise, but I will add the various royalty amounts or percentages:

Pick-up/delivery	$100 per month
Conversion	$100 per month
Mini Quik!	4% of gross revenues
Heel Quik!	4% of gross revenues
Heel/Sew Quik!	4% of gross revenues

You must also contribute 2 percent to a national advertising fund. Among your start-up costs, you must spend a total of at least $1,000 for advertising and promotion for your grand opening and during your first two months in business. Thereafter, you must spend at least 2 percent on local advertising efforts, primarily for direct mail coupons and similar traffic-building methods.

What You Get

In return, you receive the following program benefits:

- *Exclusive territory.* The fixed store locations receive these territories:

  Malls. A minimum of 30,000 population, plus a geographic density based on demographics.

  Ministores. Located in food stores and discount department stores, these are stores with at least 20,000 customers per week but no geographic territory.

  Mobile service. No territory, but you can offer your service in the same cities where other Heel Quik! stores operate.

- *Training.* You receive two weeks of training at its Atlanta headquarters and one week of training at your store. You also receive training videos, an operations manual, four regional training seminars per year, and free extra training time if you need it.

- *Preopening assistance.* You receive all site evaluation and selection and lease negotiation. Margiano asserted that the company could negotiate a better lease on your behalf than you could on your own; if you have never negotiated a commercial real estate lease, know that most are complex documents with more twists and turns than a labyrinth, and any free help you can get will help you. However, you sign the lease and remain responsible for it, so be sure to have your own attorney review it. You also receive construction plans.

- *Marketing support.* You receive Yellow Pages layouts, newspaper advertising mattes, radio scripts, billboard copy, flyers to hand out in malls, direct mail copy, and in some cases, cable TV ads.

  Your marketing plan seeks to build repeat business because at first, 80 percent of your customers are walk-ins. Males use your services every 8 to 12 weeks and women even more often, every

6 to 8 weeks, so encouraging them to return will mean that they use your services five to nine times a year.

The mini–Heel Quik! stores in grocery and discount stores and the standard stores in malls also "piggyback" or do co-op advertising with the other stores.

- *Ongoing support.* You receive field visits every four to six weeks at first and then quarterly as you progress. The company holds 20 area meetings a year, publishes a monthly newsletter, and has a six-person franchisee advisory council to represent your interests. Most important, it has a support team of current franchisees, regional distribution centers, and very knowledgeable area reps, according to Margiano. He said that these area reps, often former franchisees, offer highly credible support.

How Much Can You Make?

Each type of Heel Quik! store generates its own type of profit margins. For example, the pick-up route operation works like a regular service; you work two or three times a week going house to house and covering an efficient route. You can earn an excellent part-time income because you charge your customers retail prices, plus slightly more, but pay the service providers—a local Heel Quik! store, a dry cleaner, and so on—a wholesale price. Your gross profit is the difference. For example, for $10 worth of dry cleaning and a $40 shoe repair, you should gross about 40 percent, or $20. With several hundred regular customers, you can easily recoup your investment in a few months, and depending on your van expenses, you can net $10,000 to $20,000 per year and double your investment.

On the other hand, regular stores and Heel/Sew Quik! locations generate gross revenues in the thousands of dollars a week. Margiano said that the two best foreign stores grossed $5,000 and $4,300 per week.

The company publishes thorough projected pro formas, but does not make earnings claims. (See the three pro forma statements provided here.) They estimate net profits before debt payments and taxes for standard Heel Quik!, Mini Quik!, and

Heel/Sew Quik! stores with incomes ranging from $3,000 to $6,000 per week in most cases. The net profits range from about $39,000 to $98,800. Note that you may be able to do as well with a Mini Quik! as you can with a standard store because you have fewer start-up and operating expenses. However, the kicker in the Mini Quik! is labor; you must act as an owner-operator and do the repairs to earn those returns. If you hire a repair worker, you should use a labor factor equal to 25 percent of your gross revenues; this sharply reduces your net profits.

In conclusion, a Heel Quik! franchise can break even in a few months and recoup your investment within one year to 18 months. If you provide most of the labor for the Mini Quik! and standard franchises, you can accelerate the return. If you open a Heel/Sew Quik!, you may drag out your payback, but you generate significantly higher gross profits in the long term because so few competitors offer the additional services. Of the several important shoe repair franchises that have sprung up during the past five years, Heel Quik! gives you the widest variety of low- cost franchises and the best opportunity to find one that fits your pocketbook and your entrepreneurial urge.

HEEL QUIK!® PRO FORMA
(Projected)*

	Variable Costs	Dollar Costs On			
		$312,000 Annual Sales ($6,000 per week)	$260,000 Annual Sales ($5,000 per week)	$208,000 Annual Sales ($4,000 per week)	$156,000 Annual Sales ($3,000 per week)
Material	20%	$ 62,400	$ 52,000	$ 41,600	$ 31,200
Labor	25	78,000	65,000	52,000	39,000
Social security and unemployment (17% of labor)	4	12,480	10,400	8,320	6,240
Rent	10	31,200	26,000	20,800	15,600
Utilities and insurance	2	6,240	5,200	4,160	3,120
Advertising	4	12,480	10,400	8,320	6,240
Miscellaneous	2	6,240	5,200	4,160	3,120
Franchise royalty fee	4	12,480	10,400	8,320	6,240
Total Operating Cost		$221,520	$184,600	$147,680	$110,760
Gross sales		$312,000	$260,000	$208,000	$156,000
Net profit (before debt service and taxes)		$ 90,480	$ 75,400	$ 60,320	$ 45,240

*(Based on actual sales and cost averages.)

Total Investment Cost:
Strip Center: From $63,500 to $84,500
Mall: From $73,500 to $103,500

Up-Front Cash Requirements:
$15,000–30,000
$20,000–40,000

MICRO/MINI QUIK!® PRO FORMA
(Projected)*

	Variable Costs	Dollar Costs On		
		$130,000 Annual Sales ($2,500 per week)	$104,000 Annual Sales ($2,000 per week)	$78,000 Annual Sales ($1,500 per week)
Material	14%	$ 18,200	$ 14,560	$10,920
Rent	10	13,000	10,400	7,800
Insurance	2	2,600	2,080	1,560
Advertising	4	5,200	4,160	3,120
Miscellaneous	2	2,600	2,080	1,560
Franchise royalty fee	4	5,580	4,160	3,120
Equipment lease (5 years) ($465 per month est.)		5,580	5,580	5,580
Total operating cost		$ 52,380	$ 43,020	$33,660
Gross sales		$130,000	$104,000	$78,000
Net profit (before taxes)		$ 77,620	$ 60,980	$44,340

*Based on owner-operator plan. No labor factor is reflected in these figures. If labor other than that of owner-operator is involved in operation, a 25 percent labor factor should be used.

Total Investment Cost:
From $32,000 to $46,500

HEEL/SEW QUIK!® PRO FORMA
(Projected)*

	Heel Quik!®		Sew Quik		Dollar Cost Totals
	Variable Costs	$208,000 Annual Sales ($4,000 per week)	Variable Costs	$104,000 Annual Sales ($2,000 per week)	$312,000 Annual Sales ($6,000 per week)
Material	20%	$ 41,600	4%	$ 4,160	
Labor	25	52,000	35	36,400	
Social security and unemployment (17% of labor)		8,320		4,160	
Rent	10	20,800	8	8,320	
Utilities and insurance	2	4,160	4		
Advertising	4	8,320	4	4,160	
Miscellaneous	2	4,160	4	4,160	
Franchise royalty fee	4	8,320	4	4,160	
Total operating cost		$147,680		$ 65,520	$213,200
Gross sales		$208,000		$104,000	$312,000
Net profit (before debt service and taxes)		$ 60,320		$ 38,480	$ 98,800

*(Based on actual sales and cost averages.)

Up-Front Cash Requirements:
$20,000–30,000
$25,000–40,000

Total Investment Cost:
Strip Center: From $71,500 to $92,500
Mall: From $82,500 to $136,500

87

BATHCREST® PORCELAIN RESURFACING

Bathcrest, Inc.®
2425 S. Progress Drive
Salt Lake City, UT 84119
(800) 826-6790
(801) 972-1110

Bathcrest, Inc.,® is one of the largest porcelain refinishing franchises in the United States, with more than 180 franchises by the end of 1993. It offers a very advantageous approach for the prospective franchisee in this relatively low-cost, relatively lucrative, but highly competitive industry. As a company executive noted, some 20 franchises have tried to penetrate this market since the late 1980s, and only a handful have survived. Bathcrest is among the strongest of those survivors because it manufactures its own product line and it treats its franchisees well.

Bathcrest offers these advantages:

- No royalty payment, just a $1,200 annual renewal fee.
- No payment, besides a small deposit, until the end of the second day of training.
- Proprietary product line that it continues to develop.
- New methods with which you can cut your product costs.
- Reduced product costs. During 1993, it actually reduced its product price to its franchisees by several percentage points.

Bathcrest works so well because the company pays very close attention to its own cost. It has remodeled its 10,000-square-foot manufacturing facility, the design of which has allowed it to reduce its costs, yet hire new employees despite the recession. In fact, company executives stated that during the recession, the company became busier and busier with record sales of product to its franchisees.

The company's effort is based on its Glazecote® synthetic porcelain finish that chemically bonds to the original surface. The company gives a full five-year warranty, the industry leader. It has also introduced two very successful new product lines that add to profit margins: (1) whirlpool conversions of any kind of normal bathtub, including cast iron, porcelain steel, and fiberglass, and (2) acrylic repairs for hot tubs and spas.

How Much It Costs

You must pay Bathcrest $24,500, but unlike almost all other franchises, that includes all the costs of training travel—airfare, hotel, and meals—for one person. And the franchise fee equals only $3,500, although the company does split off the training fee of $2,500 and other costs that many other franchises include in their fee. Bathcrest stated in its UFOC these divisions:

Category	Amount
Franchise fee	$ 3,500
Material, equipment, supplies	7,845
Commission, company expenses	4,200
Training	2,500
Franchise procurement	2,300
Printing, banner, signs	1,645
Airfare, meals, hotel	1,100
Legal fees	990
Handbook, sales aids, materials	420
Total	$24,500

Additional Start-up Costs

In addition, Bathcrest estimates your start-up costs to range from $2,650 to $9,000. Both the company and I advise you to start this business from your home with your existing vehicle to reduce your start-up expenses to a bare minimum. You do not need either warehouse space or a van. The following table combines Bathcrest's and my own estimates of start-up costs to give you a clear picture of the situation:

Category	Low End	High End
Bathcrest payment	$24,500	$24,500
Vehicle	0	2,000 (a)
Operating expenses	500	5,000 (b)
Rental space	0	800 (c)
Furniture	100	1,000 (d)
Insurance	300	500
Licenses	50	200
Legal, accounting fees	100	500 (e)
Personal travel expenses	100	250 (f)
Miscellaneous	100	500
Total	$25,750	$35,250

a. Range for down payment on new van/truck purchase or using your own car.
b. Covers everything from living expenses for three months to business phone deposits, to utility deposits if you own an office.
c. Up to two months' rent on warehouse space.
d. Cost of office furniture for home office or warehouse location.
e. Payments for professionals to review the franchise documents.
f. Bathcrest covers airfare, hotel, and meals; these are for personal expenses.

Other Required Payments

Although Bathcrest does not charge either a royalty or an advertising fee, it does charge a $1,200 annual renewal fee for the first three years of the agreement. After that, although it has not done so in some time, Bathcrest reserves the right to increase the renewal fee no more than 10 percent per year.

Of course, as a product franchise, Bathcrest makes most of its income and profits by selling you refinishing chemicals, materials, equipment, and supplies. You must buy from Bathcrest, the sole supplier, its six proprietary chemicals, including filler, reducer, and etching compounds.

After your first six months in business, you must buy three quarts of Glazecote™ per week averaged during a three-month period. The company gives you that six-month grace period to use the initial inventory that you buy as part of the package. This represents a two-quart-per-week reduction since 1990, a benefit to you. However, company executives stated that they do not worry about this because their franchisees are vastly exceeding these minimums and do not need to enforce these quotas. Technically, the company can cancel the agreement if you do not meet the quotas. You must spend about $150 to $200 a week for this material.

The company estimates that these required purchases will make up about half of your total material and supplies purchases. In turn, the company earns a 30 percent gross profit on these materials; it also receives payments from the suppliers of auxiliary product lines that you buy through Bathcrest. These are the only payments you make to the company, a reasonable arrangement for this industry.

What You Get

Bathcrest offers one unusual incentive: After you pay a small deposit, you do not pay the remainder of the $24,500 until the end of the second day of training. Company executives insisted that if either you or they find that you are not fit for this business, they would rather give you your money back than have someone who is going to fail buy their franchise and damage their reputation. If you do not want to continue, you get your deposit check back and leave. Or, on occasion, the company will find that a trainee does not have the physical skills or personal temperament to succeed and will ask him or her to leave.

I endorse this approach for several reasons. First, new franchisees too often get caught up in the "glow" of buying a franchise and ignore the hard reality of running a business until it may be too late. Second, overeager—or cash-strapped—franchisors often take checks for tens of thousands of dollars without properly qualifying or caring to qualify a franchise prospect. They take the money without considering whether the person has the skills, know-how, or temperament to succeed in that business. Third, although the FTC rules force a ten-day cooling-off period between the day you receive the UFOC and the day you sign a contract, most franchise buyers remain eager to sign the contract and get started; the FTC rules do *not* give you a cooling-off period *after* you sign the contract. And most franchise agreements state very clearly that the franchise fee, once paid, is nonrefundable.

Fourth, for many new franchisees, the trip to headquarters is their first contact with actual company personnel with whom they must work every day. You may be sold by a franchise broker in your own town. You may attend a "discovery day" with the company's executives and salespeople, but not their operations people. In short, you may have little or no contact with the company's real culture, so sometimes, you decide you don't like the company, its people, or its culture. Yet, after you hand over your check, you may find yourself stuck with a franchise you don't really want or are not truly prepared to operate or make a success.

Last, the training session reveals very quickly the work you must do to succeed. Porcelain refinishing can be a messy, unpleasant job, although it does not take much strength. It takes someone with physical and technical skill to do it well. If you are a "klutz," you are unlikely to succeed with this type of franchise. Of course, you can always manage the business and hire a skilled technician or include a technically-inclined family member.

TAKEOUT TAXI FRANCHISING SYSTEMS, INC.

Takeout Taxi Franchising Systems, Inc.
1175 Herndon Parkway
Suite 150
Herndon, VA 22070
(703) 435-0882

One of the most rapidly growing markets in the food industry during the early 1990s was home delivery. Pioneered by the pizza chains, home food delivery first exploded into delivery of every different kind of food, but then exploded into a new service: a service that would deliver *any* kind of food from local restaurants. It meant that overworked two-income couples with children no longer had to feed their children take-out or delivered pizza several nights a week, and overworked singles and couples with no kids no longer had to settle for "mush in the microwave" meals. With a delivery service that brought "real" hot food from "real" restaurants, they could eat restaurant food at home and enjoy a variety of meals at a reasonable price.

To serve this growing demand, many Mom and Pop shops and several franchises popped up, but in my opinion, only one franchise has the executive leadership, financial resources, and business acumen to lead this market: Takeout Taxi.

Takeout Taxi helps ease a growing modern problem: "time famine," as Chairman Kevin Abt calls it. With more and harder working hours, more driving time, and less leisure time, few people have enough time to relax, much less cook, so they turn to home delivery services to bring quality meals at reasonable prices to their homes.

Abt added that, to his surprise, the "time famine" crosses all boundaries. He said that Takeout Taxi franchises in blue-collar areas are doing the same volume of calls as those in white collar, more affluent areas.

Furthermore, adults especially are sick of pizza. Only 8 percent of the company's total volume is pizza; 42 percent is standard American food from burgers to salads to chicken. Undoubtedly, Abt and his executives have hit a very resonant chord in the stressed-out, too-busy American psyche.

Founded by several frustrated corporate managers, Takeout Taxi is the largest franchise in this industry with more than 70 operational franchises in 23 states, Canada, and the District of Columbia by the end of 1993. And it has a very low start-up fee of $25,000.

Here's how it works: You pay a $5,000 franchise fee and $5,000 for a "marketing cell." Each basic territory has at least two cells, for a total cell fee of $10,000. The cells are based on at least 30,000 to 50,000 households within zip codes.

With your first two cells in place, you use Takeout Taxi's very sophisticated delivery scheduling systems to plan efficient and effective routes. The company trains you to apply your own marketing and sales skills and the company's very interesting incentive programs to persuade restaurants to use your services. And you use the company's sophisticated direct mail and marketing methods to send menu-laden brochures to your customers in their homes.

You earn revenue in several interesting ways: First, you pay the restaurants below-retail prices for their food, but charge the regular price to your delivery customers. The restaurants are willing to do that because you bring them incremental sales, keeping their cooks busy, but they do not need more wait staff to accommodate the increased business; thus, they save money. Second, you charge the customer an average $3 delivery fee. But—here's where it gets interesting—you also sell direct marketing services and customer incentive programs to the restaurants. The latter dramatically adds to your profits, said Abt. In fact, Abt insisted that Takeout Taxi is only a vehicle for more sophisticated, proprietary ways to sell marketing services to restaurants and others. He said, "We are a marketing company that delivers."So, the profit potential only begins with the delivery service.

By late 1993, said Abt, about 200 of the more than 1,000 cells available had been purchased, so ample opportunity still exists to profit from this market boom.

How Much It Costs

As I noted, the franchise fee is only $5,000, but you must add $10,000 to $20,000 for fees to acquire two to four cells and pay a $10,000 training fee. The company's estimated total start-up costs range from $71,650 to $91,050, as the table shows, but I added costs for training travel and additional cell fees at the high end:

Category	Low End	High End
Franchise fee	$ 5,000	$ 5,000
Cell fees	10,000	10,000
Training fee	10,000	10,000
Computer system	3,500	5,000
Signage	2,000	2,500
Rent deposits	750	1,000
Utility deposits	1,000	1,500
Training travel	500	1,500
Insurance	2,000	5,000

Radios	5,000	5,000
Office equipment	300	750
Grand opening advertising	15,000	15,000
Uniforms	500	1,000
Menus	9,000	9,000
Food bags	500	1,000
Misc. preopening costs	600	1,300
Working capital	5,000	15,000
Total	$72,050	$89,550

These costs include start-up costs for an office serving two cells with two computers and a number of delivery drivers and enough funds to launch a significant advertising campaign and carry you through the first several months in business.

Royalty and Other Fees

You pay a 4 percent royalty on gross revenues and, if the company sets up a national marketing fund, a 2 percent ad fee. You must also spend at least 3 percent of your gross revenues on advertising during your first two years and 2 percent per year thereafter. At present, the company does not have a national ad fund. At some point, you could also be required to contribute up to 1 percent of gross revenues into a regional cooperative ad fund, but none of those exists at this point.

What You Get

In return for your payments, you receive the best system in the home delivery market. You also receive these benefits:

- *Territory.* As described, at least two cells with 30,000 to 50,000 households each. Make sure that your cells have a significant number of two-income couples with and without children (demographic "dinks" or dual-income/no-kids couples) *and*, as important, numerous popular local restaurants and national chains. The key to a successful delivery service is offering a variety of American and ethnic foods that will "travel well," that is, stay in good condition while they are being delivered.

- *Term.* The agreement lasts for 10 years and can be renewed for additional five-year terms for a very low $1,000 payment.
- *Training.* You and up to two employees receive three stages of training, including five days of training at headquarters, up to five days of on-site assistance after training when company reps work with you in the field to help you sell your services to area restaurants, and for up to five more days to help you during your opening.
- *National account sales.* Takeout Taxi has a massive effort to sell national restaurant chains on this concept so local franchisees can make arrangements with the local restaurant managers. They include TGI Fridays, Chili's, Chi Chi's, Po' Folks, and the like.
- *Advisory council.* It has a very active franchise advisory council with seven committees that advise the company on all operational aspects.

In short, Takeout Taxi has developed a powerful support engine to help you grow as rapidly as you can manage.

How Much Can You Make?

As I noted, Takeout Taxi generates at least three key revenue streams: (1) up to 35 percent of the retail price for the food you deliver, or about $8 to $10 gross profit on an average ticket worth $23 to $30; (2) the $3 average delivery fee; and (3) the fees you earn for marketing the restaurants through proprietary data base services and programs.

Abt has said that some restaurants add 15 percent to 40 percent to their nightly volumes with home delivery services. My own experience shows the truth of this; when I visit the local TGI Friday's on weekend nights, a steady stream of Takeout Taxi delivery drivers flows through the restaurant, each driver carrying at least several meals. And they repeat this scene all over my city of some 50,000 people at about two dozen restaurants. Furthermore, a Friday's manager I know in a different restaurant told me that his restaurant adds $6,000 to $8,000 in gross sales on an average weekend night.

To be more specific, for every meal you deliver, you can expect to gross $7.00 to $10.00 per meal and net $1.25 to $2.00, depending on your cost controls and overhead. And that does not include your revenues from your third revenue stream.

You should recoup your initial investment within a year to 18 months and turn very high ROIs every year thereafter, building to a six-figure net income by the end of the third or fourth year with a four-cell territory. You can expect to add $20,000 a year to your bottom line with each additional cell. In sum, Takeout Taxi offers the beginning of what should become a leading-edge twenty-first-century marketing bonanza.

COMPLETE MUSIC

Complete Music Disc Jockey Service
7877 L Street
Omaha, NE 68127
(402) 339-0001

The Complete Music Disc Jockey Service franchise takes advantage of a continuing boom in disc jockey entertainment at weddings, company parties, bar/bat mitzvahs, anniversary celebrations, and dances of any type. It earned a place in this book for several reasons: First, I love to dance, and as an aging Baby Boomer, I see hundreds of people like me in my area going dancing at local disc jockey–led dances every weekend night. Second, Complete Music surveys its franchisees every year to determine their issues, and every year, they report that the company gives them excellent earnings potential, quality equipment, quality marketing materials, quick responses to their concerns, and a high level of enjoyment.

Third, you can run the business from home, and you can even start part time: You can forward your calls to corporate headquarters where its trained telemarketers will sell your bookings for you while you are at work or away.

Finally, what's not to enjoy? A Complete Music franchise gives you a way to make significant profits on a very low investment doing something that is entertaining and helps people feel happy. You can do well by doing good.

You build this business by soliciting brides-to-be to use your service at their wedding celebration and marketing your service through many advertising and promotional channels. About 80 percent of your business comes from weddings, the rest from all other party and entertainment events. You also must hire and train disc jockeys and arrange their schedules. The secret to success is excellent service at the event because word-of-mouth advertising and the wedding party's own experience with your service will determine whether or not the bridesmaids and ushers become your future customers. Company executives said that in this service business, "half the battle is marketing; the other half is keeping the promises of the first half"—in short, training DJs to give quality service that leads to referrals.

You compete with other DJ services and live bands, but you can compete successfully because you offer a higher-quality service at a competitive price, you offer a greater variety of music, you offer higher quality music than most live bands, and your DJs do not take breaks, so the party has continuous music. You also can offer auxiliary services, such as music videos and karoake music on tapes.

By late 1993, Complete Music had 112 franchise territories and about 55 owners with plans to reach a maximum potential of up to 300 franchise territories. During 1994 and beyond, the company plans to consolidate its franchises in metropolitan areas.

How Much It Costs

Complete Music has a three-tier franchise fee based on three types of territories:

- $15,500 for a primary market with a population above 200,000. President Gerald Maas noted that the company does divide major metropolitan areas, such as Chicago or Los Angeles, into several territories, but he makes sure every franchisee has plenty of room to expand.

- $9,000 for a midsized market with a population between 100,000 and 200,000.
- $7,000 for a secondary market with a population less than 100,000.

Note that the company arranges its territories by Yellow Pages coverage, so its executives often face dilemmas when one phone book serves very large territories, but under most circumstances, even if a territory has far more people than 200,000, the company grants the area as one territory. This step gives you more opportunity to build a very substantial entertainment enterprise.

Total start-up costs are very low, in a range between $10,500 and $25,000, including the franchise fee:

Category	Low End	High End
Franchise fee	$ 7,000	$15,500
Equipment (a)	2,000	2,700
Inventory (b)	100	500
Deposits (c)	250	300
Insurance (d)	250	600
Training travel	250	1,000
Office start-up (e)	700	1,400
Working capital (f)	0	2,500
Total	$10,550	$24,500

a. Required purchase of high-quality, exclusive-use Peavey Electronics sound reproduction and light display system.
b. Advertising materials and office supplies.
c. Business telephone deposits.
d. Required comprehensive business insurance policies.
e. If your local zoning laws do not allow this kind of business at home, you may have to rent a small office; this range covers lease deposits and some furniture.
f. Costs of local licensing, operating expenses, and some short-term living expenses. If you start part time, you can reduce this amount. You need a small amount to pay your DJs, but you are usually paid deposits by your customers, so the deposits can fund your DJs' fees. By the way, they work for you as part-time employees, so you do have to arrange tax payments and returns.

Royalties and Other Payments

In addition, you pay an 8 percent monthly royalty and a monthly fee for the right to use the tapes. All music is protected by strictly enforced copyright laws, so Complete Music has arranged a gross fee to the copyright agency for the right to collect the music on its compact discs and tapes. You pay your prorated share of that fee; during 1993, it equaled just $28 per month per system for almost 2,000 songs.

Although the company also has the right in the offering circular to charge an advertising fee and a supplemental training fee, it does not do so at this point, and it has no plans to do so in the near future. However, it does encourage you to spend several percent of your gross income on Yellow Pages and other advertising campaigns each year.

What You Get

In return for your fee, you receive 10 days of training at the corporate office that covers all aspects of setting up and operating your own entertainment company. Although you could do this on your own, it would take you far more money and far more time to study the music, buy the rights to it, generate your customers, and so forth. Complete Music saves you one to two years of effort and dollars at one-third the cost of buying your CDs (compact discs).

- *Exclusive territory.* As I discussed, depending on your geographic region, the Yellow Pages coverage, and demographics, you can choose from one of three territory sizes.
- *Training.* You receive 10 days of training at corporate headquarters and your own location in marketing the business, training DJs, staging the music at a party, and managing the business.
- *Field visits.* Franchise executives visit your area to help you set goals, visit local businesses, plan promotions, and conduct DJ meetings and training seminars.
- *Music library.* As important, you receive the right to use the company's library of more than 2,000 songs. You also receive a supply of catalogs that you show to customers so they can

choose the music styles they prefer.

- *Marketing programs.* The company trains you in telemarketing skills, so you can close 80 percent of your callers. Or you can pay the Complete Music headquarters telemarketing staff to do your prospecting for you. National advertising and public relations agencies generate low-cost, high-quality materials and leads for your business.
- *Marketing materials.* You receive a supply of brochures, calendars, seasonal party mailers, high school mailers, and so on. A national Yellow Pages advertising program reduces your costs by at least half compared to doing it on your own.
- *Self-termination.* Any franchisee can terminate the agreement with 120 days' written notice, no questions asked. But during the past three years, only two franchisees have either been terminated or self-terminated the agreement. This rate reflects a very happy group of franchisees.
- *Franchisee networking.* Like other excellent franchisors, Complete Music encourages its franchisees to help each other. The company also holds an annual owner's meeting to discuss new marketing programs, share ideas, demonstrate equipment improvements, recognize outstanding owners, and build relationships.

For the relatively low franchise fees, Complete Music offers a very complete package of quality service and support.

How Much Can You Make?

Complete Music does not make any earnings claims, but here is how you earn income. You charge from $250 to $500 for a wedding celebration, depending on how long it lasts—three hours is normal. The average price across the country is $350, and you book on average 40 shows per month for a gross income of $14,000 per month. You pay the DJs $75 to $100 per dance for a monthly average expense of $3,200. You pay the 8 percent royalty or $1,120, and your Yellow Pages ad will cost about $250 per month on average. That leaves you with a gross profit before overhead and operating expenses of $9,630 per month with net profits in the 30- to 40-percent-per-month range.

However, you can do even better more quickly if you add more DJs and more sound systems. You start earning a significant return when you launch a second system, and you should grow to a third system by the end of the first year. With a per-show gross profit greater than $100, you can see the very high profit potential of dozens of shows per month. And you can recoup your initial investment by the end of the first year and turn ROIs in the hundreds of percent each year after that.

In fact, the largest franchisees have 45 or more DJs at work doing hundreds of shows each month.

In conclusion, the proof of any franchise is how happy and successful its franchisees state that they are. The Complete Music survey of its franchisees stated that *all* owners said that their businesses were worth significantly more than their initial investment. Asked if they would buy the same franchise again, again *all* owners said that they would do so. Compare that result to a national average of about three quarters of all franchisees who have stated in other surveys that they would buy the same franchise again. In sum, Complete Music is a little-known gem of a franchise that has carved a significant place for itself in a growing market for weddings and party entertainment.

FLOOR COVERINGS INTERNATIONAL, INC.
PROFESSIONAL CARPET SYSTEMS, INC.
FURNITURE MEDIC, INC.

Floor Coverings International, Inc.
Professional Carpet Systems, Inc.
Furniture Medic, Inc.
5182 Old Dixie Highway
Forest Park, GA 30050

Franchise Concepts
277 Southfield Parkway
Suite 130
Forest Park, GA 30050
(800) 859-7580

PCS (800) 925-5055
FCI (800) 955-4324
FM (800) 877-9933

In a departure from the rest of this book, I have included three franchises in one section for several reasons: (1) they are owned by the same company; (2) they share the same chairman; (3) they appeal to the same consumer market for home services and shop-at-home convenience; and (4) frankly, putting them in one section meant I could include all three in the book, yet have available other sections for equally deserving franchises.

The three share some important benefits: (1) a liberal termination clause that lets you leave the system easily, (2) a money-back guarantee if you do not pass the company training course, and (3) significant ranges of opportunity in the growing home service market. Furthermore, the chairman of the company, Joseph Lunsford, said that his goal is to make these enterprises into the next ServiceMaster, a lofty but achievable pinnacle.

However, these three—Furniture Medic, Professional Carpet Systems, and Floor Coverings International—have different franchise fees and total start-up costs and probably appeal to different types of prospective franchisees. So, keeping in line with the book's structure, I will summarize the essential information for each in increasing order of their franchise fees.

Furniture Medic, Inc.

Furniture Medic is a low-cost, home-based mobile franchise that uses a proprietary method to restore and repair damaged furniture, wood veneers, and some laminates. With the price of living room and bedroom suites often higher than $5,000, more and more people would rather repair and restore rather than replace their wood furniture and furnishings. However, that is your smallest market; this service will especially appeal to hotels, insurance adjusters, antique dealers, furniture rental companies, property managers, moving companies with damage claims, and so on.

In business since only late 1992, Furniture Medic had 110 franchisees in operation by late 1993, and company officials expected to perhaps triple that total during 1994.

How Much Furniture Medic Costs

Furniture Medic charges a very low $7,000 franchise fee with average total start-up costs of $12,500 to $20,000 without the cost of a vehicle lease or purchase. In a true benefit, you pay a flat royalty of $200 per month and a $20-per-month advertising fund contribution. The table describes these costs:

Category	Low End	High End
Franchise fee	$ 7,000	$ 7,000
Opening inventory (a)	3,500	3,500
Training travel	500	3,000
Insurance (b)	500	2,000
Service van (c)	1,000	14,200
Working capital (d)	1,000	5,000
Miscellaneous (e)	100	1,000
Total	$13,600	$30,700

a. Required purchase of equipment and supplies.
b. Required business comprehensive and workers' compensation.
c. Ranges from van lease deposit and first month's payment to cash purchase with floor mats and required decals.
d. Need for operating expenses for first several months. This does not include living expenses.
e. Business licenses, professional fees, and similar costs.

What You Get with Furniture Medic

In return for your fees, you receive these services and benefits:

- *Territory.* A nonexclusive area in a designated marketing area (DMA) with a population of at least 100,000.
- *Term.* The agreement lasts ten years with the right to renew with the payment of a small fee not to exceed 10 percent of the then-current initial fee.
- *Training.* You receive an extensive three-week program, including a one-week home study course and two weeks of classroom and on-the-job training at headquarters.
- *Ongoing support.* This includes toll-free help line, newsletters, new and updated marketing materials, an annual convention, and so on.
- *$1,000 supply credit*I. On your first anniversary in business, FM

gives you an annual $1,000 credit toward supply and equipment purchases.
- *Liberal termination clause.* With 60 days' notice and a $2,400 fee, you can terminate the franchise when you wish. This clause helps prevent litigation and dissatisfied franchisees.

How Much Can You Make with Furniture Medic?

Furniture Medic does not make earnings claims. However, to earn income with Furniture Medic, you charge flat fees for repairs that can range from as low as $25 for a major hotel with hundreds of repairs to hundreds of dollars to restore an expensive antique. The secret to this business is developing volume contracts with insurance adjusters, hotels, and the like as quickly as you can. You do best to hire as quickly as you can a technician to do the work while you use your management and marketing skills to build the business. With average start-up costs between $12,000 and $17,000, you should recoup your investment during your first year and generate a comfortable middle-class income by the end of your second year.

Professional Carpet Systems

Professional Carpet Systems (PCS) is a home service franchise that offers carpet restoration and rejuvenation services, which include cleaning, dyeing, tinting, and spot coloring, and redyes faded, stained, bleached, and worn carpets to save customers up to 80 percent of replacement cost. Again, like Furniture Medic, while PCS appeals to homeowners, the volume markets in commercial properties such as apartments, hotels, hospitals, schools, restaurants, in fact, any institution or business with large expanses of expensive carpet will make up your best income sources. Very importantly, you can offer an unusual service—spot dyeing—that saves your customers far more money and trouble than the cost of dyeing the carpet. So, you can expand your market to those who simply need minor jobs, and you can add to your profits by spot dyeing some areas while you completely redye others.

In addition, you offer the full range of carpet cleaning services, such as deodorizing, flood and water damage restoration, upholstery cleaning, and so on in competition with similar franchises and companies.

How Much PCS Costs

PCS's franchise fee is $100 per 1,000 population, or $10,000 for a 100,000 population area. PCS recommends a 100,000 minimum, but you need a much larger territory to make a significant profit. In addition, you must buy an opening equipment and supplies package for $4,700, and in an unusual charge, you must pay $5,000 for two weeks of headquarters training. Total start-up costs range from $23,000 to $28,000, plus the cost of a van.

In addition, you pay a minimum weekly royalty of $45 or 6 percent of gross sales, whichever is greater. You do not pay any advertising fee. The table gives the range of start-up costs.

Category	Low End	High End
Franchise fee	$10,000	$25,000
Training	5,000	5,000
Travel	1,000	3,000
Opening package	4,700	4,700
Insurance (a)	1,000	2,000
Better Business Bureau	75	200
Working capital (b)	1,000	5,000
Miscellaneous	100	1,000
Service van (c)	1,000	16,000
Total (d)	$23,875	$61,900

a. Required vehicle, business, and workers' compensation.
b. Normal business start-up costs for professional fees, business licenses, phone deposits, Yellow Pages ads, and so on.
c. Low end covers lease deposit and first month's rent; high end covers purchase price of new van.
d. The low end is closer to the average start-up cost, while the high end would reflect a commitment to a much larger territory and rapid growth.

What You Get with PCS

In return for your fees, you receive the following:

- *Territory.* Depending on the size of your fee, you receive an exclusive territory based on zip codes within a designated marketing area.
- *Training.* In exchange for your $5,000 payment, you receive two weeks of classroom and hands-on training at PCS' Atlanta headquarters.
- *Term.* You receive a ten-year term with a ten-year renewal right in exchange for a small payment equal to 10 percent of the then-current franchise fee.
- *Support.* PCS also provides complete start-up marketing materials, a toll-free help line, a monthly newsletter, and an annual convention as well as a technical support staff.
- *Liberal termination clause.* Somewhat like FM, you can terminate with 60 days' notice, but you have to pay a fee equal to the larger of $2,340 or 6 percent of your previous 12-months' gross income. However, the company's mid-1993 UFOC reported a relatively high failure rate of 86 franchisees, about 14 percent per year. This includes 29 canceled by mutual agreement, 30 for nonpayment of royalties, and 28 reacquired for many reasons. Company executives explained that most of the reacquisitions stemmed from the company's desire to buy back portions of large territories that the original franchisees had not developed so the company could develop those areas with new franchisees.

How Much Can You Make with PCS?

Like the other two, PCS does not make earnings claims. But if an average new carpet costs $1,500, you would charge about $300 to redye the old one and $25 to $50 or so to spot-dye stains. You would charge competitive rates for carpet cleaning, damage restoration, and similar services. It appears that with one vehicle and a 100,000-population territory, you can recoup your total cash investment and earn a middle-class income within two years. Or you can grow the business with technicians and multiple vans in a larger territory and develop very high long-term returns on equity and an affluent income.

Floor Coverings International

The flagship franchise of Lunsford's growing conglomerate, Floor Coverings International (FCI), is a mobile, shop-at-home service that offers affluent and middle-class consumers the convenience of buying new carpet, wood and vinyl flooring, and related products at home. An excellent franchise for women, FCI is actively encouraging their participation as franchisees. Furthermore, unlike FM and PCS with their owner-workers, FCI seeks out people with strong sales and marketing backgrounds who can sell the products and services and hire installers to do the actual work. FCI also encourages husband-and-wife teams so the strengths of each spouse can complement the strengths of the other.

By late 1993, FCI had more than 300 franchised areas, many with more than one FCI van on the road. Company executives said that they are adding 10 to 15 new franchisees per month.

In an important development, in early 1993, FCI joined with Montgomery Ward to set up FCI kiosks in many Montgomery Ward stores to sell carpet and flooring to Montgomery Ward customers. In essence, Montgomery Ward turned over its carpet marketing to FCI in exchange for a percentage fee of each sale. The kiosks generate leads that FCI franchisees follow through with shop-at-home appointments with the customer. Company executives said that the potential for this service is in the thousands of customers per year and tens of millions of dollars in new income for franchisees.

How Much FCI Costs

FCI has the highest franchise fee, $29,000, for an "executive franchise" with 50,000 qualified households within a DMA, plus 70 cents for each additional household. A "standard franchise" with just 10,000 qualified households has a $14,000 fee and a charge of 70 cents for each additional household. An "executive franchisee" must also pay $5,500 for an opening equipment package while the standard one costs $4,500. In addition, an executive franchise pays a minimum weekly royalty equal to the larger of $75 or 5 percent of gross sales; the standard franchise pays a minimum of $45 per week or 5 percent. For advertising fees, the executive pays $25 or 2 percent of gross sales per week; the standard pays $15 or 2 percent. The table shows the approximate start-up cost ranges; company executives said that the average is about $34,000.

Category	Standard	Executive
Franchise fee	$14,000	$29,000
Opening package	4,500	5,500
Van cost	1,000	16,500
Travel training	1,000	3,000
Insurance	1,000	2,000
Better Business Bureau	75	200
Working capital	1,000	5,000
Miscellaneous	100	1,000
Total (a)	$22,675	$64,200

a. The high end represents cash purchase of a vehicle.

What You Get from FCI

FCI executives stated that you get the largest and fastest-growing mobile carpet retailer's successful system. Of course, what you receive in fact varies with the type of franchise you buy. With an "executive" package, you get a territory large enough to build up to four or five vans with your own salespeople growing the territory while you manage the business. The "standard" package limits you to a one-van operation that you will need to work on your own.

The executives also stated that they are committed to helping you reach your ultimate personal and business potential. In concrete terms, in addition to the territories described earlier, here are the benefits you receive:

- *Training*. Very thorough, the training includes a two-week, at-home study course, two weeks at corporate headquarters, and

one week with the best franchisees who act as regional directors. After formal training ends, support staff stay in constant
touch with you for the first two or three months.

- *Opening package.* It includes all you need to fully equip your
  CARPETVAN® and gives you a $500 to $1,000 allowance for
  initial marketing or direct mail and a $500 credit toward the
  down payment on the van.
- *Term.* The agreement lasts 10 years with a 10-year renewal for
  a payment equal to 10 percent of the then-current franchise
  fee.
- *Liberal termination clause.* It includes the same escape clause as
  the other two. FCI reports a relatively high average failure
  rate, a total of 150, including 65 by mutual agreement, 54 for
  nonpayment of royalties, and 32 reacquired and resold
  through transfer, death, and similar personal reasons. This
  high rate shows how difficult this business can be during a
  sharp recession. However, to reduce this rate, the company
  has tightened its selection procedures by requiring each
  prospect to have additional financial resources and to go
  before a review committee to discuss their sales and marketing backgrounds.
- *Franchisee-based support system.* FCI turns its best franchisees
  into regional directors who train and support new franchisees.
  In return, FCI splits the royalty with these directors.
- *International quality suppliers.* FCI works with among the very
  best carpet and floor covering manufacturers in the world so
  you can offer high quality at reasonable prices.
- *Fully loaded van.* When you leave training, FCI provides a fully
  loaded van that you can use the next day to start your business.

All in all, these services give you enough support to build
your business quickly.

How Much Can You Make with FCI?

Company executives cited figures from the American Floor
Covering Association that stated that based on industry averages,

you can expect to achieve a 35.5 to 38 percent gross profit on each sale before your operating expenses. If an average carpet sale totals $1,500 to $2,000, then before your operating expenses, you can expect to earn $532.50 to $760 and net in the 20 to 25 percent range, or $100 to $500, depending on how well you control your expenses.

Of course, you want to encourage high-volume commercial sales because the occasional sales to homeowners require a lot of time, effort, and coordination for the lowest payoffs while commercial work generates lower margins, but much higher dollar profits.

As you will see in the Decorating Den discussion in Chapter 5, selling interior decorations is a very tough, highly competitive business, so it requires total dedication and hard work to build a prosperous business within several years. The carpet side of the business is especially difficult because people only buy carpet once every so many years, so you must constantly search for new business. FCI wisely seeks people with strong sales and marketing experience to expand its franchise.

If you have those skills and want a low-cost start-up with long-term equity growth, you should invest in an "executive" franchise or grow into one so you can add new vans and trained salespeople.

FOUR SEASONS SUNROOMS

Four Seasons Sunrooms
5005 Veterans Memorial Highway
Holbrook, NY 11741
(800) 521-0179
(516) 563-4000

Four Seasons Sunrooms was one of the 1980s' leading franchise success stories that continues to succeed into the mid-1990s. From a $2,000 investment by a construction worker, Four Seasons has grown to 272 franchised showrooms worldwide. It has nurtured a very positive, upscale image with a pervasive national and regional advertising campaign and a very sophisticated lead generation program for its franchisees.

During the late 1980s and early 1990s, the company transformed what had been a market strategy aimed at energy-conscious consumers into a highly successful strategy aimed at making a sunroom or solarium a remodeling "necessity" for a home, restaurant, or office. If you need any more evidence, visit any local fast-food restaurant built since the late 1980s, and you will probably find a solarium or sunroom enclosure.

The market for home remodeling itself is enormous, about $112 billion during 1993, with $6 trillion in homeowners' equity. With more than 40 million homes at least 25 years old, and some 3.5 million homes resold each year, you can see that the market for this product has only begun to be tapped. Equally important are the commercial and office remodeling markets, which could grow at 10 percent or more per year during the rest of the decade. Many suburban office park complexes use solariums for worker cafeterias or fitness clubs.

Four Seasons franchises are based on the "remodeling center and showroom" concept. You open a showroom that builds Four Seasons' products into the structure or you put them inside the structure to display your residential and commercial product lines. You also make direct sales calls to architects, developers, and major construction firms. Company executives said that restaurants, nursing homes, government facilities, company cafeterias, any facility where health and social environment issues are important make ideal markets. To reach homeowners, you use Yellow Pages ads and direct marketing techniques. However, you can expect your business to divide like this: 60 to 75 percent in residential new construction and remodeling and the rest in commercial work.

As important, they stated that you need to look at the United States not as a country, but as regions where jobs, home equity, cost of living, disposable income, life-styles, and so on differ and so the demand for sunrooms will vary from region to region. But since the gas-filled, treated, double-paned glass both blocks out heat in summer and retains heat in winter, you can sell the same product line in Maine or Florida. You can sell energy conservation, added value, beauty, and appearance regardless of location.

You offer a broad product line that includes nine models of wood- and aluminum-framed solariums, several patio sunrooms, a line of wood and glass doors, and related products, including skylights, windows, and store fronts. Some franchisees sell luxury add-ons, such as spas, ceramic tile floors, and the like.

What It Costs

Four Seasons has reduced its franchise fee since 1990, but still offers three types of franchises based on market potential and population:

- $7,500 for a level 1 rural franchise such as Great Falls, Montana.
- $10,000 for a level 2 small-city franchise such as Utica, New York.
- $15,000 for a level 3 large-city franchise such as Boston, Massachusetts.

But company executives noted that the best opportunities are available in the small-city and rural areas.

Included in the franchise fee is a $2,500 advertising allowance for your initial advertising and promotional efforts.

Four Seasons requires a minimum showroom space, whether a building or in a warehouse area, and expects you to devote full-time effort to the business. You sell and market your products and hire subcontractors to do the installations. The company also encourages rural franchisees to add the sunroom business to an existing business, such as home remodeling, new construction, or pool and spa businesses. Thus, total start-up costs, including the fee and a required start-up product package, can range from $15,250 to $65,250. Four Seasons includes the franchise fee, displays, signage, leasehold improvements, product package, lease deposits, training travel, furnishings and fixtures, and working capital. The start-up product package should cost about $15,000.

You may incur other costs:

- Zoning variance approvals for your showroom center;
- Legal and accounting fees related to the franchise;
- Office supplies and equipment;
- Construction fees, if any; and
- Site selection fees, if any.

Beneficial Royalty Payments

You pay *no* royalties on your sales because you must buy the sunroom products from Four Seasons. You pay a small 2.5 percent royalty on nonsunroom sales sold through the franchise. You do not pay an advertising fee, despite Four Seasons' effort to spend at least 2.5 percent of its own revenues on its superb national advertising campaign. In addition, Four Seasons gives you a 5 percent advertising allowance on your purchases from Four Seasons, but you must use the co-op credits, or you can lose them, company executives insisted.

Your largest ongoing cost will be required purchases from the company that equal about 55 percent of your gross revenues. In short, Four Seasons works like an auto dealer: To call yourself a Ford dealer, you can sell only Fords.

What You Get

In exchange for the franchise fee and start-up product package and marketing package, you receive a complete turnkey showroom:

- *Exclusive territory in a strong demographic area.* Look for territories with numerous restaurants, office parks, middle-class and upscale homes, and professional office space.
- *Superb lead generation system.* All Four Seasons' ads aim to generate coupon responses. It automates and sends to the local franchisees all the hundreds of thousands of leads it receives each year. The company also sends each lead a full-color catalog with the franchisee's name and number.

- *Cooperative advertising allowance.* As noted, you earn a 5 percent allowance on local ads.
- *Training.* Three to five days of headquarters training.
- *Professional marketing tools.* A sophisticated sales presentation system.
- *National accounts program.* The company aggressively pursues national accounts among hotel chains, supermarkets, fast-food franchises, major commercial developers and builders, and so on.
- *A 10-year term on the franchise agreement with additional 10-year terms easily available with no additional franchise fee.*
- *International brand-name recognition among the upper middle class.*
- *Site location and showroom construction assistance.*
- *Ongoing field support and telephone hotlines.*

In short, the Four Seasons' headquarters operation is truly one of the most impressive in franchising.

How Much Can You Make?

Although the company does not make volume earnings claims, figures reported in the late 1980s remained consistent with the early 1990s, thanks to the recession that depressed prices for remodeling. However, that reflects both lower subcontractor costs and stable product prices, so franchisee profit margins did not suffer. Average franchisees reported gross revenues ranging from $600,000 to $750,000, with net profit margins in the 25 to 35 percent range.

Here's how you calculate it for each sale. The average residential solarium sells to the homeowner for $10,000 (including assembly). Your cost for the product that you sell for $8,000 is $4,400 or 55 percent. Your cost for assembly is $1,400, or 17.5 percent. If you use a commissioned salesperson, he or she receives 8 to 10 percent of the gross or $800 to $1,000, leaving you a gross profit before office expenses equal to $3,300 or 33 percent of your gross revenues. If you sell the sunroom yourself, you pocket the additional 8 to 10 percent, for a gross profit margin of 42 percent. Most franchisees tend to control their expenses and make their own sales, so their pretax profits fall in the 35 to 42 percent range. But I use conservative estimates so you will gain a more realistic picture.

However, if you emphasize commercial sales and market dozens or hundreds of sunrooms to real estate developers, you can arrange for Four Seasons to ship the sunrooms to their job sites and let their workers do the installation. Your per-sunroom selling price and profit are less, but your gross revenues and net profits are higher because these sales do not incur advertising or installation costs, and you reduce your per-unit overhead. In short, if you have a solid background in marketing, sales, or management, you could find Four Seasons Sunrooms an excellent opportunity to build a significant business with healthy ROIs within three years.

FOX'S PIZZA

Fox's Pizza
204 West Long Avenue
Dubois, PA 15801
(800) 992-3697
(814) 371-3076

I have found it very difficult to discover any profitable fast-food franchises that you can start for less than $100,000. However, I found a few excellent ones, and one that especially strikes a chord is Fox's Pizza. Established 23 years ago, Fox's Pizza makes it possible for you to become the Domino's, Subway, Blimpie, and Pizza Hut for the small towns of America at an amazingly low cost of about $65,000 or less. Ranked 13th of the top 25 pizza franchises—none of those ranked higher costs less than $100,000 to start up—Fox's offers take-out and home delivery menus with All-American fast food: pizza, salads, and wedgies, hoagies, or subs (depending on what you call them where you live!) in small and medium-sized towns or on the ex-urban fringes of major metropolitan areas. These towns range in population from 1,500 to 8,000, usually about 5,000. In short, Fox's Pizza has found a way to succeed where the major franchises choose not to tread. A Fox's Pizza brings high-quality food to small communities that otherwise must settle for poorly run Mom and Pop shops.

With a Fox's franchise, you bring a professional, sophisticated approach to customers who rarely experience the virtues of modern fast-food operations. And, as you do, you earn very significant short- and long-term returns on a comparatively low investment. An equally good reason to buy a Fox's franchise is the probable shakeout in the fast-food franchises with high start-up costs, high overhead, and low profits that Fox's executives predict for the 1990s. As a small company, they said, Fox's can react quickly to market changes to meet local needs and help you keep your overhead down and your profit margins up. For example, before the introduction of the "Bigfoot"-style pizza, Fox's introduced its own 21-slice "Big Daddy" pizza at a comparable price, yet with their lower overhead, Fox's franchisees' profit margins were slightly higher.

By late 1993, the company had 135 franchisees in the Northeast and Midwest and expected to expand to the Sunbelt states during 1994. It was planning to increase its presence in all those areas during the next several years.

How Much It Costs

The Fox's Pizza franchise fee is only $8,000, but required training, sign use, and equipment installation fees add $11,000, so you pay $19,000 directly to Fox's. As the table shows, total start-up costs approximate $67,000 for a turnkey shop; however, company executives say average start-up costs total about $65,000, and conversions of existing Mom and Pop shops cost far less.

Category	Low End	High End
Franchise fee	$ 8,000	$ 8,000
Training fee	5,000	5,000
Sign use fee	3,000	3,000
Equipment installation (a)	0	3,000
Equipment, fixtures (b)	32,500	38,500

Opening inventory (c)	6,000	7,000
Security deposits (d)	800	1,200
Insurance premiums	1,000	1,200
Working capital (e)	5,000	10,000
Total	$61,300	$76,700

a. Fox's does not now charge a $3,000 installation fee that it has in its offering circular.

b. Includes all-new package of "everything" you need to open your doors in most locations from pizza oven to can opener.

c. Includes all food stuffs and inventory for the first three months of operation; you can probably reduce this as your cash flow increases.

d. Includes lease deposit, business phone, local utilities, and so on. Fox's suggests that you rent an 800- to 1,200-square-foot store; in rural areas, you can probably rent space relatively inexpensively, for $500 to $750 per month compared to up to four or five times that much in an affluent suburban area.

e. Three months' operating expenses, including advertising, employee salaries, utilities, and so on. Add more if you need to have living expenses available during the same period.

Flat-Fee Royalty Payment

In one of Fox's significant advantages, it charges only a fixed $200 per month royalty payment. As you read this book, you should be able to discern that I strongly favor franchises with fixed royalties because with flat fees, you sharply increase your profit margins as your revenues increase. Fox's also does *not* charge an advertising fee, although you should spend a small percentage of your revenues on advertising—direct mail coupons, doorhangers, home delivery coupons, local newspaper ads, and so on. Although the company does require you to buy items that carry the company's trade and service marks from approved suppliers, the company does *not* earn income from these approved suppliers. But Fox's president, James R. Fox, does own a half interest (50 percent) in Fox's Pizza Commissary, Inc., the primary supplier, and he earns income when the commissary makes a profit.

All in all, Fox's offers a very straightforward deal in which the benefits far outweigh the costs.

What You Get

For your fee, you receive the following benefits and programs:

- *Exclusive territory.* Depending on your area, it may take one of three forms:

    Five-mile radius of retail shop in rural area;

    An appropriate political subdivision—township or
      borough—of a suburban area; or

    A customer base of not less than 25,000 people in a
      designated section of a larger city.

The UFOC notes that for the third type, the primary consideration is the estimated number of potential eat-in, carry-out customers living or working within the area.

As important, you may also enter into a multiple-store area development agreement to open more Fox's Pizza stores in your geographic area. In fact, several franchisees own several shops, but you cannot open a second one until the first one succeeds.

- *Five-year term.* You receive a five-year license, but you can renew for additional five-year terms for a payment of just 10 percent of the then-current franchise fee.
- *Training.* Fox's works much like other flat-fee franchises: It hires existing franchisees to train you; they train you only at your own store location and they begin the day you open for business. The training lasts for 10 days and consists of in-store instruction in all aspects of running a Fox's store. Note that you should be able to hire employees with fast-food experience to make the process somewhat easier.
- *Marketing.* Fox's provides a new advertising program each month, but its "keep-it-simple" philosophy means that you use $35 3-feet by 12-feet banners to announce special promotions and $26-per-1000 flyers to give to customers.
- *Inventory.* You can purchase foodstuffs and inventory from the commissary at rates generally much lower than you could get on the open market. You also gain national account status with leading vendors who otherwise would not even deliver to your town.

- *New product development.* Just as the company responded quickly to the "Bigfoot" pizza thrust, it constantly monitors the pizza and sandwich market to offer new products and variations that match or exceed those from its major competitors.
- *Quality.* Fox's distinguishes itself from its local competition with consistent product quality and a high-profile operation.
- *Support.* Although small, Fox's corporate staff is always available at a toll-free number to help you increase sales, save money on supplies, add new products or promote existing ones, and counter competition in your area.

Most important, it puts you in business in the two high-growth segments of the pizza and fast-food market: home delivery and carry-out.

How Much Can You Make?

Before you consider how much you can make, consider that Fox's franchisees rarely fail. During 1993, only three of 135 failed, and two of those failures were caused by divorces. In the five years between 1989 and the end of 1993, the total terminations were 29, or about 6 per year, a rate much lower than the national average for franchises in general and fast-food franchises in particular.

The low rate holds because Fox's franchisees make significant net incomes that give them affluent life-styles in small towns. This franchise would be perfect for a retired manager or military officer who enjoyed small-town living and who wanted to supplement a retirement income and build an inheritance for his or her children. Or middle-aged managers could leave the urban rat race and build minichains of Fox's Pizza stores and make more money than they now make in their corporate jobs.

Although Fox's does not make an earnings claim, systemwide sales totaled $24 million during 1992 for average gross revenues per store of $208,000. Subtract 35 to 38 percent for food costs, 20 percent for labor costs, and 15 to 17 percent for overhead, including rent, utilities, and advertising, and your net pretax profit margin would range from 25 percent to 30 percent, with an average of $53,000. If you borrow money to begin, you subtract loan payments from that amount.

The size of the town does not have much to do with your profits either; among the stores with the highest gross revenues are Fox's franchises in towns of 3,500 or less population that do not have many fast-food operations. Undoubtedly, if you want to earn high profit margins in fast food, and you do not have much cash, a Fox's Pizza is an excellent choice.

5

Franchises with Fees from
$8,001 to 11,499

DECORATING DEN SYSTEMS, INC.

Decorating Den Systems, Inc.
7910 Woodmont Avenue
Bethesda, MD 20814–3058
(301) 652-6393

Decorating Den Systems, Inc., offers a mobile interior decorating franchise; that is, its franchisees—98 percent of whom are women—offer in-home interior decorating services to middle-class and affluent homeowners. These women come from many occupations, including teaching, health care, management, retail sales, homemaking, and so on. Many have spouses as their business partners. When they buy this franchise, the Decorating Den franchisees receive training, national buying power, and a well-known name and avoid the cost and difficulty of opening a retail showroom. The franchisees transport the showroom to their clients in a specially equipped ColorVan with more than 5,000 samples of window treatments, wall coverings, furniture, floor coverings, carpets, and accessories. This mobile franchise has significant appeal to busy two-income couples, working singles, or divorced individuals who do not have time to do their own coordination.

Dozens of leading manufacturers and brand-name companies supply Decorating Den franchisees with quality products. In turn, Decorating Den franchisees offer their customers a clear advantage because they can arrange shipments. Further, as a franchisee, you sell home decorating products, offer the design consultation free, and coordinate product installation; you do not do any installation or heavy work.

Franchisees earn income on retail markups on customer purchases; unlike many professional interior designers, you do not charge additional fees for your consultation. Gross retail markups range from as low as 40 percent to as high as 70 percent, with 50 percent as the average range. The company reports that an average client purchase totals more than $1,500.

By the end of 1993, Decorating Den reported that it had approximately 1,200 franchisees worldwide in the United States, Canada, and several foreign countries. During 1992, the company reported systemwide sales in excess of $60 million, a 12 percent increase over 1991, and 1993 sales totaled about $70 million, a 16.6 percent increase.

The system works through some 50 regionally owned franchises that functions like this book's definition of a master franchise. The regional franchisee sells the individual franchises and trains and supports the local franchisee before and after corporate training. The individual franchisee signs a three-party agreement that makes both the regional franchisee and Decorating Den corporate responsible for carrying out the agreement terms.

The typical franchisee is a woman who would like to own an interior decorating business, but who wants a proven business development plan that covers all aspects of sales, marketing, and business expansion. Some do not have the know-how to open a showroom or the desire to go through interior decorating school and an apprenticeship to obtain professional credentials. Decorating Den, instead, trains each franchise in its systematic approach to provide interior decorating services to middle-class and affluent Baby Boomers.

How Much It Costs

Decorating Den offers two kinds of franchises:

Associate Franchise

For a fee of $8,900 (a $2,000 increase since the first edition of this book), an associate franchisee operates in a zip code area owned by either a senior franchisee or a regional director, whichever applies. She has no developmental rights in her zip code, but she has promotional rights that permit advertising within that zip code area. You also pay higher royalty percentages depending on sliding scale percentages that decline from 15 to 11 percent of gross sales. You would have to make significantly higher sales to reduce your royalty percentages to the same level as a senior franchise. The following table illustrates these fees:

DECORATING DEN ROYALTY RATES

Senior Franchise

Annual Total Paid ($)	Percentage (%)
$0–100,000	11%
$100,001–300,000	10%
$300,001–600,000	9%
$600,001–1 million	8%
More than $1 million	7%

Associate Franchise

$0–100,000	15%
$100,001–300,000	14%
$300,001–600,000	13%
$600,001–1 million	12%
More than $1 million	11%

An associate assigned to a small one-van territory must fulfill a minimum sales quota of $30,000; senior franchisees with larger territories must fulfill higher minimum quotas during their second and subsequent years in business. Note further that if a senior franchisee does not meet her sales quota, the company retains the right to put an associate franchisee in her territory.

Senior Franchise

The franchise fee for a senior territory ranges from $8,900 to $23,900, an increase since the first edition of this book. In return, you receive an exclusive marketing territory based on zip codes and the relative retail sales potential of that geographic area. The territory limits are determined by ColorVan potential, which ranges from one to at most four. The territory is also determined by number of households, median income, gross retail sales, and similar factors that determine the buying power of the households in your area.

As a senior franchisee, you also must meet stiff performance quotas that increase each year. A one-van territory stays at a $30,000 minimum throughout the ten-year agreement, but the minimum for a four-van territory increases from $30,000 in the first year to $120,000 for each year from the fourth through the tenth. Clearly, Decorating Den gives you room to grow, but it does require performance. "Use it or lose it" appears to be the company's attitude.

Start-up Costs

After the fee, your total start-up costs will be relatively low, especially if you lease your ColorVan, because you should run this business from your home to minimize your initial investment and ongoing overhead costs. The following table describes a high-low range:

Category	Low End	High End
Franchise fee	$ 8,900	$23,900
Colorvan (a)	1,000	1,000
Insurance	1,150	1,150
Working capital (b)	8,000	12,000
Living expenses (c)	5,000	5,000
Total	$19,050	$38,050

a. The low end represents the approximate lease down payment, first months' payment, and miscellaneous costs.

b. Decorating Den includes initial advertising, telephone answering service, Yellow Pages ads, business telephone deposits, training travel expenses, and so on in this figure.
c. The company stated that living expenses are variable, but I add this amount for living expenses if you must support yourself or your family before you begin to earn an income. In this business, even with deposits, you do not earn money until after the customer's order has been installed and the customer is satisfied.
d. This wide range varies according to associate or senior status.

In addition to the foregoing requirements, you must pay a 2 to 4 percent advertising fee or a set monthly minimum. And you must buy materials and supplies from company-approved suppliers. Note that the company does receive commissions and fees from these suppliers for distributing their products, but the company uses these commissions and fees to fund retail sales contests for franchisees throughout the year.

What You Get

For your fees, you receive a very broad and deep training program and other benefits:

- *Territory.* As noted, you receive an exclusive marketing territory under specific conditions discussed in the agreement. Senior franchisees are supposed to develop their territories and expand their businesses with more decorators according to a schedule worked out with the regional director. Associate franchises do not receive exclusive territories and must meet the minimum quota to keep their licenses.

- *Training.* Perhaps the most significant advantage, Decorating Den has a six-month training program. First, for three and a half to four weeks before you attend corporate training, you work through business planning, marketing planning, and positive mental attitude lessons, according to President James S. Bugg, Sr. Then, you attend "total immersion learning" for 10 days at Lifestyle University, which teaches you everything you need to know to begin. Then, during your first 12 weeks in the field, you work with the regional director at his or her center one day a week.

And the company offers continuing education credits to earn a certified decorator rating, Bugg added. Earning this certificate requires at least two years of study and a two-and-a-half-day test. In fact, only 30 of the 1,300 Decorating Den franchisees have received this certificate, making them the elite. Bugg noted that during 1992, 15 people took the test, but only 1 passed.

- *Term.* The franchise agreement lasts ten years, and you may renew at the then-current terms for a small 2 percent fee.

- *Preferred suppliers.* You receive the benefit of direct access and wholesale pricing from dozens of national brand names.

- *Advertising.* The company provides a start-up package of advertising planning and programs. A grand opening promotion lasts three weeks and includes direct mail, media advertising, and special promotions from approved suppliers. The company also runs national TV commercials and provides ongoing marketing materials.

- *Services.* Decorating Den also provides a national buying service, a merchandising service for promotions and discounts, advanced training programs, and counseling.

- *Support.* You receive direct support and frequent visits from your regional director (master franchisee) who helps you improve and grow your business.

The Turnover Controversy

During the past several years, Decorating Den has been criticized by some government observers for its relatively high turnover rates. One report showed that within five years, a very high percentage of new Decorating Den franchisees had failed.

Replying to this criticism, Bugg stated, "In eight years, I have never seen a single person fail who followed our system. The trick is to convince people to follow the system. When they don't follow our advice and our methods, they fail, and then, they seek to blame the system for their failure. This is not the case."

He said that many new franchisees believe that Decorating Den is going to be a romantic, glamorous business that they can do part time with little effort. He noted that when new franchisees find that it requires hard work and long hours, it shocks them. They find that they don't want to work that hard, so they drop out of the system after a few months. In fact, he said that 20 percent of his franchisees do "fantastically well," 20 percent do poorly, and the rest do moderately well depending on their effort and motivation. Bugg added that the company spends most of its service and support effort motivating this middle 60 percent. But he asserted that the same percentages hold true in any sales/service enterprise and that Decorating Den's experience with failures is normal.

Bugg insisted that although the company allows part-time franchisees, they cannot expect to earn high incomes. "Succeeding in this business takes a lot of hours and very hard work to build a customer base for the first year and a half to two years. They should have developed enough referral and repeat business that they need to add a new ColorVan and grow their business even more. It often takes two to four years to make significant returns."

However, although the company spends 60 to 90 days in an extensive five-step interview and qualification process of all franchise candidates, some franchise observers questioned whether Decorating Den should tighten its eligibility requirements even more with tougher screening procedures to prevent the "romantics" from entering the system. After all, the purpose of franchising is to give novices a system that increases their chances to succeed compared to their chances to succeed on their own.

On the other hand, the "romantics" have a responsibility to "take off the blinders' when they investigate a franchise and find out exactly what they face. They, too, share the burden for making a choice that better fits their willingness—or lack thereof—to work hard. In short, if you are considering Decorating Den, remember that you will have to work very hard to produce significant returns on investment; if you don't want to do that, then find another franchise.

How Much Can You Make?

Interior design is a very competitive business, especially during the cost-conscious 1990s. You compete against everyone from professional ASID designers at the high end to major retailers and thousands of small firms at the low end.

If you assume a moderate start-up cost of about $30,000 and an average gross revenue per purchase of about $1,500, you must make 30 to 40 sales during your first year to recoup your initial investment.

Consider that with systemwide sales of $70 million and 1,200 franchisees (800 of whom are actively selling full time), that means the average franchisee grosses only $87,500 per year. However, note that one remarkable first-year franchisee survived a serious illness and overcame her foreign status to gross more than $146,000, according to a company newsletter. She attributed her recovery from her illness to the support of her regional director and her own drive to succeed.

You may not have to duplicate her effort, but with gross profit margins in the 40 to 60 percent range, you should be able to net a middle five-figure income within two to three years. But remember to avoid the image of glamour and face the reality that this is a difficult business that requires hard work.

WORLDWIDE REFINISHING SYSTEMS

Worldwide Refinishing Systems, Inc.
1020 North University Parks Drive
P.O. Box 3146
Waco, TX 76707
(800) 583-9900
(817) 756-2282, ext. 2359

Worldwide Refinishing has more than tripled the number of its U.S. franchisees since franchising magnate Don Dwyer bought it in 1988. By the end of 1993, the total exceeded 450 as the company now proclaims that it is the largest refinishing business in the world. Like Mr. Rooter and Rainbow International, Worldwide is another piece in Dwyer's puzzle to build a 10,000-franchise worldwide empire.

It has become a very highly rated piece, too, receiving number one rankings in its category in *Entrepreneur* magazine for four years in a row.

Worldwide offers a very simple, inexpensive, low-overhead business that competes with several other very good companies in this book: refinishing all kinds of services from bathtubs and sinks to any surface made of porcelain, formica, ceramic tile, fiberglass, wood, steel, and cultured marble. Worldwide Vice President Charles Wallis noted that the bulk of franchisees' business comes from bathtub, countertop, and ceramic tile repairs and refinishing.

Its simple process involves heating the old surface to a high temperature and coating it with the company's special chemicals. The company claims that its new finish offers the highest quality and durability on the market; to show this to customers, franchisees must offer a one-year warranty and may offer a ten-year one. In fact, the industry-standard warranty is five years, so you probably must offer that just to stay competitive.

Although you sell the service primarily as an inexpensive home remodeling alternative—saving homeowners up to 80 percent of replacement cost—you also establish commercial accounts. Wallis estimated that residential business accounts for 60 to 70 percent of your income, while commercial makes up the rest, but it varies by area and by your emphasis. The average cost of refinishing a tub equals about $400. This figure varies widely from region to region and with the local competition. For example, I have seen prices in the Washington-Baltimore area in the $279-per-tub-range, less, of course, for commercial accounts.

Worldwide suggests that you start your business from home and build it up to about $200,000 gross volume before you open an office. You will need to hire technicians to do the work while you market and manage the service.

How Much It Costs

Worldwide has a two-tier franchise fee:

- *Exclusive territory.* It costs $9,500 for a minimum 100,000 population to which you can add more population for $95 per 1,000 people. You can add as much population as you want at this level. You work as a single owner-operator at this level.

- *Limited-exclusive territory.* It costs $19,000 for a population base of 200,000. This applies only to major metro areas, and it is granted only after the company studies the market and determines the number of franchises it may grant in the area.

The low-end fee has increased $2,000 since 1990, and the second tier has been added.

Most new franchisees choose the limited-exclusive tier for several reasons. First, with more population, you have greater potential to reach more customers more quickly. Second, if you run out of other options (bank loans or family and friends), you may finance a portion of the fee, so you can buy more bang for the bucks you bring. Third, if you are a veteran, you can get a 25 percent discount or automatically finance half of the fee. In fact, Dwyer was the leader behind VETFRAN, a discount program through which some 175 franchisors offer special discounts, low- or no-fee franchises, or special financing arrangements to veterans or "excessed" members of the Armed Forces. Finally, you can obtain a regional director agreement that allows you to add more territory for $95 per 1,000 population. However, the catch is that Worldwide reviews and renews your regional director status each year. You act as an area developer, selling small territories to other franchisees and providing marketing and technical support to them.

The following table estimates a range of start-up costs from both Worldwide's UFOC and my industry knowledge:

Category	Low End	High End
Franchise fee	$ 9,500	$19,000
Equipment and supplies (a)	5,126	5,126
Van down payment (b)	750	850
Training travel	450	1,350
Van decal package	385	385
Working capital (c)	2,000	20,000
Total	$18,211	$46,711

a. Price has increased $1,510 since 1990, a 41.8 percent jump.

b. Worldwide's UFOC lists only purchase prices. Most new franchisees buy used vans and add Worldwide signs and logos.
c. Worldwide lumps together all remaining business start-up expenses, including business phone, start-up advertising, business liability and auto insurance deposits, Yellow Pages, contractor payments, and so on, and living expenses for three months while you build your initial cash flow.

Note that unlike many franchises, Worldwide does *not* include the original equipment and chemicals in the franchise fee, raising your start-up costs by more than $5,000.

Royalties, Fees, and Purchases

You must pay a weekly 5 percent royalty on gross sales; although the company reserves the right to charge a 2 percent advertising fee, it was not doing so by the end of 1993. Worldwide also has a sales quota with a minimum royalty: at least $600-per-week minimum gross sales within six months of training, or you must pay a royalty fee of at least $30 per week or face losing your license.

You must also buy your chemicals from the company; that should equal about 15 percent of your gross annual sales.

You must also do local marketing and have a Yellow Pages ad that meets company specifications.

What You Get

In return for your fees and royalties, you receive the following services and privileges:

- *Exclusive territory*. Be sure to develop an area with middle-class households and many commercial businesses that might require your services.
- *Support system*. Worldwide offers a variety of support programs, including regional meetings, advanced training, a national convention, and telephone support from the marketing director.
- *Ten-year term*. With an original ten years, you can renew for additional ten-year terms at no charge, a valuable benefit. But the contract does not allow for franchisee termination.

Although Worldwide reported that 88 terminations had occurred since 1988, Wallis explained that 46 of those were resales, 11 were multiple territories consolidated into single units, only one was canceled for quality control problems, and some 30 were abandoned; that is, the franchisee simply walked away. With the company's rapid growth, the 31 true failures represent a below-average percentage, a positive sign.

- *Training.* Worldwide has doubled its training from one week to two weeks to give you more management and marketing skills. Wallis noted that this additional training had helped new franchisees double their revenues during their first months compared to new franchisees under the old training period. You spend more time in both the classroom and the field with Waco-area crews.

  Since January 1993, Worldwide has also offered advanced training courses at three levels: (1) independent owner-operators; (2) owner-operators with helper(s); and (3) managers who hire technicians, but do no refinishing labor.

- *Technician training.* At a cost of $500 per week for each person, Worldwide will train additional technicians.

- *New product division.* It has added a new division to help you increase revenues: *Bath-to-whirlpool conversions.* For a retail price between $595 and $1,000, franchisees can now convert existing bathtubs to whirlpool baths and earn gross profit margins of about 50 percent. Again, the whirlpool conversion saves the homeowner at least 50 percent of the replacement cost.

With these new services, you can increase your gross revenues and expand your business. Clearly, many home service franchises have realized that "one-trick ponies" cannot generate enough revenue to make a thriving business, so many are adding new services. By the same token, the company can sell more tools, equipment, chemicals, and so on to its franchisees.

Of course, you also receive marketing programs, toll-free hotline, and ongoing research.

How Much Can You Make

Extrapolating from the company's financial statements, during 1992, systemwide sales totaled about $7 million, or only about $28,040 per franchise, but most of those franchisees were only a year old or less. Furthermore, Wallis noted that 22 franchises did not report their earnings, that 20 percent work only part time, that the figure includes those being resold, and that some low-producing franchisees were "inherited" from the franchise that Dwyer acquired during the late 1980s. Wallis has been quoted in a published report as saying that after two to three years, an owner-operator can build a $70,000 to $100,000 gross income and net about half of that.

In a very successful case, a man-and-woman team built their business to a gross volume of more than $500,000 in just three years after they invested $50,000 (plus living expenses for a year) to get started. It took them more than a year to break even, but now they employ 14 full-time workers and expect to gross $1 million a year by 1996.

Although Worldwide used to publish very detailed operating costs estimates, it did not do so for this update. The company did report that most franchisees earn $50- to $80-per-hour gross with a typical refinishing job costing between $325 and $400 and the average ceramic tile job priced at $387.

Materials cost about $50 per tub, and technicians earn $50 to $80 for a four- to five-hour job. If they can sell add-ons, they earn a commission, but boost the gross revenues to $500 to $1,000 per job. After expenses, you can have a gross income before overhead and taxes ranging between $200 and $600 per job.

If you do the work yourself, you may build up to three to five tub jobs per week, or a pretax income after expenses between $30,000 and $100,000 a year after two to three years.

In short, you can recoup your initial investment within the first year (especially if you are a veteran), and begin to earn 200 percent ROIs by the end of the third year.

THE MAID BRIGADE SYSTEMS, INC.

Maid Brigade
850 Indian Trail Road
Atlanta, GA 30247
(404) 562-2400

Maid Brigade was selected for this book because its franchisees have contributed significantly to the company's development and because the company offers a low start-up cost, yet supports its franchisees with a thorough training program and support network. I also know the couple that acts as one of the company's 10 regional coordinators and that couple's leading franchisee through a local franchise group to which we all belong. All of them impress me as honest businesspeople sincerely interested in their franchisees' and their own success.

As a cleaning franchise, Maid Bridge also uses the team cleaning method with two- or three-person crews. Its executives said that franchisee crews clean four to six houses a day with an average charge of $60 per house for a gross average daily income ranging from $240 to $360. With maximum per-crew gross annual revenues between $100,000 and $180,000, you need to develop several crews to generate high five-figure net incomes. The average Maid Brigade franchise has two to three crews, and its owners earn significant net profits on a lower than average investment.

Unlike some cleaning franchises, Maid Brigade provides practically nonstop training from the time you sign the agreement until you sell your franchise. Like the best cleaning franchises, Maid Brigade has a declining scale royalty with which you keep more money as you make more money.

By late 1993, Maid Brigade had 140 U.S. territories and about 100 individual franchisees with 90 more territories in Canada. Company executives said that the company offers significant growth opportunities throughout most of the United States.

How Much It Costs

Maid Brigade offers one of the lowest franchise fees of the six leading maid franchises, $9,500, with among the lowest start-up costs that average $25,000. The table shows an estimated low-high range:

Category	Low End	High End
Franchise fee	$ 9,500	$ 9,500
Computer system	1,400	2,000
Equipment (a)	0	1,000
Security deposits (b)	200	800
Automobile (c)	500	1,000
Insurance and bonding (d)	500	2,000
Advertising/Yellow Pages	5,000	6,000
Training travel	500	1,000
Working capital (e)	2,000	5,000
Living expenses (f)	0	10,000
Total (g)	$19,600	$38,300

a. You may work from home at first or set up an office. This category ranges from an office-at-home to a small office with lease deposits, signs, and some preopening expenses.
b. Utility deposits, telephone deposits, furniture rentals, or lease deposits.
c. Some franchisees let employees use their own vehicles at first, but you may prefer to lease an automobile for your crew.
d. Cost of required comprehensive business insurance, employee bonding against theft, and so on.
e. Basic operating expenses for the first one to three months, but this franchise does generate cash flow as quickly as you attract customers.
f. If a spouse does not work, you need to have enough capital to cover basic living expenses for three to six months.
g. Average start-up costs total about $25,000.

Royalties and Fees

In addition, you must pay a declining scale royalty that begins at 7 percent and declines to 3 percent for the best producers:

Royalty Rate	Gross Annual Income
7%	Up to $200,000
6%	Between $200,000 and $300,000
5%	Between $300,000 and $400,000
4%	Between $400,000 and $500,000
3%	More than $500,000

You also pay an advertising fee of 2 percent per week into a separate fund managed by a Board of Directors consisting of three franchisees, one subfranchisor, and three corporate managers. This board controls the ad fund and must spend 85 percent of the fund total to help build the local franchisees' business with national, regional, and local ad campaigns. It can devote the remaining 15 percent for test marketing, surveys, market research, and so on. Furthermore, each franchise must spend at least 1 percent of its gross revenues on local advertising efforts.

What You Get

In return for your fees and expenses, you receive a very thorough training program, a large territory, a reasonable term, and a very strong support network:

- *Territory.* You receive a territory with at least 15,000 qualified households. The company defines these households as those with total incomes above $50,000 with people between 30 and 45 years old in larger market areas with an ethnic and cultural mix so you can find an adequate labor supply.

Although the company's offering circular has a minimum weekly revenue quota of $1,000 by the end of the first year and $3,000 per week during the second and future years, company executives said that they see these requirements as goals and have never terminated a franchise that did not meet a quota.

- *Agreement term.* The agreement lasts 10 years with free renewals, except for administrative costs.

- *Training.* Maid Brigade's quality program includes three stages:

    Pretraining start-up manual with videos and separate manuals for advertising, marketing, and operations. The manuals are also on line through a computer network link to company headquarters.

    Five days of initial training at company headquarters in Atlanta, both classroom and on the job.

    Support for 120 days. For the first four months after you

begin, an experienced franchisee acts as your assigned start-up specialist who stays in close contact with you and to whom you can turn for help.

This "designated trainer" helps you blend very easily into the company's support network.

- *Support network.* You join a group of franchisees in the same region working with a regional coordinator or subfranchisor. This group helps each other with personnel recruitment, operations problems, marketing and advertising co-ops, and so forth.

  The company provides a toll-free hotline with technicians available for all kinds of advice and ongoing training seminars around the country throughout the year.

- *Termination rates.* The company reports very low termination rates and very high rates of successful franchisees who sell their existing operations for substantial returns on equity. During the three years between 1990 and 1992, the company reported only 4 terminations and 12 transfers or sales.

  Company executives stated emphatically that they do not believe in terminations. "We are in the relationship business, and we have to accept a lot of responsibility if someone fails. We train thoroughly and we give high levels of support, so if someone does not follow the system and fails, we cannot prevent it. But in our minds, we still feel somewhat responsible. If someone is not happy, we encourage them and help them to sell the business and recoup their costs," asserted President Don Hay.

With this very positive attitude among company executives, franchisees have a much greater chance of success.

How Much Can You Make?

Maid Brigade does not make earnings claims, but published articles and information I have learned from franchisees shows that during 1993, the average experienced franchisee grossed between $250,000 and $300,000 a year with net profits meeting industry standards of 20 to 25 percent.

For example, according to a 1992 report in *Executive Female*, Emily Adams in suburban Washington, DC, developed six teams within two and a half years and was grossing $300,000 a year. However, she sold her franchise for $50,000 (a more than 200 percent return on her initial investment), but then bought a regional franchise including two states, part of Virginia, and all of the District of Columbia. By late 1992, she had sold 27 individual franchises in her region; she received part of the franchise fee for each sale and receives a portion of the continuing royalties.

Adams's regional franchisor experience may be unusual, but her personal franchise experience is average for a Maid Brigade franchisee after two to three years. But you cannot achieve those results unless you develop several full-time teams and charge between $49 and $69 or more per cleaning, depending on the house size. The largest Maid Brigade that I know grosses some $12,000 a week; however, company newsletters report that the top award winner for 1992 exceeded $13,000 per week in sales on occasion. Furthermore, the Pacific region of ten franchisees had 1,000 customers and a total of $1.5 million in sales for average gross earnings of $150,000 per franchise. Overall, it appears that the average franchise can quickly build up to $3,000-per-week gross sales.

In short, you should double your initial investment during your second or third year and earn a middle to high five-figure income with the potential to earn a six-figure income as your franchise grows. Even better, you can develop significant long-term equity compared to your initial investment.

HUNGRY HOWIE'S PIZZA AND SUBS, INC.

Hungry Howie's Pizza and Subs
35301 Schoolcraft Road
Livonia, MI 48150
(313) 422-1717

Hungry Howie's is the 12th largest pizza franchise with more than 250 franchises by late 1993 with systemwide sales exceeding $83 million. And, like Fox's Pizza, it is one of the very few pizza franchises with total start-up costs below $100,000. Besides a low start-up cost between $75,000 and $85,000, Hungry Howie's offers several key differences compared to its major competitors:

- The original Flavored Crust Pizzas; customer surveys have shown that these flavored crusts have the highest customer loyalty of any pizza and that customers will drive farther to buy a Hungry Howie's pizza than any other type of pizza in its area. It offers eight flavors: original, sesame seed, buttered, cajun, poppy seed, rye, butter cheese, and garlic.

- Low-cost, but highly effective and aggressive local marketing programs. The programs are designed to emphasize your community service and connect you with local organizations with large numbers of customers: high schools, scout troops, PTAs and PTOs, children's athletic leagues, and the like.

- Terrific taste and product quality compared to its major competition at competitive prices, according to company executives and survey results. The company also created in 1991 the very popular and profitable "Fruzza," an eight-inch round of dough topped with cherry or apple filling, cinnamon, sugar and streusel, and introduced the "Pantangle," a rectangular deep-dish pan pizza, in 1992. It chose not to follow the "Bigfoot" phenomenon, the executives stated, because their three-pizza deal gave more pizza with more toppings at a lower price.

- Locations next to or close to strip center anchor stores, such as a major grocery store chain or a large video store.

- Two increasingly popular distribution methods: take-out and home or office delivery with an option for more expensive sit-down locations.

The only limitation to Hungry Howie's at this point is that by the end of 1993, you could find the franchise in only ten states, mostly in the Midwest, Florida, and California. Company executives said that the company plans strategic regional growth of 20 percent per year during the next five years. They plan to move into a new area and fill it in before they move onto the next area, unless a substantial area developer with the resources to build 20 stores should approach them with a viable growth plan. However, if you are in a state near a state where Hungry Howie's already has a presence, you could work with them to open your territory.

Hungry Howie's is also making a significant push into so-called arena marketing; in late 1993, it was named the official pizza of the Palace of Auburn Hills (an 18,000-seat stadium), the Detroit Pistons basketball team, and Pine Knob Music Theatre. As these programs expand, you should be able to take advantage of them in your areas.

How Much It Costs

Hungry Howie's has a very low $9,500 franchise fee, very reasonable start-up costs, a graduated royalty fee that helps you make more money as you begin, and a unique advertising fee structure, all advantages compared to its major competitors. The table lists the anticipated start-up cost range:

Category	Low End	High End
Franchise fee	$ 9,500	$ 9,500
Real estate lease (a)	800	2,500
Security deposits (b)	2,000	4,000
Leasehold improvements	5,000	25,000
Signage (c)	1,000	3,000
Equipment/fixtures (d)	40,000	65,000
Start-up inventory (e)	4,500	4,500
Start-up advertising	1,500	2,500
Training travel	1,000	2,500
Working capital (f)	10,000	10,000
Total (g)	$75,300	$128,500

a. First month's rent on a 1,000- to 1,200-square-foot strip center store.
b. Lease deposit, business telephone, utility, and other deposits.
c. Exterior and interior signs.
d. Preferably new equipment package, but all inclusive.
e. Standard purchase amounts for first 60 days of operation.
f. Employee salaries and operating expenses for first two to three months, although you probably will not need this much because pizza shops turn a posi-

tive cash flow very quickly.
g. Hungry Howie's executives said that the average start-up costs tend to come in at the lower end of this range.

A required purchase is Hungry Howie's pizza boxes that you must buy from a distribution company owned by company executives, and you must also buy all your other supplies (wearables, spices, and so on) from either an approved supplier or an affiliated distributor.

Royalty and Advertising Fees

In a benefit for the new owner, Hungry Howie's charges an increasing royalty on this scale:

Year 1	3% or $300 monthly minimum
Year 2	4% or $400 monthly minimum
Year 3 and after	5% or $500 monthly minimum

However, you pay an advertising fee of *only* 3 percent on the number of pizza boxes that you buy from the distributor at a rate of 15 cents for a single box. You *do not* pay any ad fees on your beverage, sandwich, and salad sales. If you are in a region with 12 or more locations, you must contribute your 3 percent to a regional advertising co-op. If you are not in a region, you do not pay the 3 percent. In either case, you must also spend at least 5 percent of your gross revenues on local advertising.

Company executives explained that new owners appreciate the lower royalty because it helps them build their profit margins more quickly, and established owners who have reached the 5 percent royalty level do not mind paying the increase because they realize the value they receive.

What You Get

In return for your fees, you receive a significant support package:

- *Exclusive territory*. You receive an exclusive territory with a one-mile radius from another Hungry Howie's franchise. In practice, no one is ever that close. Actually, company executives encourage you to locate near a major competitor; across the street is best, they asserted, because the major competitor's advertising draws people to the location, and your quality attracts them to your store. As important, your territory rights do not depend on your meeting any minimum sales volume.

- *Training.* You receive a very complete four-week training program, including a week in a classroom and several weeks working with a designated franchise trainer at an operating franchise close to your location. Training does not begin until after you have chosen your site and your contractor has begun construction.

- *Start-up assistance.* You receive the usual package of services including help with site location, lease negotiation, floor plans, construction advice, and the like.

- *"Soft" grand opening.* Wisely in my view, Hungry Howie's requires a one-week "soft" opening (no advertising except for box-topping) so you can work out the kinks and train your new employees. The company recommends that you have a formal grand opening when weather permits and your staff feels comfortable enough to accommodate a sales rush.

- *Marketing and new product development programs.* The company also provides grand opening and ongoing advertising and promotion programs for your local efforts. Its test kitchen also follows market trends to produce new products that attract more customers and increase your average ticket per sale.

- *Ongoing support.* You receive store visits from a field representative or the director of operations every 60 to 90 days. They can help you with operational problems and report problems to headquarters. In short, you receive a thorough program to help you start with success and grow, but as you know, the secret to this pizza business is location. With a good location and a well-managed operation, you can quickly build a very profitable business.

Even better, Hungry Howie's reports a very low failure/termination rate. Only 1 of more than 250 stores was terminated during 1993, and only 3 or 4 stores a year change hands. And the company has never had any litigation. This means the franchise has a very high number of happy, profitable franchise owners.

How Much Can You Make?

Like most franchises, Hungry Howie's does not make any earnings claims of how much money you can make with this franchise. However, the pizza industry has developed very accurate estimates that indicate that for net profits, you just cannot beat the pizza business; perhaps Chinese food gives slightly higher profits, but with a Hungry Howie's, you can net pretax profits in the 20 to 30 percent range, more if family members help manage the store.

You can expect rent costs to range from 4 to 8 percent, advertising at 5 percent, labor costs from 18 to 24 percent, supplies from 30 to 35 percent (including paper goods), operating expenses (gas/electric), and total royalties and fees from 5 to 8 percent. Total those and your net profits will range from 20 to 38 percent.

You can expect to break even at $3,400 to $3,500 per week, but expect gross revenues from $6,000 to $7,000 per week.

Hungry Howie's stores on average gross $325,000 to $350,000, with established stores grossing $500,000 to $1 million (for 115-seat restaurants in the Orlando-Tampa, Florida, area). So, within two years, your net profits should easily range from $65,000 to $105,000 a year, very good results.

However, if you are truly smart, you will find a territory for which you can sign a "multiple-unit agreement" (MUA) and build your own minichain of six or more Hungry Howie's within three years. After you establish the first, or first two stores, local banks may loan you the money to open the rest. Even paying managers, each store should still spin off net profits for you in the $25,000 to $35,000 range, so you can triple and quadruple your net profits, and build enough equity to generate very high returns on investment. In short, Hungry Howie's is a very interesting rarity in modern franchising: a low-cost, yet highly profitable and successful fast-food franchise.

DURACLEAN INTERNATIONAL

Duraclean International
2151 Waukegan Road
Deerfield, IL 60015
(800) 251-7070
(708) 945-2000

For almost 65 years, Duraclean has been one of the best cleaning franchises in the country. During 1993, Duraclean had more than 650 active franchises in the United States, Canada, and 22 foreign countries. It has been in business since 1930, making it the oldest franchise in continuous, successful existence, and the son of the original founder continues to manage the company.

However, far from being a stodgy firm, Duraclean has transformed itself during the past several years into a multiple-market, multiservice cleaning concept called Duraflex. Marketing Director Michael Higgins said that Duraclean had "blossomed" into a total cleaning company offering nine services for one simple reason: The more services that a franchisee can offer, the more revenues he can generate. As important, each service complements the other, allows add-on sales to the same customer, is easy to perform, and best of all, costs very little to begin. These nine services and the cost of their equipment packages are described in the next section.

Note that you can mix and match services depending on whether you emphasize residential or commercial cleaning or you set up separate cleaning crews within your area. The carpet cleaning, upholstery and drapery, fire and water restoration, and ultrasonic cleaning fit well in a residential mix, while the rest allow you to build a commercial business.

Duraclean recommends that you build your carpet business first and add the other services as your customer base and cash flow permit. Or if you have the money, you can add other services immediately, but most build and use cash flow to grow. It also suggests that you sell to both residential and commercial markets, but clearly, you will need different crews to do the different tasks. Note, too, that with the additional services, you compete head to head with other leading franchises, some of which this book discusses.

How Much It Costs

Best of all, the initial franchise fee is very low, just $9,900 (which has not changed since 1990), and you can finance $6,000 of that at a reasonable interest rate. At the end of 1993, the monthly payments were about $139, $38 less than in 1990.

Of the $9,900, Duraclean applies $4,800 to the license, trademark, territory rights, and training and $5,100 for a complete initial equipment package. When you investigate a cleaning franchise, determine whether the franchise fee does or does not include an equipment and supplies package. If it does not, your initial costs will be much higher.

In a very favorable point, the fee also includes all the cost of travel, lodging, and meals for your five-day training at headquarters.

Each equipment package for each additional market costs the following:

- *Market B*—Upholstery and Drapery, $4,315—you can pay $1,726 down (40 percent) and finance the rest at 13.9 percent. Or you can add a furniture cleaning only package for $464.

- *Market C*—Ceiling and Walls, $2,095—to enter a commercial arena.

- *Market D*—Fire and Water Restoration, $2,095—to appeal largely to insurance adjusters for their clients.

- *Market E*—Janitorial, $9,900—for a different, heavy-duty equipment and supplies package to offer cleaning services to office buildings and professional offices.

- *Market F*—Hard Surface Floor Cleaning, $3,500—to provide services for hospitals, institutions, shopping malls, and any major business with hard flooring.

- *Market G*—Ventilation Ducts, $7,500—to take advantage of a growing new industry concerned with indoor air quality.

- *Market H*—Pressure Washing, $2,200—for both residential exteriors and commercial-industrial interiors and exteriors.
- *Market I*—Ultrasonic Cleaning (vertical blinds, crystal, china, golf clubs, and so on), $10,000—with very sophisticated, new equipment for an upscale residential market.

Additional Fees

Duraclean's royalty is called a CAP (Cooperative Assistance Program), which pays for a plethora of ongoing training, services, and support. Every two weeks, you pay a minimum of $79 (a 19.4 percent increase since 1990) on gross receipts up to $640 (a fairly steep minimum royalty rate of 12.3 percent or more, but this is less than the 1990 rate). After that, you pay a declining scale:

8 percent of revenues between $640 and $2,200 ($51.20 to $176);

6 percent of revenues between $2,200 and $4,000 ($132.06 to $240); and

2 percent of revenues greater than $4,000 (at least $80.02).

You also agree to buy $850 per year's worth of Duraclean's proprietary chemicals, a minimal amount. And you must have business liability insurance for which the company has arranged a very-low-cost group program for between $70 and $170. You will also need workers' compensation insurance and auto insurance for a required van. The company also offers a group auto insurance program that costs $67 to $89 per month. You must have a business telephone line and a mail box, if you choose to work from home, how the vast majority of new franchisees begin.

Of course, with such a low-cost initial investment, you can begin part time and work into full-time status. Most franchisees do this, but some are quite comfortable with remaining part time. The following table gives a low and high range of start-up cash requirements:

Category	Low End	High End
Franchise fee (a)	$3,900	$ 9,900
Additional markets (b)	0	9,900
Insurance down payments	200	500
Telephone deposit	200	400
Office supplies (c)	100	200
Van lease (d)	0	600
Office leases (e)	0	600
Working capital (f)	1,500	5,000
Total (g)	$5,900	$27,100

a. Low end equals down payment; high end equals full cash payment.
b. Low end starts with only residential and commercial cleaning; high end adds various other markets or commercial janitorial.
c. Includes cost of mail box rental and office supplies.
d. Low end if you use your own vehicle; high end represents first- and last-month van lease payments.
e. At high end, deposit and first month's rent for small office.
f. Low end figure good if you work part time from home; high end if you work full time from an office to cover operating and living expenses.
g. Low end total more usual as new franchisees begin part time from home while high end represents an ambitious full-time start-up.

What You Get

Like many cleaning franchises, Duraclean does not give exclusive territories, but it does promise to avoid encroachment on your primary marketing area as long as you are building your business. You would use a better strategy as you grow by picking market niches available in your region.

You do receive extensive training through a four-phase, continuous process:

- *Phase I*—in-home study program with complete manuals and videotapes before headquarters training.
- *Phase II*—in-field training for two days with a cooperating franchisee who gives you a hands-on introduction to the work.

- *Phase III*—six-day comprehensive training at its Success Institute (including the cost for you, your spouse, and a partner. If you drive, this includes a car mileage allowance of 27.5 cents per mile up to the cost of one round-trip airfare). Compared to other franchises, this benefit can save you up to $2,000.

- *Phase IV*—continuing education through regional meetings, graduate courses, conventions, technical bulletins, and more.

Major New Support Program

Perhaps more important to your success in the long term, Duraclean has a top-notch staff of support managers, each of whom works directly with you to improve your business. First, a Business Development Manager helps you evaluate your market areas, your services, and your financial goals. He helps you develop a marketing and business plan so you can reach your goals. Next, a Market Development Manager helps you expand your services, hire and manage employees, and develop new customers. And, with support staff from chemists to mechanics, a Technical Development Manager helps you or your employees do the work properly and efficiently. The company also provides computer, accounting, and similar programs. It also has an advisory council that meets twice a year to discuss important issues. Some of its members are elected by franchisees, and some are appointed by Duraclean. In short, Duraclean's training and support programs are among the best in franchising, not only the cleaning industry.

The company also has a very low failure rate—less than 3 percent per year. Higgins reported that at most 20 franchisees had ceased operations during 1992 and 1993, and most of those happened because of death, retirement, acquisition, and other personal reasons. The company terminated only a few for non-payment of royalties. Higgins insisted that Duraclean "has a tendency to work long and hard to solve problems before they reach that stage."

How Much Can You Make?

Although it does not provide specific earnings projections, Duraclean is far more open than most franchises about how much you can make. The accompanying exhibit shows average income and expenses for four income ranges for 1992, the latest year available. Of course, your experience would differ from these averages. Note that average gross sales range from about $28,100 to $329,725 with gross profits (after direct expenses) ranging from about $18,400 to $171,900, for gross margins of between 65.5 and 52.1 percent. At the high end, the increased volume and labor costs reduced the margin, but increased the profits by about ten times. Note, too, that the best source of sales is repeat business, so good customer service makes or breaks your business.

Information from this book's first edition also showed that Duraclean franchisees also make very high profit margins on each type of service: 75 percent on carpet cleaning, 70 to 90 percent on fire and water restoration, 46 percent on draperies, and 62 to 78 percent. Even better, these services include royalties and labor and materials costs, so your own pretax profit margins should range from 37 to 55 percent.

Note, however, that the commercial cleaning industry is much more competitive, and your gross profit margins will fall; however, the increased sales volume may more than make up for that difference. You can sell add-on services, such as soil retardants and stain resisters, and additional markets, such as hard surface cleaning, to boost your commercial margins.

Clearly, if you work steadily and start part time, you can easily recoup your very low initial investment in your first year. But be careful about the number and type of payments you assume: You could have a franchise payment, a van lease payment, an equipment finance payment, and others that will sharply reduce your ability to earn both a cash income and a good ROI.

The cleaning industry—both residential and commercial—is very, very competitive, but it is also growing rapidly, so you do best to go with leaders. And with 63 years' experience, Duraclean has long been one of the best. Its recent innovations show that it plans to remain a leader.

DURACLEAN, INC.
ANALYSIS OF FRANCHISE SALES FOR THE YEAR ENDING DECEMBER 31, 1992

Franchises submitting monthly and year-to-date reports through December 31, 1992, have provided us with overviews of some financial characteristics.

For your examination, we have divided those reporting franchises into four financial groups: those with annual sales over $200,000, those with sales averaging between $100,000 and $200,000, those with sales averaging between $40,000 and $99,000, and those averaging between $18,000 and $39,000 in annual sales. Within each group we have, by average, compared common characteristics.

Factors	Over $200,000	% of Total	$100,000–200,000	% of Total	$40,000–99,000	% of Total	$18,000–39,000	% of Total	Combined Averages Amount	% of Total
Sales	$329,728	100.0%	$123,656	100.0%	$62,795	100.0%	$28,112	100.0%	$544,291	100.0%
Direct expense:										
Production supplies	11,914	3.6	13,567	11.0	4,923	7.8	1,675	6.0	32,079	5.9
Vehicle maintenance	16,391	5.0	5,666	4.6	3,082	4.9	1,798	6.4	26,937	4.9
Wages (to others)	100,491	30.5	30,455	24.6	7,899	12.6	1,217	4.3	140,062	25.7
CAP payments	11,458	3.5	6,801	5.5	4,948	7.9	2,825	10.0	26,032	4.8
Yellow Pages	6,562	2.0	7,336	5.9	2,976	4.7	1,468	5.2	18,342	3.4
Advertising	11,009	3.3	1,338	1.1	1,517	2.4	710	2.5	14,574	2.7
Total direct expense	$157,825	47.9%	$65,163	52.7%	$25,345	40.4%	$9,693	34.5%	$258,026	47.4%
Gross profit	$171,903	52.1%	$58,493	47.3%	$37,450	59.6%	$18,419	65.5%	$286,265	52.6%
Number of jobs	1309		820		412		240		2,781	
Jobs per week	25.17		15.77		7.92		4.62		53.48	
Average job	$251.89		$150.80		$152.42		$117.13		$195.72	
Source of sales										
Repeat	$206,579	62.7%	$76,072	61.5%	$34,349	54.7%	$16,386	58.3%	$333,386	61.3%
Referral	$60,280	18.3%	$23,172	18.7%	$10,869	17.3%	$5,372	19.1%	$99,693	18.3%

Yellow Pages	$ 30,211	9.3%	$ 19,856	16.1%	$ 6,644	10.6%	$ 3,654	13.0%	$ 60,812	11.2%
Other advertising	$ 30,658	9.8%	$ 4,556	3.7%	$10,933	17.4%	$ 2,700	9.6%	$ 50,400	9.3%
Return on Ad Dollar										
Yellow Pages	$4.67		$2.71		$2.23		$2.49		$3.32	
Other advertising	2.93		3.41		7.21		3.80		3.46	
Commercial	$ 35,073	10.6%	$ 39,453	31.9%	$ 15,449	24.6%	$10,944	38.9%	$100,919	18.5%
Residential	294,655	89.4	84,203	68.1	47,346	75.4	17,168	61.1	443,372	81.5

These figures are based on 1992 monthly analysis reports submitted by 104 Duraclean franchises. Of the 104 reports, 59 were either not complete or did not fit the parameters of this summary. All Duraclean franchises, including the dealers upon which this data is based, are offered the same products and services by Duraclean. These franchises offered substantially the same services to the public as will be offered by any franchisee.

These sales, profits or earnings are averages of specific franchises and should not be considered as the actual or potential sales, profits, or earnings that will be realized by any other franchise. The franchisor does not represent that any franchisee can expect to attain these sales, profits, or earnings.

Substantiation of this data will be made available to the franchisee upon reasonable request.

MOLLY MAID

Molly Maid, Inc.
540 Avis Drive
Ann Arbor, MI 48108
(800) MM MOLLY
(313) 996-1555

Molly Maid was growing rapidly during the mid-1980s, but started to falter after David G. McKinnon, president and CEO, left in 1989. Concerned about the company he founded, McKinnon returned, vowing to help Molly Maid reach its fullest potential. Molly Maid has righted its course, restored founder and chairman David G. McKinnon to his former position, and moved forward aggressively to reestablish its industry position. With 100 U.S. franchises by late 1993 and more than 320 worldwide, Molly Maid plans to add one new U.S. franchisee per week during 1994 and beyond until it reaches a core of some 400 territories, according to company executives. Its long-term plan includes up to 2,500 territories based on current demographics. Although the number of its U.S. franchises declined during McKinnon's absence, it remains the second largest in its category and is well positioned to become the leader, asserted company executives.

The residential cleaning market continues to be one of the fastest growing in the United States. Although that may be a sad commentary on the state of U.S. industry, the reality creates a significant opportunity for you to build your own business.

In this booming industry, company executives added, finding customers is not the challenge: Customer satisfaction, that is, keeping your customers happy, is the challenge. And the key to this satisfaction, they stated, is a professional approach to house cleaning. That approach includes making a virtual fetish of professionalism and recruiting and motivating the best available housekeepers. McKinnon insisted that the only factor that limits franchises' growth is their ability to manage and motivate their staffs.

Molly Maid's key advantage remains its serious attitude toward an upscale professional image for its franchisees and their employees. Raising image to almost a fetish, company executives said that the franchisees wear business suits, their employees wear traditional maid uniforms, and all drive distinctively marked dark blue cars with the company's pink logo. This approach gives their two-income-family customers a level of comfort that other maid services cannot offer.

The executives also asserted that they have raised the occupation of "maid" or housekeeper to that of professional cleaning person. Franchisees must recruit the best available people and pay them more than average to retain them. This reduces costly and high turnover rates, saves training and recruitment costs, gives customers service continuity, and reduces long-term labor costs. And the company structures its payroll so that it rewards performance by paying its maids on an incentive plan for both the quantity of houses and the quality of the work that they do each week.

For both franchisees and their employees, Molly Maid offers a Monday through Friday, 9 to 5 job, which has far more appeal than either retail or fast-food businesses. The executives challenged the long-held misperception that cleaning services are a second-class business, but they noted that as more corporate refugees enter the industry and understand the profit potential, the stigma is diminishing. More and more sophisticated businesspeople have discovered that residential cleaning is a $4.5 billion business, yet all the professional franchise companies hold only a 5 percent share of that huge and rapidly growing market. So, the potential for expansion and consolidation is immense.

The executives' recognition of this market's potential, their dynamic professional approach, and their drive to build their franchisees' revenues set Molly Maid apart from their competitors.

How Much It Costs

Molly Maid has significantly changed its franchise fee structure. The fee now consists of three sections:

$4,900 fixed cost fee;

$1 per qualified household within a territory, with a minimum of 5,000 households, or a minimum of $5,000; and

$2,000 for an equipment package.

The minimum total franchise fee, including supplies, equals $11,900, but the actual average fee ranges from $11,900 to $16,900 (the latter for a 10,000-household territory).

Most importantly, Molly Maid defines "qualified household" by customer demographics: two-income households, even blue collar, whose adults do not have the time or desire to spend five to six hours a week cleaning the house. The executives noted that although you might think affluent households would be the best markets, many of the company's most successful franchises are in blue-collar, middle-income neighborhoods.

They added that with a full territory, you can expect your total start-up costs to range from $25,000 to $30,000 with the following table showing reasonable high-low ranges.

Category	Low End	High End
Franchise fee	$ 9,900	$14,900
Equipment package (a)	2,000	2,000
Computer system	0	4,500
Auto lease (b)	800	1,000
Office equipment (c)	200	1,000
Phone deposit	200	500
Insurance deposits (d)	1,500	2,500
Initial advertising	2,000	5,000
Training travel	250	1,500
Office space lease	200	800
Licenses/permits	100	200
Legal/accounting fees (e)	250	500
Working capital (f)	2,000	5,000
Total	$19,400	$39,400

a. Enough equipment, supplies, uniforms, and so on to furnish two two-person crews.

b. Lease down payments and first month's payment for two vehicles.

c. You will have to rent an office in keeping with the company's professional image, so you will need some furniture and furnishings.

d. You must have "honesty" bonds for your employees and buy insurance that meets Molly Maid's minimum standards.

e. Fees for your accountant and attorney to review the franchise agreement.

f. If you need to pay salaries and/or personal expenses during your first three to six months in business, you need a nest egg. Molly Maid includes only business expenses for the first month in its UFOC.

Other Fees and Required Purchases

The franchise royalty fee is among the lowest in the industry.

Annual Gross Income Range	Royalty
Up to $300,000	6%
$300,001–600,000	5%
$600,001–900,000	4%
More than $900,000	3%

However, you must also make minimum weekly royalty payments after your first six months in business:

Months 7–12	$ 60 plus $0.003 per QH*
Months 13–24	$120 plus $0.006 per QH
Months 25–36	$180 plus $0.009 per QH
Months 37–48	$240 plus $0.012 per QH
Years 5 and up	$300 plus $0.015 per QH

*QH = qualified households in territory. For example, if you have 10,000 households, you would pay between $30 and $150 more.

Although Molly Maid's offering circular provides for an advertising fee, in a major change since 1990, it does not now collect it, but it does require you to spend at least $5,000 or 3 percent, whichever is greater, of your local gross revenues on advertising each year to promote your business. These may include Yellow Pages, door hangers, coupons, newspaper inserts, and so on.

Furthermore, as you expand, you must lease a new vehicle from a lessor for every two-person crew you add and buy it's uniforms, signage and the like from the company. But Molly Maid does not profit from these purchases.

What You Get

You obtain all the benefits that Molly Maid's professional image brings to this competitive market. The problems that surfaced at the time of the joint venture in the mid-1980s led many franchisees to drop out of the system. Molly Maid has since built a strong foundation and is growing rapidly. Now, the company is more selective with regard to franchise partners; during 1992 and 1993, only one franchise was terminated, and that occurred because of a personal problem. Thus, Molly Maid has not only returned to its earlier high success rates, but has improved on them.

For your franchise fee, you receive the following:

- *Exclusive territory.* As noted, it will include between 5,000 and 10,000 qualified households.

- *Agreement term.* Your initial agreement lasts five years, relatively short, but you can renew automatically with only a $500 renewal fee. Very importantly, you have a 60-day cancellation clause through which you can drop out of the system. The executives stated that it helps no one to have unwilling franchisees stay in the system, so they make it easy to leave. They believe that the franchisees' success will keep them in the system.

- *Training program.* It has been dramatically expanded to include the first six months of your business. You go through 30 days of at-home training before you attend 5 days of headquarters training; at home, you develop a business plan and complete a market study. At headquarters, you do three days of classroom work and two days in the field. Then, you enter the five-month "Right Start" program in which field reps visit you after eight to 10 weeks to help you "fine tune" your operations and evaluate your efforts according to seven key statistical results.

In short, Molly Maid wants to help you make sure that you generate a positive cash flow quickly. The executives stated that since "Right Start" began in January 1992, new franchisees have improved their results by 50 percent.

Other benefits include low-cost financing programs and ongoing support through workshops, conventions, conferences, and so on.

How Much Can You Make?

Unfortunately, as is typical in the industry, Molly Maid no longer publishes actual results. But the executives did state that, on average, the franchisees gross far more than the average income of their competitors. The industry average appears to equal about $180,000 while Molly Maid franchisees average about $290,000 per year with 15 to 25 percent net profit margins.

You figure the potential like this: Molly Maid charges $47 to $57 per house—and does not offer discounts. Part of its professional image is to maintain its price point. A two-person team should earn $1,000 to $1,200 per week, or clean about four or five houses per day.

Company executives asserted that you should look at the financial potential this way: First, look at the system and its professional approach and compare it to the franchise competition. Second, you should consider the company's financial model and royalty structure that creates a remarkable long-term ROI during a 10-year plan. In that plan, you can save $10,000 a year in royalties with the company's declining scale percentage. Finally, they asserted that you should consider the people with whom you work and their dedication to your success.

Clearly, since the turnaround began, company executives have reasserted Molly Maid's leadership in this industry. The franchisees' average gross incomes exceed both industry and franchise averages, and the ROIs on a $30,000 investment should exceed hundreds of percent per year within three years.

CERTA PROPAINTERS

Certa ProPainters
10871 N.W. 52nd Street, Suite 8
Sunrise, FL 33351
(800) 462-3782
(305) 748-3808

Certa ProPainters is the full-blown version of a 22-year-old successful franchise called College ProPainters that, since 1971, has made franchisees of college students who painted houses during the summer. Now, with Certa ProPainters, the company has turned the full-time residential painting service into a professional, systematic activity.

By late 1993, Certa ProPainters had about 50 active franchisees (College ProPainters had more than 850, but that is a seasonal summertime business only).

Before Certa ProPainters made its move, house painting had been done primarily by craft workers or small, local firms. With structured marketing and organized systems, Certa ProPainters brings all the traditional advantages of franchising to this fragmented business.

Certa ProPainters has positioned this franchise as an opportunity for managers; it does not want painters. Vice President Thomas W. Wood said that franchisees spend half their time marketing the business and selling jobs and the other half managing on-site crews. You hire six to 10 full-time employees to do the work while you build the business.

Wood cited these advantages:

- Consumers can trust a reputable company with national recognition with two-year guarantees and a high level of customer service.

- Franchisees receive complete training in all aspects of a business that Certa ProPainters executives pioneered.

- Franchisees increase their profit margins with national wholesale discounts for paints and materials. Wood said these discounts should save on average $8,000 to $10,000 a year.

- The low start-up costs (between $20,000 and $30,000) give many people the chance to build a tangible business with low-risk entry and easy sales. You do not have to risk your home or retirement funds.

In fact, so far, most franchisees come from among middle managers laid off in high-technology industries who like the informal atmosphere the industry provides. As Wood notes, the most difficult part of this business is motivating and supervising painters; selling the service is actually easy because it is usually in high demand. However, the low start-up costs, the potential for significant long-term returns, and this franchise's appeal to those "stuck in the middle" of the corporate crisis qualified Certa ProPainters for this book.

How Much It Costs

The franchise fee ranges from $10,000 to $15,000, depending on several factors:

Regular franchisee	$15,000
Previous College Pro franchisee	10,000
Military veteran (through VETFRAN)	10,000
Painting contractor conversion	(varies) 10,000

However, with a $7,000 down payment, you can finance either $3,000 or $8,000 for three years at about 10 percent interest—the rate is negotiable.

Total start-up costs add $10,000 to $15,000 to that total. You can work from home and use a truck or van, the cost of which will range from $1,000 down payment to $8,000 for a used van. You need $2,000 for start-up marketing and $5,000 for miscellaneous expenses, such as business phone deposit, insurance, and Yellow Pages ad. And you need some working capital for operating expenses; note that all salaries for your painters are paid from revenues received from the jobs they do. Add more to the $15,000 if you need a cushion for three to six months' living expenses.

However, Wood contended that with the company's telemarketing and direct mail programs, your business starts very quickly and generates cash flow just as quickly.

You must also subscribe to an answering service and a paging system and agree to extend a two-year warranty on every job. These services will mean additional start-up and monthly operation costs, and the warranty could mean that you spend time and money correcting mistakes.

In addition, you pay an annual flat fee royalty of $12,000, or $1,000 per month. This flat fee means that the more you earn, the more you keep. Even better, you do not pay any royalty for the first 90 days, so your first-year royalty totals only $9,000. That's it; no ad fee, no percentage royalty.

What You Get

In return for your fee, you receive the following benefits:

- *Exclusive territory.* Based on area demographics, you receive a territory with between 18,000 and 20,000 single-family homes with household incomes above $50,000. On average, homes need painting every six or seven years, more often in the Sunbelt, but Wood said that those also tend to be smaller jobs compared to the jobs in other regions.

- *Three-year term.* The initial term lasts only three years, but you can renew for additional terms for free. But at renewal, the company can adjust the flat fee royalty up to 30 percent for the first renewal and up to 15 percent more for the second.

- *Training.* You receive two weeks' training at corporate headquarters in marketing, estimating prices, managing crews, and hiring employees. You spend the first week on classroom work and the second painting and supervising crews on actual job sites.

- *Operating assistance.* You receive ongoing assistance with national discount paint buying programs, hiring and training employees, planning and executing telemarketing and advertising programs, and so forth.

All in all, this seems like a very straightforward and simple operation.

How Much Can You Make?

It may be simple, but you can make substantial returns on your low investment. Although the average independent painter grosses $60,000 a year, Wood said, the average Certa ProPainter franchisee can expect to quickly build a gross volume of $200,000 or more. The average residential painting job costs the customer $1,400 in Florida (smaller homes), $1,800 in the Mid-Atlantic states, and $2,500 in New England, so you need to have three full-time crews with two or three painters each constantly moving from one job to another. You pay the painters $10 an hour each.

Wood estimated that labor would equal 45 percent of your gross, materials 10 to 12 percent, the flat-fee royalty about 6 percent, and operating expenses another 10 to 15 percent for net pre-tax margins in the 20 to 25 percent range. You should net $40,000 to $60,000 per year within two years.

Fortunately, this opportunity is wide open. Certa ProPainters exceeded its first-year goal of selling 40 franchises and plans to sell 35 to 40 more each year for the next several years. If you want a simple, tangible franchise with easy marketing and an easy, low-cost, low-risk way to start, Certa ProPainters would make an excellent choice.

VIDEO DATA SERVICES

Video Data Services
30 Grove Street
Pittsford, NY 14534
(716) 385-4773

With more than 270 franchises, Video Data Services (VDS) is the largest and most successful videotaping service franchise. The company has 128 franchises in 34 states and 142 affiliates or dealers in 16 states, but all new licensees will be franchises. VDS has been rated consistently the best video franchise each year for 10 years, and it usually qualifies in the top 100 of all franchises.

VDS receives these accolades because its president, Stuart Dizak, is considered one of the most open and forward looking of all franchisors. He has testified before Congress on several occasions about how to improve franchising and make franchise agreements more equitable. In fact, the House of Representatives Small Business Committee is using the VDS franchise agreement as one of its model agreements.

Further, when I attended its 1993 annual convention, I found that VDS franchisees ran the convention, led the discussions, conducted all training sessions, and more. The experienced franchisees went out of their way to help the newcomers "jump start" their businesses. I also found that Dizak has a very small staff and prefers to limit his corporate staff and expenses so he can keep his annual royalty payment very low.

That annual payment remains just $500—no percentages—as it has been since 1984. Not only does VDS have a fixed royalty, it does not charge an advertising fee, and it continues to offer a very rare money-back guarantee. These characteristics show that VDS is a franchise worth consideration.

VDS is a very simple, inexpensive service business in which you can easily quadruple, even sextuple, your original investment during your first two years in business. Working with truly state-of-the-art professional video equipment, you videotape all kinds of events—from weddings to trials to legal depositions to business sales training or marketing tapes to children's dance recitals to speeches to conventions to workshops and to many more market niches. In fact, the most successful franchisees choose market specialties: One monopolizes the dance recital and children's gymnastics market in his town; another has no interest in weddings or children, but specializes in industrial training and business marketing videos; and a third concentrates her efforts on the booming legal market, particularly mock trials and pretrial practice sessions.

You can also provide very-high-profit-margin services, including film-to-tape transfers for up to 14 cents per foot. (The average 8mm reel is 400 feet long, yet your equipment does practically all the work, so you net practically all of the fees.) One franchisee reported that he charges on average $65 for film-to-tape transfer jobs, but his costs total just $5, so he makes a 1,200 percent profit on a 95 percent profit margin.

Best of all, you can begin the service part time from your home and keep your overhead costs very low. You can use your own car or minivan and your current personal computer for your administrative work.

VDS is an excellent franchise for women, and many of VDS's leading franchisees are women who work full time. Certainly, it is one of the few businesses in which women earn the same fees as men and can reach six-figure incomes quickly.

If videotaping services are so lucrative, why can't you do it on your own instead of buying a VDS franchise? You can do it on your own if you want to do all the legwork, to spend a year or two learning how to sell your services, and to learn how to buy the right equipment and to pay less than the retail price for it. In short, you can do things the hard, expensive way, or you can buy a low-cost franchise that gives you all the equipment you need and a national network of supportive franchisees to help you get started.

Money-Back Guarantee

With 15 years in this industry, I find that VDS remains the only franchisor that offers a no-questions-asked money-back guarantee. If you are dissatisfied after your training session and want to drop out, VDS will refund all your money. Some franchises refund a portion of your money, some will refund your money if you flunk out of their training classes, but very few give you the choice. Dizak said that he follows this policy first and foremost because it alleviates any suspicions that a reluctant prospect may have. He also wants to avoid two problems: (1) lawsuits over the franchise fee, and (2) unhappy, unsuccessful franchisees creating dissension in the system. On the other hand, most franchisors state in their agreements that they will not refund any of their fee after your sign the agreement, a practice that could trap unwilling and unable people in the system.

How Much It Costs

Compared to the very high short-term income potential, VDS remains very inexpensive. The total payment to VDS equals $17,950, of which about $10,000 is considered the franchise fee. The rest includes all the equipment, including a professional low-light camera, two videocassette recorders, a graphics generator, a microcomputer, and all other equipment to put you into business. The following table estimates your total start-up costs:

Category	Low End	High End
Franchise payment	$17,950	$17,950
Lease deposits (a)	0	1,200
Office equipment	250	1,500
Initial advertising	1,000	2,000
Vehicle	0	2,000
Insurance (b)	600	600
Working capital (c)	2,000	5,000
Additional equipment (d)	3,000	5,000
Total	$24,900	$35,250

a. Nothing if you start at home, the recommended step; about $400 per month for 400 square feet in warehouse-type office space. VDS recommends that size office.
b. VDS has arranged an inexpensive general liability group policy, but you can buy a policy from any source.
c. If you begin part-time and your spouse pays your household expenses, then you can reduce this to zero, but you still need to pay for business stationery, arrange for a business phone line, and make similar purchases to set up an office. You also may need to include a month or two of living expenses before you begin to receive income from your work.
d. VDS estimates that within your first six months in business, you will probably want to add at least $3,000 for a second camera an a special effects generator.

Other Fees and Payments

You pay a flat $500-per-year fee that pays for all ongoing services, including an excellent monthly newsletter filled with practical tips and equipment reviews. Although VDS could charge a 1 percent advertising fee, it never has done so and does not plan to do so.

That's it; as a wholesaler of video equipment, VDS makes most of its income selling equipment to its franchises. It encourages you to buy its equipment and gives excellent prices, but you do not have to do so. In fact, many VDS franchisees sell used equipment and services to other franchisees. For example, if you do not want to buy a special effects generator, you can call someone who has one and negotiate a price for the work. You ship the tape to the other franchisees; he or she does the work and ships it back to you. You can also ask other franchisees to visit with you and help you learn how to develop a production or do a job you do not know how to do now.

What You Get

Obviously, the two most important aspects of this business concern marketing and the equipment package. The equipment package includes a professional video camera, a VHS editor with low-level special effects, a color monitor, film-to-tape transfer equipment, an electronic editor, a graphics generator, two VCRs, and many accessories.

The marketing program teaches you how to identify and sell five important targets, all of which you learn during the three-day training program:

1. Conventions, exhibits, seminars, and speaking engagements
2. Home, school, and industry conversions to tape for quick income
3. Weddings, receptions, birthdays, retiree parties, anniversaries, and other social occasions
4. Legal depositions, trials, and mock trials
5. Dance recitals

The training program begins with two weeks of study at home. A three-day classroom session at headquarters follows. You complete your training with six weeks of at-home study with training tapes and materials as you begin offering your services. The three-day classroom session emphasizes marketing and using the equipment.

You also receive an exclusive territory that includes about 200,000 people in two or more contiguous zip codes. Be sure that your territory includes numerous affluent households, major hotels, a county or district courthouse with many lawyers near by, insurance agencies, real estate agencies, medium-sized businesses, and similar high-potential customers.

The initial agreement lasts 10 years with the right to renew for an additional 10 years. Although VDS reserves the right to charge a renewal fee, it was not doing so at the end of 1993.

In addition, as I stressed before, VDS provides very strong support by basing that support on franchisees helping each other. If you call Dizak for help, he is just as likely to refer you to two or three other franchisees as he is to answer the question. According to the offering circular, Dizak could charge for telephone consultation, but never has charged anyone.

Concerning franchise failure rates, Dizak reported that most often, the few franchisees who have left are no longer with VDS because they were not working out and for whatever reason lost interest. He only terminates a franchise when you do not pay the $500 annual royalty. Since you can work part or full time and make as much or as little as you want to earn, the annual payment is very reasonable. It also avoids messy recordkeeping and auditing problems.

How Much Can You Make

With VDS, you can create multiple opportunities to earn income. Virgil Miller began his business in 1987 after recovering from an injury as a sheriff's deputy. After two years, he was earning a six-figure income, and by late 1993, had continued to increase his income. Another franchisee came from a blue-collar job and has become one of VDS's leading trainers and income earners. Six-figure incomes are apparently quite common among VDS franchisees within two to three years.

You earn income in many ways. VDS reports that its franchisees charge between $600 and $1,200 for the average wedding. Others charge far higher fees to tape legal depositions and mock trials. Business training tapes often cost $2,000 to $7,500 or more for a complete production.

Recall the 95 percent profit margin on film-to-tape transfers. You can offer auxiliary services for other local videographers who do not have the same equipment—graphics, special effects, music, and so on—and negotiate fees for them. You can charge $20 to $30 each to copy tapes, yet your cost is about $2 for a tape.

At least, if you work part time and do one taping per week, VDS stated that you can earn $20,000 or more per year.

Apparently, the average VDS franchisee starts part time and earns a moderate income during the first year, then goes full time during the second year and dramatically increases his or her income. Net pretax profits range from 60 to 80 percent because you keep your overhead low. Be aware, however, that you can waste your profits by buying lots of new equipment or renting fancy office space you do not need. In sum, videotaping is a lucrative opportunity, and VDS is the best franchise to teach you how to earn very high ROIs in this growing industry.

Novus Windshield Repair

Novus Franchising, Inc.
10425 Hampshire Avenue South
Minneapolis, MN 55438
(800) 328-1117
(612) 944-8000

With a dramatic change in franchise strategy, Novus Franchising has shifted its focus from single owner-operators to more sophisticated, more experienced managers who want to build a business providing windshield repair services to large fleets and insurance industry. With more than 550 franchises in all 50 states, and 2,000 dealers in 52 foreign countries, Novus remains the world's largest windshield repair and commercial scratch removal franchise.

The number of Novus franchises declined by 19 percent during the recession from a high of 688 in 1990 to a low of 554 in 1992, but company executives attributed this decline to the recession's severity, the company's change in emphasis, and the desire of many part-time franchisees to leave the Novus network.

However, President Robin Smith noted that the company began a dramatic turnaround during 1991 and 1992 with these steps:

- Twenty new products added to the basic franchise package;
- Some $750,000 worth of new marketing programs and promotional materials;
- Expanded and extended training program;
- The new Novus First marketing concept that works through insurance companies to generate automatic referrals to local franchisees through a toll-free central telephone system;
- In-field training and sales development with Novus staff after classroom training at company headquarters;
- Uniform signage, uniform, and image package;
- Significant new version of its scratch removal package;
- New lines of chemicals and resins, essentially reinventing the company's line to accommodate new auto glass technologies;
- New auto glass crack repair system;
- New "headlamp saver" product that saves several hundred dollars to replace the complex new headlight assemblies becoming popular on new cars; and
- New operations manuals to help you manage the franchise.

In short, despite declining royalty income and product sales during the recession, Novus has devoted significant resources to change its strategy and preserve its leadership in this industry.

Smith reported that in 1992, Novus was rated the 14th largest dealership/franchise in the world, and its franchisees and dealers grossed systemwide sales of about $50 million during 1993.

Most important for prospective franchisees, Novus now seeks experienced sales, marketing, and management professionals who can manage a rapidly growing business. It also seeks area developers who want to obtain large exclusive territories and maximize the available market. Smith noted that Novus wants individuals with the motivation, capital, and resources to manage this growth.

In turn, Novus has "upped the ante" by raising its franchise fee and total start-up costs.

However, the basic business remains the same: providing windshield repair and scratch removal for the consumer and area fleet vehicle owners and branches of major fleet owners, such as car rental firms, telephone companies, utilities, delivery services, and so on. Novus estimates that the total market exceeds $2 billion a year with more than 8 million cars and trucks. Its key selling point remains that insurance companies and fleet owners find it much less expensive to repair a crack or scratch than to replace a windshield that costs hundreds of dollars. In fact, most insurance companies now waive the deductible and pay the full cost for windshield repairs. Commercial scratch removal also saves the cost of new glass, new sign lettering, alarm system rewiring, and the like.

How Much It Costs

With all these changes, Novus' franchise fee now totals $11,000 with an additional $1,305 training fee and various amounts for repair materials, equipment, vehicle identification, and promotional materials. The company estimates a total start-up cost of $23,000; the following table illustrates a reasonable low-high range:

Category	Low End	High End
Franchise fee (a)	$11,000	$11,000
Misc. equipment (b)	2,290	2,290
Training fee	1,305	1,305
Training travel	500	1,000
Resins and materials (c)	420	500
Franchise I.D. package	675	675
Equipment maintenance kit	115	115
Promotional materials	295	295
Insurance/misc. expenses (d)	2,600	5,000
Working capital (e)	3,000	7,500
Total	$22,200	$28,680

a. You can buy additional territories under a development agreement if you pay a nonrefundable franchise fee equal to $2,500 times the number of Novus businesses that you must open under the agreement terms. Then, you pay a declining initial franchise fee for each franchise that you open in the territory: $8,500 for the first one, $6,500 for the second, $4,500 for the third, and $2,500 for the fourth and each additional one.

b. In addition to the franchise fee, you must pay $1,530 for the windshield repair equipment and $760 for scratch removal equipment. If you buy only windshield repair, you can deduct the $760, but it would be unwise to leave out the important profit center of scratch repair.

c. The resin and materials for each franchise cost $195 for windshield repair and $225 for scratch removal, but delete the $225 if you leave out the latter service.

d. You will need liability insurance, workers' compensation, and various other required insurance policies. You must also have a business telephone line with an answering or pager service, and you may need furniture and equipment for an office at home.

e. If you must have three to six months of living expenses, add that. If you plan to hire employees, you need to include enough to cover their salaries until you begin to generate cash flow.

In addition, you must pay a 6 percent monthly royalty from the beginning, but after the end of your first year, you must pay either 6 percent or a minimum of $185 per month, whichever is greater. You must also pay a 2 percent advertising fee into a company-managed ad fund, but the company waives the ad fee for the first 12 months you are in business.

You may also lease equipment from Novus for $33 per month for 60 months for the windshield repair package and $60 per month for the same term for the scratch removal package.

Fortunately, you can work from your home and you can use your own car, truck, or van, or your employees or independent contractors can use their trucks or vans. You need to reduce your overhead as much as possible as you begin this business; Novus even recommends that you avoid financing and make sure that you have enough working capital on hand to carry you through the first few months.

Like most product franchises, you must also obtain replacement materials and equipment from approved vendors, including Novus.

What You Get

In return for your fees, you receive a minimum seven-and-one-half-day training program at Novus headquarters; the company has extended and toughened its training requirements to make sure you understand the more complex technology and know how to manage and expand the business. Smith noted that Novus will extend the training to ten days and beyond if the need arises.

As important, Novus Chairman Gerald Keinath is the "founding father" of this industry and offers his more than 20 years' experience. Further, the company provides its 20 new products, new marketing strategies, and new advertising programs to help you build your business more rapidly.

Novus grants exclusive territories to individual franchisees who enter into an area development agreement. Otherwise, it does not grant exclusive territories, but does grant "authorized areas" outside of which you should not compete. In return, the company states that it does not intend to open any new franchises within a one-mile radius of another fixed location or to establish more than one franchise for every 100,000 of population, except in rural areas where a 50,000-population area may be set up. However, the company has now imposed an annual minimum gross revenue requirement of $25,000 in windshield repairs and $5,000 in scratch removal (for those with both). If you fail to meet these minimums, Novus reserves the right to terminate your franchise.

These represent significant changes since 1990; the minimum requirement was $15,000 for windshield repair and $5,000 for scratch removal. Clearly, the company had to expand the territory to make them more viable for more sophisticated franchisees. Further, you receive a 10-year agreement, instead of five years, so you have more time to build the business and build some equity. You can renew for an additional 10-year term. You do not have to pay a new franchise fee, but you must pay any royalty percentages and other charges current at the renewal.

Unfortunately, a very promising deal with Sears to open Novus repair facilities in its auto stores failed because Sears refused to allow mobile services in the areas around Sears' stores. As Smith maintained, windshield repair is a mobile service that fleet owners expect you to bring to them. Other customers said they were not willing to drive their vehicles to Sears' stores.

How Much Can You Make?

First and foremost, Novus executives made it clear that the company does not make any earnings claims. The estimates of profit margins and potential income and profits are my own.

As the Sears deal fell through, Novus replaced it with a new profit center called Novus First. Working through a central toll-free referral service, Novus franchisees receive calls to fix the damaged windshields of insurance company policyholders. Smith asserted that this program has been very successful in those states where state regulations allow it. In Wisconsin, for example, a participating Novus franchise tripled his insurance business with just one insurance company.

In general, however, from Novus's 1992 financial statements, you can calculate that the average franchisee grossed more than $50,000 a year, a significant increase since 1990. So, it appears that while Novus has fewer franchisees, they may be earning more money.

You earn income by charging an average of $45 per repair (up $10 since 1990, too). The cost of materials equals about 4 percent, and the royalty and ad fee total 8 percent, so your gross profit before labor costs equals 88 percent. Hiring employees or independent contractors should cost between 30 to 40 percent, and if you keep your overhead low, you should net 30 to 40 percent of each job. If you emphasize fleet business, your per-job price falls to $30 to $35, but you reduce your labor costs and you overhead per job: The technician batches the jobs at each location, so he avoids travel and downtime.

If you focus on building the business and hiring others to do the work, you should build a high five-figure or low six-figure gross income within two to three years and net in the mid-five figures ($30,000 to $50,000) per year.

CHEM-DRY CARPET CLEANING

Chem-Dry Carpet Cleaning
Harris Research, Inc.
1530 North 1000 West
Logan, UT 84321
(800) CHEM-DRY (243-6379)
(801) 755-0099

Chem-Dry Carpet Cleaning is among the best carpet, upholstery, and drapery cleaning franchises in the country with more than 2,600 U.S. franchises and some 1,100 more in 35 countries, including Russia. Its founder, Robert Harris, has patented a unique carbonated cleaning method that gives his cleaning process many advantages: (1) the product gets rid of very difficult stains, including red dyes and pet stains; (2) it dries very quickly; (3) it does not leave soapy or sticky residues; and (4) the service offers a money-back guarantee.

The company plans to continue its current growth until it reaches 5,000 worldwide. It had planned to do so by 1993, but the worldwide recession slowed its growth.

Chem-Dry was selected for the first edition of this book because it has a relatively low total start-up cost and offered a reasonable package of services and benefits for the franchisees. It appears in this edition because of its new all-natural, safe, nontoxic product line "The Natural" and its relatively high profit margins. It continues as a very good opportunity for people who do not have significant funds, but who do want to exert the time, energy, and effort to build their businesses, especially military retirees, "outplaced" military officers, and corporate "refugees."

Chem-Dry also encourages its franchisees to start from home and keep overhead low, but it does not represent a "get-rich-quick" scheme. You will have to devote several years of hard work to market the business and develop reliable cleaning crews to earn substantial returns.

Defining the Territory

Chem-Dry awards a nonexclusive territory with an average population of 60,000 and a maximum population of 110,000. Chem-Dry defines these boundaries, but does not grant exclusivity, a relative shortcoming in the industry. It uses these three factors to define its territories:

1. County boundaries and population characteristics
2. Telephone directory coverage that prevents overlapping of two marketing areas
3. *Rand McNally Marketing Atlas and Guide,* a reference source that provides statistical information of business, economic, and geographic data about an area

Although Chem-Dry does not grant master franchises or area development agreements, it does give you the right of first refusal to develop an adjacent territory if someone else wants to buy it. In fact, it would seem the smart course for you to try to expand into adjacent territories as your business expands, but Chem-Dry has granted so many territories, you might be hard-pressed to find a territory without nearby competition. You might have to buy adjacent or nearby territories from existing franchisees that could be expensive. Or you can take over territory from a trouble franchisee.

How Much It Costs

Offsetting its tough territory rules, Chem-Dry has relatively low start-up costs, but still well within the industry averages:

Category	Low End	High End
Franchise fee (a)	$11,400	$11,400
Equipment package (b)	3,550	3,550
Vehicle lease (c)	1,000	1,500
Vehicle insurance (d)	200	500
Phone deposit (e)	100	350
Business licenses (f)	100	200
Insurance payments	100	300
Legal/accounting fees	250	500
Training travel (g)	0	0
Commercial space (h)	0	800
Computer system (i)	2,000	6,000
Working capital	5,000	10,000
Total	$23,700	$35,100

a. Includes marketing package, training videos, operations manuals, complete start-up support package.
b. Required start-up equipment, cleaning materials package.
c. If you need to lease a minivan or small truck, expect lease down payments of at least two months' payments. If you already own a vehicle you can use, eliminate this expense.
d. Down payment or six-month payment on van or truck.

e. Varies according to phone company and area.

f. Varies by municipality. Be careful, too, if your town does *not* allow you to run a business from your home or park your marked vehicle in your driveway in violation of zoning laws.

g. Chem-Dry has a new training facility at its new international headquarters building with a video and stereo sound system. It holds training for new franchisees each month.

h. If you work from home, eliminate this expense. Rent small industrial warehouse office space at low rents. The high figure covers a month's deposit and the first month's rent.

i. The low figure includes software costs; the high end includes costs of buying a complete hardware and software system. Chem-Dry no longer sells these systems, but you have the option of working with the independent contractor who bought the system rights to obtain this system.

Chem-Dry also offers optional equipment packages, but I advise you to start with the basic package, generate some cash flow, and then consider buying the optional packages as you see the direction your business is heading. These packages include the following:

Water damage extraction	$3,700
Drapery and upholstery	2,995
Carpet repairs	1,275
Interior auto detailing	285
Leather and vinyl repair kits	283

Therefore, a more sensible start-up cost range includes a variety of expenses that you might not otherwise consider; however, the start-up range remains a reasonable total compared to the three-year ROI you can expect.

Financing and Royalty Payments

Fortunately, Chem-Dry also offers a financing package. You can pay $4,950 down and finance the balance of $10,000 for five years (60) months at *no interest*!

More important to your long-term profits, Chem-Dry charges a flat monthly royalty fee equal to just $175—no percentage royalties or advertising fees—regardless of how much revenue you generate. In short, the more you earn, the more you keep.

However, Chem-Dry has steadily increased this monthly payment from $104 in 1989 to $175 during 1993, a 68.3 percent increase for *new* franchisees in four years, after only a 4 percent increase between 1986 and 1989. A franchisee who bought a license in 1989 with a monthly fee of $104 paid only $117.43 during 1993, a 12.9 percent increase, less than the increase in the cost of living during the same period. Each franchise's agreement guarantees that his fees will not increase more than the increase in the consumer price index (CPI). However, fortunately, Chem-Dry has never increased its fees by that amount, and in many years, it has not raised the fee at all.

You also must buy the cleaning solutions from the company. That will amount to about 15 percent of your total costs.

What You Get

In exchange for your franchisee and package purchases, you get the nonexclusive territory rights, complete headquarters and video training, 30 miniconventions (regional training workshops), ongoing telephone support, operations manuals, newsletters, and the like. In the materials package, you receive enough supplies to clean about 45,000 to 50,000 square feet of carpet, or about $15,000 in gross revenues.

As noted, the company does five days of training at its new international headquarters. It still provides its training videos and manuals—that you can also use to train employees—because the tapes are of such high quality that you can easily brush up on your skills without help. The company supports its videos and manuals with toll-free phone lines, a "911 HELP" program for those struggling with marketing, and technical assistance. Company executives also visit hundreds of franchisees each year both to help those who are struggling and to learn from those who are succeeding.

How Much Can You Make?

Chem-Dry does not publish earnings estimates, but you can talk to successful franchisees, and they can tell you how much you can expect to earn. Like most service businesses, Chem-Dry is labor intensive, but it has low overhead and materials costs. Therefore, you need to consider how much you want to earn per hour—if you plan to work in the business—how much you can afford to pay workers, and what size net profit you want to earn before you decide whether or not Chem-Dry would be your choice.

You earn income by charging by the square foot for your service. However, unlike the cut-throat competition that advertises very cheap prices for carpet cleaning, you take the high road. Company executives maintained that one of Chem-Dry's best advantages is that you can promise no hidden charges and offer a money-back guarantee. They said that the company refuses to practice bait-and-switch tactics that will harm their franchisees' reputations. They asserted that many customers tell them that the customers are glad that Chem-Dry was straightforward and honest about their charges. With this honesty, you receive the best advertising of all—word of mouth and referrals.

Depending on the competition's intensity in your area, your price per square foot may range from as low as 10 cents per square foot for major commercial projects to as high as 25 cents per square foot, with 16–18 cents considered a national average. On this basis, you would charge $240–270 for an average 1,500-square-foot home with wall-to-wall carpet.

You also may have to market your service at first with discount coupons to develop your initial customers, and that will reduce your gross revenues and profit margins until you develop a reputation and following. But the company recommends that you never lower your prices, and many franchisees charge premium prices during peak seasons.

Chem-Dry executives stated that an average one- or two-person crew can clean three to five homes per day, depending on house size and travel time. You should gross between $540 (three small homes) and $1,080 (three large homes) per day. Even better, Chem-Dry franchisees report that they earn net margins of 40 percent to 60 percent after all expenses, including labor. If you have one crew busy six days a week, you can gross between $160,000 and $325,000 and a net pretax income between $65,000 and $130,000. You can expect to reach this range within three to five years of building the business. Long before that, however, you will have begun to earn significant ROIs on your cash investment. This franchise offers significant opportunity to those who want to build it up.

Company executives noted that Chem-Dry franchisees range from 15-year-old Mom and Pop operations making a comfortable middle-class income to thriving businesses with 15 trucks going full speed six days a week. The executives said that they encourage their franchisees to set a goal of building a business with three to five crews and trucks so the franchisees can manage and market the business, yet reap significant profits.

Good Profits with Strong Equity

Actual Chem-Dry franchisees have reported gross revenues ranging as high as $2 million a year, but the average is probably in the under-$200,000 range. You also build significant equity over time. During mid-1993, for example, a Chem-Dry in Hawaii sold for $250,000, and during 1993, several Chem-Dry franchises sold for between $50,000 and $100,000. In terms of ROI on your initial cash investment, these resale values show that by building the business, you can earn a significant annual income, generate a very high annual ROI, and then sell to reap the equity you have built up.

Further, Chem-Dry has a very strong research and development program and plans to continue its technological leadership of a very crowded market.

6

Franchises with Fees from $11,500 to 15,999

KITCHEN TUNE-UP

Kitchen Tune-Up
131 North Roosevelt Avenue
Aberdeen, SD 57401
(800) 333-6385
(605) 225-4049

Kitchen Tune-Up (KTU) is one of those highly successful franchise services that takes a seemingly innocuous idea—in this case, restoring wood surfaces—and touches a nerve with consumers that creates out of nowhere a booming company. I have interviewed President Dave Haglund several times and I work with many of his local franchisees, and found that the Haglund family truly cares about their franchisees and encourages them to work together to solve problems and increase their sales.

Since early 1993, Kitchen Tune-Up has boomed, adding more than 75 new franchisees during 1993, and soaring past 250 franchise areas. As important, the results of existing franchisees in this five-year-old system continued to show impressive results, with many doubling and tripling their sales. Haglund said that systemwide sales have continued to more than double every few months as the new franchisees have completed their first wave of jobs.

This growth occurs in a very simple business: restoring dirty, weathered, greasy wood to its original luster on kitchen cabinets, paneling, desks, doors, office furniture, any interior wood. Although it began as a homeowner's service, KTU has quickly expanded its business into many new commercial and homeowner services. First is KTU Wood Care Services for commercial customers such as law firms, banks, hospitals, executive suites, anywhere in business that uses a lot of wood furniture or decorative wood.

Second, to its basic nine-point "scrub attack" for residential wood care services, is the addition of two more divisions: (1) Kitchen Fronts, which puts new, relatively low-cost kitchen doors on existing cabinets, and (2) Woodinit Furniture Care, which repairs and touches up damaged wood furniture. In short, KTU is quickly adding new revenue streams so its franchisees can expand their businesses more rapidly.

KTU's restoration services bring these benefits to either businesses or homeowners:

- *Huge cost savings.* A $300 to $400 KTU job can save a homeowner $2,000 to $10,000 to replace or refinish kitchen cabinets. This especially appeals to homeowners—and their real estate agents—who want to add value to, or at least improve the look of their homes as they prepare to sell them.

- *Preventive costs.* KTU commercial services can prevent businesses from spending thousands to replace expensive commercial woodwork because it has not been maintained.

- *Image boost.* Prestigious businesses, such as banks, law firms, and the like, want to maintain a high-profile image, and restored wood can enhance that image. Of course, commercial work nets much higher profit margins than does residential work, too!

- *No muss, no fuss.* The very safe KTU process does not use any dangerous or toxic chemicals, and homeowners can use their kitchens immediately after the franchisee does it. The savings of days or weeks of time, inconvenience, and mess that refinishing or replacing kitchen cabinets causes makes homeowners very happy with the service.

These make nice benefits for the customer, but for the franchisee, KTU offers a very-low-cost, low-risk way to start your own business that has a potential for long-term growth into a multiple-employee enterprise.

How Much It Costs

KTU has a $11,500 franchise fee. It also requires the purchase of a substantial $3,400 equipment and materials package, which should include enough material to recoup about half or more of your investment—not only tools and materials, but also sales presentations, marketing brochures, business stationery, training videos and tapes, and so forth. The following table lists the specifics of the total start-up costs that range from as low as $17,900 to $31,500.

Category	Low End	High End
Franchise fee	$11,500	$11,500
Equipment/materials package	3,400	3,400
Additional tools (a)	50	600
Office start-up (b)	500	2,800
Vehicle expense (c)	0	700
Insurance (d)	250	500
Training travel	200	1,000
Working capital (e)	2,000	5,000
Living expenses (f)	0	6,000
Total	$17,900	$31,500

a. You should have most of these in your basement or garage.

b. KTU allows you to work from home, but more and more, the company is encouraging new franchisees to open a small office to avoid home-bound distractions and to build a full-time, active business. The high end covers all the costs of opening an office.

c. Most use their current vehicles; the high end represents a down payment on a leased van.

d. You must have normal business liability insurance and any additional office and/or vehicle insurance policies.

e. This includes business start-up costs for initial advertising, Yellow Pages, business telephone line, and other business expenses during the first few months.

f. KTU's UFOC states that you should have enough savings or income from your family to pay your living expenses for the first three to six months, so I add this consideration to the high-end figure to represent three months at $2,000 per month.

Royalty Fees

In addition to these, you must also pay KTU a royalty of 7 percent per month on your gross revenues; however, to help you build cash flow, KTU waives the minimum royalty for the first 90 days you are in business. The company does not charge a national advertising fee, but its franchisee advisory council does on occasion seek contributions for national public relations and advertising programs.

You can also buy approved products and materials from KTU or approved sources, and KTU does make money from these sales. But it also charges prices and makes available products at discounts that would be difficult to find elsewhere.

In a further benefit, existing franchisees can buy additional adjacent territories for only half the current franchise fee, a significant break that should encourage many franchisees to expand their areas. In fact, a large number, perhaps a majority, do own more than one territory.

What You Get

In return, you receive these programs and benefits:

- *Exclusive, or protected, territory.* KTU offers two types of territories, depending on the proximity of the closest franchisee.

An exclusive territory gives you a population of around 100,000, and no one can open another KTU franchise in that territory. A protected territory allows KTU franchisees to sell their services in a larger metropolitan area, but it also allows KTU to put another franchisee in that area.

As KTU grows more rapidly and more adjacent territories are sold to different franchisees, the legal language in its offering circulars could cause confusion, so be sure to ask about how they administer this fairly and avoid encroachment.

- *Ten-year term.* You receive a generous 10-year term—most low-cost service franchises limit it to five or fewer years and the right to renew for additional 10-year terms at no cost.

- *Mutual termination.* Although many franchisors practice mutual termination, few put it in their offering circulars as a contractual right for the franchisee. KTU does so, I think wisely, because it prevents unnecessary disputes and lawsuits. In any case, KTU has reported very few failures, only 14 between 1990 and 1993, even as the system grew very rapidly.

- *Training.* You receive five days of training at corporate headquarters in restoring the wood—no experience necessary—and marketing and managing the business. After the formal training, Haglund informally puts you with successful nearby franchisees; you meet with them often to discuss problems and network with them for help on tough jobs, do joint advertising, or receive general advice on business building.

- *National marketing program.* In a significant move, KTU has agreed with two of the largest wood care chemical companies to use their numerous sales reps to work with and help local franchisees. This assistance and seminars at conventions will help franchisees do more and more profitable commercial work and expand into the Woodinit Furniture Care service.

- *Market and service development.* KTU now has four major divisions—Kitchen Tune-Up, KTU Wood Care Services, Kitchen

Fronts, and Woodinit—each a new revenue stream and profit center for franchisees.

- *Support services.* KTU also offers a caring and quality support staff and has hired new support staff to help cope with the rapid growth. Encouraging franchisees to help each other also relieves some of the burden from the corporate staff.

In short, KTU offers a very thorough package of benefits and support designed to help you grow fairly quickly.

How Much Can You Make?

You earn income by charging flat fees for "tune-ups" of kitchen cabinets, usually in the $350 to $400 range. At least, in late 1993, Haglund was encouraging his franchisees to increase their prices from what had been an average price of $292, a very undervalued service compared to the $2,000 to $10,000 cost to refinish or replace the cabinets.

However, you add to your profits by selling new cabinet hardware for 100 percent markups, usually $70 to $100 for hardware that costs $30 to $50. You build your profits by suggestively selling add-on services: "While I'm here, would you like me to restore that lovely antique desk," or "I can restore this door the kids have scratched up for just a few dollars more." These extra restoration services, which may take a few minutes, cost the homeowner an extra $50 to $100 or more, but most of that is pure profit because you avoid selling costs.

On the commercial side, you charge significant fees for work that may take a day or longer. By late 1993, the average commercial job price was about $900 to $1,000, but some franchisees were charging $6,500 or more to restore all the wood in churches in their area. Others were charging several thousand dollars to do an entire floor of executive suites in corporate office buildings.

In some figures published in KTU newsletters, it appears that you can quickly increase your gross revenues from $1,700 to $2,000 a month to more than $5,000 to $9,000 per month. The company was urging its franchisees to set a goal of adding commission salespeople to develop $100,000 in additional revenues *each* to net $20,000 to $30,000 more per year for each salesperson.

In general, new franchises, often married couples working together full time or with at least one spouse helping on weekends, usually work from home for at least the first year or so. They begin to expand fairly rapidly during their second year. They recoup their initial investment early in their second year and begin to build significant ROIs during their third year. You should begin to net a middle five-figure income ($40,000 to $60,000) a year by the end of the third year, perhaps much more if you spend your off hours marketing the business, following through with customer referrals and building the commercial side.

L.A. SMOOTHIE

L.A. Smoothie
700 Canal Street
New Orleans, LA 70130
(800) 643-3910
(504) 522-5588

L.A. Smoothie represents a unique combination of "smoothie" frosty fruit drink bar; salad, soup, and sandwich fast-food restaurant; and nutrition and health center. The "smoothie" is a combination of fruit, vitamins, supplements, and shaved ice blended at high speed to produce a healthy, cold drink that resembles a milk shake without the drawbacks of milk, fat, cholesterol, or many calories. They were formulated with the help of a doctor and a dietician. Although this "smoothie" is unique, other franchises serve frozen fruit drinks and have similar concepts. Note that a "smoothie" is not frozen yogurt or ice cream shakes.

I hesitated to put this franchise in the book because the concept and the company are relatively new; however, by late 1993, it did have two corporate stores and half a dozen operating franchises with plans to open 12 more around the Southeast during 1994. The company plans to expand from its Southeastern base through the Sunbelt during the mid-1990s, but it also plans to make sure that it does not spread its resources too thin.

Its experienced managers added new revenue streams during 1993 to transform L.A. Smoothie into a thorough concept aimed at health-conscious but relatively young adults with middle to upper middle incomes. The concept includes (1) frosty fruit "smoothies"; (2) healthy salads, soups, sandwiches, breads, and "guilt-free goodies"; (3) contemporary activewear (jogging and aerobic outfits, tee shirts, and sweats); (4) nutritional supplements; (5) a health reference library of exercise audiotapes, videos, and books; and (6) ecologically sound products, such as air and water purifiers and recycled paper products. These six revenue streams appear to significantly increase your profit potential as you locate your stores in "power strip centers" with major discount stores or supermarkets as anchors. This is an unusual beverage/fast-food store that can complement the others in these centers.

Furthermore, unlike almost all the ice cream and frozen yogurt franchises, you can offer all that an L.A. Smoothie has to offer for less than $85,000 start-up costs, a relatively small amount by fast-food standards.

How Much It Costs

The franchise fee is only $12,500, and total start-up costs range from about $60,000 to $90,000. The table breaks down the costs:

Category	Low End	High End
Franchise fee	$12,500	$12,500
Equipment (a)	17,500	22,000
Leasehold improvements (b)	15,000	35,000
Inventory and supplies (c)	10,000	15,000
Working capital	10,000	15,000
Miscellaneous (d)	2,500	5,000
Total (e)	$62,500	$104,500

a. Includes all smoothie machines, convection oven, meat slicer, and refrigerated prep table for salads and sandwiches.
b. Varies widely depending on whether you rent existing space or raw space and the amount of "build-out funds" you can negotiate with the landlord. A typical store will be 1,000 to 1,300 square feet with minimal seating.
c. Start-up food, clothing, nutritional products, and so on.
d. Includes lease and utility deposits, professional fees, insurance, permits and licenses, and so on. It appears that the miscellaneous category is too small to accommodate all the costs that the company put in that category. So, if I were a franchisee, I would plan to increase my working capital to include some of these start-up costs as well as working capital for operating expenses.
e. The average start-up cost is in the $75,000–80,000 range.

Royalty and Purchases

L.A. Smoothie charges a very reasonable 5 percent royalty and 3 percent advertising fee. Both added to my interest in this franchise because you can focus on building your local market yet keep most of your revenues.

However, you must buy some items from the company and sell L.A. Smoothie–distributed or –approved products. Primarily, these include logo items and labeled products that promote the company name and from which you may earn higher profit margins.

What You Get

In return for your fees, you receive a very generous franchise program:

- *Exclusive territory.* The UFOC only grants a one-mile-radius territory, but as a new franchise, the company is highly unlikely to encroach on your area any time soon. However, the company does reserve the right to haul a mobile L.A. Smoothie trailer to special events within your territory and sell products. Company executives said that they reserved this right because they take a trailer to the many outdoor events in New Orleans, such as the jazz festival and Mardi Gras, to promote the company name, and they did not want to lose that right when someone bought a franchise that included any of those areas. The company is highly unlikely to do the same anywhere else.

- *Ten-year term.* The company offers a generous 10-year term and a 10-year renewal with no renewal fee; however, when you renew, you must update your store to match the then-current store style.

- *Training.* You receive seven days' training at headquarters and a company store and another seven days at your location as you open.

- *Preopening assistance.* Before you open, the company helps you locate a site and negotiate the lease and provides standard construction plans.

- *Ongoing support.* In one of its best aspects, the company's rep makes monthly site visits and calls you on the phone several times a week to check on your progress and answer questions. The company also publishes a periodic newsletter with new products and pricing information.

- *Multiple-unit development.* As you succeed, or if you have a previous successful track record, L.A. Smoothie will consider an area development agreement. But the executives insisted that above all, they want to avoid failures, so they grant development agreements very cautiously, another wise step, in my opinion.

The company also has a fairly liberal policy through which the franchisee can terminate the franchise if, together, they cannot find a suitable site. And the company will refund 75 percent of the franchise fee, keeping 25 percent for site location and demographic expenses.

L.A. Smoothie executives appear to have identified all the key elements that help a franchisee prosper.

How Much Can You Make?

The company does not make earnings claims, but using results from the company stores does allow them to offer a range of operating costs and income projections. In general, the company estimated that a standard 1,000-square-foot store will have fixed costs

L.A. SMOOTHIE
Pro Forma Projection*

	A	B	C	D	E	F	G	H	I	J	K
1	%/Sales	$160,000	$170,000	$180,000	$190,000	$200,000	$210,000	$220,000	$230,000	$240,000	$250,000
2											
3	Smoothie	88,000	93,500	99,000	104,500	110,000	115,000	121,000	126,500	132,000	137,500
4	(55%)										
5											
6	Food	32,000	34,000	36,000	38,000	40,000	42,000	44,000	46,000	48,000	50,000
7	(20%)										
8											
9	Yogurt	9,600	10,200	10,800	11,400	12,000	12,600	13,200	13,800	14,400	15,000
10	(6%)										
11											
12	Coffee	4,800	5,100	5,400	5,700	6,000	6,300	6,600	6,900	7,200	7,500
13	(3%)										
14											
15	Snacks	9,600	10,200	10,800	11,400	12,000	12,600	13,200	13,800	14,400	15,000
16	(6%)										
17											
18	Gifts	8,000	8,500	9,000	9,500	10,000	10,500	11,000	11,500	12,000	12,500
19	(5%)										
20											
21	Vitamin supplements	8,000	8,500	9,000	9,500	10,000	10,500	11,000	11,500	12,000	12,500
22	(5%)										
23											
24	Subtotal	$160,000	$170,000	$180,000	$190,000	$200,000	$210,000	$220,000	$230,000	$240,000	$250,000
25	(100%)										
26											*(continued)*

L.A. SMOOTHIE
Pro Forma Projection*

	A	B	C	D	E	F	G	H	I	J	K
27 Less: Fixed cost		(86,600)	(86,600)	(86,600)	(86,600)	(86,600)	(86,600)	(86,600)	(86,600)	(86,600)	(86,600)
28											
29 Less: Cost of goods		(61,920)	(65,790)	(69,660)	(73,530)	(77,400)	(81,270)	(85,140)	(89,010)	(92,880)	(96,750)
30											
31 Net profit		$11,480	$17,610	$23,740	$29,870	$36,000	$42,130	$48,260	$54,390	$60,520	$66,650

The aforementioned figures reflecting sales, income, and gross or net profits were prepared by L.A. Smoothie Corporation for its own projections and should not be considered as actual or probable sales, income, and gross or net profits that will be realized by franchisee. The franchisor does not represent that any franchisee can expect to attain such sales, income, and gross or net profits.

192

of about $86,000, including rent, utilities, payroll, insurance, and other operating expenses. Your markups on your major products will range from as low as 100 percent on vitamins to as high as 500 percent on coffee. With very low food preparation costs, you will make markups on salads and sandwiches far higher than those for a normal fast-food restaurant. The accompanying table shows a nonbinding pro forma projection for stores with gross sales ranging from $160,000 to $250,000. With moderate success, you should have pretax net profits ranging from $35,000 to $65,000 by the end of the second year, if you manage the store most of the time.

Note that these are relatively conservative estimates because I know a franchisee who owns a yogurt and salad store in a major regional shopping mall; he bought it when it had depressed revenues of $275,000, and he boosted those revenues significantly. A turkey sandwich and salad franchise in the same mall grossed more than $500,000. Your revenues may not reach $500,000 in a "power" strip center, but your rents will be about one-half to one-third the amount you would pay in a mall, so your net profits should be about the same or higher if you promote your other revenue streams.

In conclusion, L.A. Smoothie has a very interesting concept that should appeal to the increasingly health-conscious consumer; if you are interested in that lifestyle, you should consider the franchise one worth serious consideration.

SERVICEMASTER

ServiceMaster Residential/Commercial Services L.P.
855 Ridge Lake Boulevard
Memphis, TN 38120
(800) WE SERVE (937-3783)
(901) 684-7500

With more than 3,000 U.S. franchisees and a total of 4,100 worldwide, ServiceMaster is a granddaddy of all cleaning franchises, with more than 45 years in business. ServiceMaster

Residential/Commercial Services (Res/Com, for short) is the franchising arm of a $4 billion colossus that owns Merry Maids, Terminix, and numerous other franchises *and* a huge commercial cleaning enterprise that specializes in major buildings and institutions.

In the future, the industry will consolidate because of ever stricter and more expensive regulations that govern the use of industrial cleaners and disposal and recycling of wastes. As the industry becomes more technical, more complex, and more regulated, only larger, well-financed companies will survive, according to company executives.

Thus, ServiceMaster's size is an asset to any potential franchisee because it can provide the training, expertise, and support that anyone needs. Furthermore, the company's franchise structure can accommodate both part- and full-time franchisees. Executives stated that the company continues to offer "tremendous" opportunity because it has five types of low-cost cleaning franchises that you can build as large or as small as you want. You can begin with one and expand into another, or you can expand the one with which you feel most comfortable and successful; you can start part time and work to become full time within a year or so—the course most new franchisees follow. Or you can remain small and earn a reasonable part-time income.

The five types and their franchise fees include the following:

- Window and Carpet Cleaning, for homes and small office buildings—$14,150.

- Contract Services, for professional janitorial services for commercial or institutional buildings (except hospitals)—$23,350.

- Small Business Services, for small-building maintenance in office and institutional buildings of 5,000 square feet or fewer—$12,350.

- Small Market Services, for professional building maintenance, carpet and furniture cleaning, and disaster restoration services in small territories—$14,250.

● On-Location Services, for disaster restoration and carpet and furniture cleaning—$23,350.

In sum, with any of these, you offer varied cleaning services for homes and/or businesses in huge markets that, despite the presence of numerous major franchises, remain fragmented. The total commercial cleaning market equals almost $31 billion. The segments range in size from $1.8 billion for small-office commercial cleaning to $1.9 billion for residential carpet cleaning to $4.0 billion for disaster restoration to a whopping $23.0 billion for janitorial, office, and institutional cleaning. Of this total market, ServiceMaster, by far the largest player, has less than a 10 percent share. No other franchise has even close to 1 percent.

How Much They Cost

In addition to the franchise fee, you must pay $7,500 for an equipment package for each separate operation. You can earn a 5 percent discount for cash, or if you are a minority member or someone with industry experience, you can receive a $4,000 discount for contract services and on-location franchises and $2,000 discount for the other three. In addition, you can finance up to 70 percent of the fee and the equipment cost. In late 1993, the company charged 11 percent interest and offered two installment plans, one with increasing payments and the second with equal or level payments.

The table shows the range of total start-up costs depending on which of the five opportunities you select:

Category	Low End	High End
Franchise fee	$14,150	$23,350
Equipment package	5,000	10,000
Vehicle lease/purchase (a)	1,283	3,000
Insurance (b)	1,000	1,000
Truck-mounted unit (c)	995	12,000
Working capital (d)	7,500	12,500
Total (e)	$29,928	$61,850

a. Low end covers three payments on lease; high end covers down payment on van or truck.
b. Covers vehicle and comprehensive business insurance down payments.
c. Ranges for low-end lease down payments of truck-mounted carpet and window cleaning units to cash price to buy the units new.
d. Includes all other start-up costs, such as professional fees, home office equipment, business phone deposits, advertising, and so on. It does not include any funds for living expenses for the first three to six months; ServiceMaster assumes many will start part time and hold a full-time job. Add more funding if you plan to start full time.
e. High end would be a full-time, major territory operation that you planned from the beginning. Most start-ups fall in the lower end of the range.

You should reduce your start-up costs by working from home and by buying or leasing used vehicles and extra equipment. A large resale market exists in these products.

Royalty Fees

ServiceMaster charges different royalty rates for its different service franchises:

- *Contract service.* Declining scale fee from 7 percent to 4 percent, depending on the service provided. No royalty for the first four months, but a $100 monthly minimum thereafter.

- *Other four services.* A 10 percent royalty.

They also have different advertising fees:

- *On-Location, Small Market, and Window and Carpet Cleaning services.* One percent paid to national ad fund and at least 4 percent on local advertising.

- *Contract and Small Business services.* One-half of 1 percent paid to the national ad fund and at least 1 percent on local advertising.

What You Get

In return for your fees, you receive these benefits:

- *The ServiceMaster name.* ServiceMaster is known nationwide for its success and its quality franchise operation.

- *Training.* ServiceMaster has a very thorough 11-phase training program that lasts for the first 18 months you are in business. The first four phases include reviews of start-up manuals and self-study programs. Next, you spent two weeks in on-the-job training with your area distributor, and only after that, you spent a week at the company's Academy of Management. Next, you develop a marketing and sales plan and set up your office, review your financial resources and identify your short- and long-term goals. In the last two phases, you go through a first-anniversary review and periodic reviews during your first 18 months. During your headquarters training, the company pays the cost of transportation and lodging; it does not pay for other travel training costs. Most people who buy ServiceMaster franchises are doing their first entrepreneurial experience, so they need this continuous and serious training to help them understand how to manage and expand a business.

- *Computer software and forms.* The company gives you book-keeping, accounting, and management software so you can generate reports and financial statements.

- *Continuous support.* You receive ongoing support from one of 75 franchisee-distributors who oversees your area. Both the company and its distributors hold regular training seminars and conferences four to six times a year, a regional conference, and a convention every two years. You also receive four visits from the distributor each year, technical updates, and toll-free telephone support.

- *Territory.* You receive a nonexclusive territory, but within it, you will have a primary area of concentration that the company promises not to oversaturate with other franchisees.

- *Five-year term.* The first agreement lasts five years, and you can renew for as many terms as you want very easily and at no cost.

- *Termination.* The company offers a liberal mutual termination clause in its contract. During the three years between April 1, 1990, and April 1, 1993, the company terminated 348 franchises, but this total includes retirements, unrenewed agreements, and failure to pay debt, in short, all reasons. Even so, it represents a very low termination rate of 2.5 to 3 percent per year. Executives said that the company "does not not renew" any franchise, and the company acts to terminate for very specific contract violations that the franchisee does not remedy after repeated urging and offers of help.

How Much Can You Make?

ServiceMaster does not make earnings claims, and its franchisees are so diverse—from one-person part-timers to multiple-truck operations with three dozen crews—that it is very difficult to estimate returns on investment. Clearly, you can make of this opportunity what you want to.

Most start with the carpet cleaning or janitorial service franchise and expand from that point as their income and customer base increase. They tend to shift from part time to full time during their second year, so by the end of their third year, they are earning middle-class incomes in the middle five figures. By then, they have recouped their average $30,000 investment. From that point, they progress as they want to. People with management experience who want to build their truck fleets and add crews can reach six-figure incomes by the fourth or fifth year and build equity worth many times the original investment.

Mini Maid Franchising

Mini Maid Franchising
1341 Canton Road, Suite C-1
Marietta, GA 30066
(800) 627-6464
(404) 421-1588

Mini Maid's founder, president, and CEO, Leone Ackerly, pioneered the team cleaning concept in 1973 and began the team cleaning franchise industry in 1976. Although some maid franchises have now surpassed Mini Maid in the number of franchises, Ackerly continues to claim the lead in service to her franchisees. For example, Mini Maid is the only company in this industry included in the book, *The Service Edge, 101 Companies That Profit from Customer Care.*

Furthermore, Mini Maid's $12,500 franchise fee remains among the lowest in the industry. Third, it continues to offer a flat monthly fee instead of a percentage royalty so you keep more of your income as you grow your business. Fourth, it does not charge an advertising fee. Fifth, it gives you a very large territory of 20,000-plus target households with annual incomes above $35,000 to make sure you have an adequate market to reach. And, sixth, it respects its franchisees enough to not automatically debit their checking accounts for royalty fees.

By late 1993, Mini Maid had 106 franchise territories with 53 franchisees in 29 states. The company reported systemwide revenues of $13 million during 1992, but one franchisee accounted for $800,000 of that. Thus, some 53 franchise owners, including new ones, divided $13 million or average revenues of about $250,000.

During the 12 months before October 3, 1993, seven more franchise owners joined the network.

This trend shows a decline in both owners and franchise territories since the book's first edition, but Ackerly has said that she strives to preserve the intimate and family feeling that the company offers, so she and her franchisees can help and encourage each other. She added, "We have an informal mentor program so experienced franchisees can help the newcomers. This has helped many new people succeed."

Mini Maid franchises are concentrated on the Eastern Seaboard and in the South and Midwest, so many excellent territories remain available to the individual owner. Within your large territory, the company expects you to develop one effective four-person team within the first four to six weeks and to grow your business to three teams as quickly as you can.

How Much It Costs

In addition to the $12,500 fee, you can expect your start-up costs to range from $8,000 to $10,000, among the lowest in the industry. This includes a down payment on a required minivan or wagon, which must be painted in Mini Maid's pale blue. You will also need a business phone, auto insurance, business liability insurance, bonds for your employees, and an answering service. Above all, you need working capital to pay your employees while you train them and generate your first customers. You also must expect to pay $1,000 to $2,000 to local vendors for an initial advertising campaign in your territory.

Further, Mini Maid charges a declining royalty that does not begin until you have been in business for three months. You pay 6 percent of the first $100,000 in gross revenues during each calendar year, 5 percent on the next $100,000, 4 percent on the third $100,000, and 3 percent on all revenues above $300,000. As good, it does *not* charge an advertising fee, but you must spend at least 2 percent of your gross revenues on local advertising, including the Yellow Pages, weekly newspapers, doorhangers, and direct mail coupons. Ackerly noted that an effective spot for ads is the local newspaper's society or lifestyle section. Mini Maid also saves you hundreds of dollars with a national Yellow Pages purchasing program.

What You Get

For the franchise fee, you receive the following:

- *Start-up equipment and supplies for two four-person cleaning teams, which includes uniforms.*

- *The largest exclusive territory in the industry (20,000-plus target households).*

- *Three weeks of training.* Includes one week at Atlanta headquarters, one week of previsit videos and workbooks, and one week of postvisit training with more videos and workbooks. Again, you can use them to train your employees.

- *National accounting services through Paychek.*

- *National Yellow Pages program.*

- *Auto leasing advice.*

- *Field consultations as needed.*

- *Newsletters and management bulletins.*

- *National convention and meetings with service vendors.* Insurance agents, voice mail vendors, marketing experts, and so on.

Perhaps best of all, Ackerly said that she is always available to speak with any franchisee about any matter.

How Much Can You Make

Mini Maid franchisees operate volume cleaning businesses that work most efficiently when one four-person team cleans seven to nine houses per day. Each team can clean a house in about 55 minutes with a charge between $49.50 and $69.50 per house, depending on the region. The average is $59. Your profit margin depends on how well you control your labor costs, which make up 35 to 40 percent of your overhead. One crew working to maximum capacity could earn $472 per day ($59 times 8 houses) five days a week.

But the company makes no earnings claims, and Ackerly asked that this author make that specific statement. These calculations are my own. Nonetheless, even with a $100,00 year gross, you can earn a significant ROI on your low cash investment of less than $25,000. By the end of your second year, you should be grossing about $100,000 a year with a net income in the $35,000 to $50,000 range, depending on well you control your costs.

If you want to work with a team-oriented company with an industry pioneer and earn a significant return, you should consider Mini Maid.

MERRY MAIDS

Merry Maids
11117 Mill Valley Road
Omaha, NE 68154
(800) 798-8000
(402) 498-0331

Merry Maids, consistently the most highly rated maid service franchise, was purchased by the $5 billion-a-year ServiceMaster giant in 1988. This acquisition gave Merry Maids access to the financial and marketing resources to withstand any downturn, grow more rapidly, and offer more services than it has in the past. (ServiceMaster is featured earlier in this chapter.)

By the end of 1993, Merry Maids had grown steadily and exceeded more than 782 franchises worldwide, including more than 700 in the United States, 50 percent more than in 1988. This number exceeds the total number of all its leading competitors combined.

With its long-term track record for growth and successful franchisees, Merry Maids is an excellent relatively low-cost franchise for both men and women, married couples, and partners. About one-third are owned by women, one-third by men, and the rest by couples. It has a very reachable five-year goal of adding 100 franchises per year to exceed 1,200 franchises worldwide; it added 94 each year during 1991 and 1992 and more than 100 in 1993.

Unlike other services, Merry Maids continues to use a two-person team that can only clean three to five houses a day. However, with a two-person team, you can field twice as many teams and cover a broader geographic area.

Like the rest of the industry, Merry Maids is benefiting from a very strong demand among two-income professional and managerial households between the ages of 35 and 55 with no time and no desire to clean. Company executives stated that the company has territories available across the country, particularly in the Southeast and Florida. Or you can buy part of existing large territories granted to franchisees who now find that they cannot develop all of them, so they want to sell part of their rights. Or you can buy an existing franchise with a business base.

How Much It Costs

Merry Maids has increased its franchise fee by 17.1 percent to $20,500 since 1988 for full-sized territories. The small-market franchise fee is just $12,500. However, in one of the primary benefits that Merry Maids offers, you can now finance up to $11,500 of your fee through ServiceMaster Acceptance Corporation at prevailing interest rates and loan terms. Thus, you can reduce your cash requirements by 30 to 40 percent.

Total start-up costs range between $19,000 and $36,000. In return, you receive an exclusive territory, complete training, and enough equipment to outfit two two-person teams. See the following table for a division of start-up costs.

Category	Low End	High End
Franchise fee	$12,500	$20,500
Training travel	500	1,000
Computer system (a)	1,500	2,000
Utility deposits (b)	200	750
Insurance deposits	1,000	2,000
Office rent deposits	250	800
Office furniture, supplies	500	1,000
Working capital (c)	1,500	3,000
Total	$17,950	$31,050

a. Low end for software and additional equipment if you own an IBM PC or compatible; high end for total new system.
b. Includes phone and utility deposits for office space rental.
c. A relatively low figure at both ends if you and a spouse plan to do this full time. This applies only if you can rely on another income for living expenses.

Other Fees and Costs

You must also pay a weekly 7 percent royalty or "service fee" on your first $500,000 of annual sales, but only 5 percent on any amount over that. You must maintain a full-time telephone with a 24-hour answering service and advertise continually in the local Yellow Pages; you save on that by participating in local co-op ad groups.

After the first 90 days in business, you must pay a weekly software license fee until your gross sales reach $3,000 a week.

However, as a notable benefit, Merry Maids does *not* charge an advertising fee. The company has negotiated national rates for franchises with the nation's largest direct mail suppliers, Val-Pak,

ADVO, and Money Mailer (the last is featured in this book). To gain low-cost national advertising, Merry Maids' marketing executives negotiate promotional and incentive tie-ins with national manufacturers, including Dial, Handi-Wipes, and Montgomery Ward. The company has documented the huge free advertising boost that a local franchise receives and that attracts new customers. Nationwide, these promotions bring in millions of dollars worth of new business each year, they stated.

Required Sales Quota

Merry Maids retains a tough weekly sales quota: You must achieve a weekly sales volume of $2,000 per week ($104,000 per year) by the end of your first year. The small-market quota is $1,500 per week. Otherwise, Merry Maids has the right to terminate the franchise. However, very few franchises fail to achieve this level, and this minimum indicates how well you can do if you follow the system. It serves more as a goal to help push you to develop more teams, market your services more widely, and build your customer base.

One thing is clear: Merry Maids wants its owners to be full-time managers of rapidly growing businesses. Although they do not tend to do as well over the long haul, owners can hire full-time managers who spend all their time managing their teams. Of course, hiring a manager will sharply reduce your ROI.

What You Get

You receive an excellent package of benefits and support:

- *Exclusive territory.* It will have a minimum of 10,000 "qualified households," that is, middle- and upper middle-class households with potential customers. The secret to success is owning a precisely targeted territory full of affluent, two-income professional and managerial households. For example, among the most successful Merry Maids franchisees is the one in Columbia, Maryland, an affluent area of two-income professional and managerial households with average household incomes well above $50,000 a year.

- *ServiceMaster Quality Service Network.* The parent company sponsors a toll-free 800 number service that unifies under one roof all inquiries for any of its services. It refers all calls to the franchisee closest to the customer. Anyone can call 1-800-WE SERVE for everything from maid service to pest control to lawn care to home warranty to carpet cleaning to disaster restoration services.

- *Five-year term.* The original agreement lasts five years, but you can renew for additional terms at low cost.

- *Training.* You receive five days' training at company headquarters that emphasizes team management, marketing, and professional cleaning service management. The company holds at least seven national and regional training seminars per year and a national convention that more than 80 percent of all franchisees attend. You can also use a complete video library to help train your team employees and learn advanced techniques.

- *Data management system.* The company has a very sophisticated computer system that manages the difficult aspects of your operation: scheduling, labor costs, and customer tracking.

- *Staff support.* Company executives said that by late 1993, the company had more than 39 support staff employees and 21 franchisees who act as regional coordinators. The corporate staff includes eight former franchisees. In fact, the fourth largest franchisee retired, sold the business to his son, and went to work in franchise support at headquarters.

- *"Buddy Program."* Merry Maids encourages you to work with your neighboring franchisees through a formal "buddy system." The "buddies" monitor your progress and help you improve your operation. Although not unique, this is very unusual in franchising and a very positive sign.

- *Low termination rates.* Merry Maids continues to have one of the lowest involuntary termination rates in the industry. Many are sold by their owners who have built up the business and want to take out their equity. Merry Maids franchises often sell for $100,000 or more, so you can triple your investment when you sell out, after you have garnered high ROIs for many years.

How Much Can You Make?

Merry Maids' company publications indicate a significant level of success. For example, more than 100 franchise owners, or about 15 percent, received a four-day trip for producing at least $6,000 in weekly sales between October 21 and December 26, 1992. At an annual pace, their gross income would exceed $300,000. More significant, the highest total weekly sales exceeded $40,000, or $2 million a year.

From these experiences and other company reports, you should plan to build your teams rapidly to boost your revenue growth. You pay your labor $7 to $9 per hour, but charge $59 to $65 per house. If you pay a 7 percent royalty, 25 percent for overhead, 4 percent for supplies, 35 percent for labor, and 4 percent for advertising, you should net about 23 to 27 percent in pretax income.

You should exceed $2,000 per week during your first year with a gross income between $100,000 and $200,000 by the end of your second year. You should break even within six months to a year. You should have approximate net incomes of $20,000 during your first year and $40,000 to $50,000 during your second.

Merry Maids remains among the top three maid service franchises, and it is poised for steady growth during the 1990s.

THE SPORTS SECTION, INC.

The Sports Section, Inc.
3120 Medlock Bridge Road, Building A
Norcross, GA 30071
(800) 321-9127
(404) 416-6604

I learned firsthand about how The Sports Section works and how profitable it can be. During summer 1993, my stepson played county league baseball, and the local Sports Section franchisee took his team pictures. However, the franchisee and an assistant spent just one morning taking pictures of dozens of baseball players, most of whom spent at least $15 for a package that included individual photos and a team photo. The processing cost for these photos equaled about 40 to 50 percent of the retail price. After his expenses, this local franchisee netted at least 20 to 30 percent, or $5 per player. And he was doing it as a full-time summer job because he was a part-time high school football coach and full-time Sports Section franchisee. When I experienced this operation firsthand, I knew it could become a very profitable full- or part-time franchise.

By late 1993, The Sports Section had plenty of territories still available. The company awards territories based on the number of people in an area. Look for areas with a high number of youngsters and high parental interest in youth sports.

As I indicated, The Sports Section provides team and individual photographic services for schools and sports leagues. They range from Little League to youth soccer, hockey, football, basketball, lacrosse, summer camps, karate schools, dance and gymnastics groups, and swim teams—some 300 different types of sports or youth groups. Of course, the major sports act as the mainstays of the business. You do not need any photography experience because the company teaches all the photographic skills you need to operate the business.

The best Sports Sections franchisees have a full-time salesperson and a primary photographer with several other dependable part-time photographers and numerous assistants. The owners keep overhead low with part-time labor and by paying sales commissions.

This franchise also represents a very simple "soft sell" in which gregarious people who enjoy youth and sports may do very well. It may help to have a connection to your local leagues, perhaps as a coach, a coordinator, a parent, and so on. But to make this a success, you must understand that it is like any other type of selling—it is a numbers game in which you must contract with so many teams and leagues and take so many pictures to first reach breakeven and then make significant profits.

Even more important, you attract add-on sales because you offer 120 types of photographic layouts, sizes and types of photos, and auxiliary products. They range from a basic "MemoryMate" with a 5 × 7 group , 3 × 5 player photo, and wallet-size photos to packages with several individual 8 × 10 photos, 5 × 7 photos, and many wallet-size ones to personalized sports cards, pennants, key chains, magazine covers, photo mirrors, calendars, statues, I.D. cards, posters of various sizes, a collector series of individual photos, and many more. You can gently or aggressively upsell these products to the players or their parents to increase your profits.

This franchise can be very enjoyable and rewarding, but you also must run it like a business to make a significant return on your investment.

By the end of 1993, The Sports Section had awarded 88 territories in this home-based, recession-resistant, cash, low-overhead business.

How Much It Costs

The company offers three types of franchises with different fees based on different-size territories. Each also has minimum sales quotas and different equipment packages.

- *Plan A*. Requires a $14,500 franchise fee for a territory with up to 500,000 population. Five-year term, with field training, but no financing. You receive a complete outdoor photography equipment package, in-field sales and photo training, and corporate support. You are expected to generate $15,000 in processing fees (wholesale prices that the franchisor charges you to develop the photos) during your first year and $20,000 during each year after that. You must pay a $1,000 renewal fee when the agreement expires. You also pay a 15 percent premium over the base wholesale processing fee that reduces your gross profit margins.

- *Plan B*. Requires a $19,500 franchise fee for a territory with a population up to 750,000 people. Five-year term with no financing and sales and photo training in the field. You receive a complete outdoor photography equipment package and support services. You pay a 10 percent premium above the base wholesale processing cost. You are expected to generate $15,000 worth of processing fees during your first year and $20,000 during each year after that. You pay only a $500 renewal fee when the agreement expires. Company executives stated that 60 to 70 percent of all franchisees begin with this plan.

- *Plan C.* Requires a $31,500 franchise fee ($29,500 if paid in cash) with $20,500 cash payment and four installment payments: $2,000 in 30 days and $3,000 each on the 60th, 90th and 120th days after the agreement begins. You receive a 1-million-population territory, a five-year term with the financing option, and a complete outdoor and indoor photography equipment package. Training includes extended instruction in equipment use and marketing and business development. You must also generate $15,000 in processing fees during the first year and $20,000 a year thereafter, but you pay no renewal fee. Even better, you avoid any add-on charges to the base wholesale price for photo processing, so your gross profit margins increase.

In short, the more you pay, the more territory you can buy to expand your market area.

The table shows estimated start-up cost ranges:

Category	Low End	High End
Franchise fee	$14,900	$31,500
Equipment/supplies	2,500	4,000
Film (a)	100	1,500
Advertising	0	350
Deposits (b)	100	1,000
Answering machine (c)	50	250
Working capital (d)	250	5,000
Total	$17,900	$43,600

a. You receive an initial supply; this represents additional purchases.
b. If you work from home, you only need a deposit for a business phone line; if you open an office, you must add lease security deposits and perhaps utility deposits. Almost all franchisees work from home.
c. Required by franchisor; a voice mail service may work, too.
d. Low end for at-home operating expenses; high end includes cost of opening and running an office for two to three months before you reach break even.

The company does not charge any royalties or advertising fees, but it does require you to use its production facility to develop your photographs. The company essentially charges you wholesale prices to which you add a substantial markup that you determine according to the price the competition charges in your area and your own ability to negotiate a fair price with your clients. For example, an average purchase may include an 8 × 10 group photo and a 5 × 7 individual photo, both in a matte-embossed frame, and eight wallet-size photos. The company charges you about $7.00 and you charge $14 to $16, or a 100 percent or more markup and a 50 percent gross profit margin.

What You Get

As the discussion of the individual franchise plans indicated, you receive a protected territory, a five-year agreement term with an inexpensive or no renewal fee, an equipment package, and a package of support services. In general, you receive in-field training, including a day or two making sales calls and a day or two conducting a photo shoot in your own territory. All packages give you about six days of training.

Everyone can attend two or more training seminars per year, use the toll-free hotline, and work with field representatives who pay occasional visits to your area.

The company also reports a very low termination rate, only three in one year, and two of those were terminated because of each franchisee's family problems; another ten operations were sold or transferred when partners split up, franchisees sold out for a profit, or part-time owners took full-time jobs in other areas.

How Much Can You Make?

Like most franchises, The Sports Section does not make earnings claims, but it does provide price sheets that show how much it charges its franchisees for photo processing services. These price sheets show that, as I noted, you can earn very high gross profit margins on individual items. These margins range from 40 to 70 percent. To maximize your profits, you determine how much you can charge and strive to keep your overhead low.

For example, with a $16 average purchase across the country, in a one-day photo shoot, you can photograph 400 kids (approximately 80 to 90 percent will purchase a package) with one setup, two cameras, and one photo assistant. You shoot one team every 10 to 15 minutes (it's true; I saw them do it very easily and quickly). You take the parents' checks before you shoot the photos, and you may gross more than $4,200 during that day. After you pay for production and other costs, you may net $800 to $1,300 for that day's shoot.

Of course, you must also devote time to selling the leagues, managing the operation, maintaining customer relationships, and the like. During the peak months, you should have photo shoots often and generate a significant return on your initial investment after you have developed the business for two or three years.

If you are a sales-oriented person who enjoys developing and maintaining relationships with amateur and school athletic league coordinators and coaches, you should find this a very lucrative franchise that offers far more product variety and more support than any similar enterprise.

JACKSON HEWITT TAX SERVICE

Jackson Hewitt Tax Service
4575 Bonney Road
Virginia Beach, VA 23462
(800) 277-FAST (3278)
(804) 499-3007

I admire Jackson Hewitt's moxie: In its franchise packet, it shows an aerial view of its oldest and largest location where its major competitor has put not one, but two, offices, one next door and one across the street. Yet, Jackson Hewitt executives said that their office increased its volume 7.2 percent during that tax season.

Humorous notes aside, Jackson Hewitt Tax Service has leaped ahead of its stodgy competition to embrace the hottest trend in tax return preparation: electronic tax return filing and refund anticipation loans for people who want their money quickly. During 1993, Jackson Hewitt filed more than 380,000 electronic returns, a market share of about 3 percent of all electronic returns, by far the largest share of any tax return preparation franchise. Yet, franchisees need know nothing about tax returns, electronic filing, and the like. Following the company's system, you hire part-time and seasonal tax return preparers who do the work while you manage and market the business. In fact, company executives said that of their more than 800 franchisees by the end of 1993, one-third were accountants, certified public accountants (CPAs), or attorneys; one-third were tax preparers; and one-third had no previous tax experience.

Although the franchise was among the fastest growing in the country during 1992 and 1993, the executives stated that they screened prospects very carefully to find the best people with these characteristics: "people person," flexible personality, above-average intelligence, modest means, risk-taking ability moderated by an ability to follow a system, seeker of American dream, and one who can provide good customer service.

To find these paragons, Jackson Hewitt puts prospects through the most thorough review procedure that I have ever found in the franchising industry. First, you file a detailed application. Next, you go through a one-hour telephone interview with a regional director/business partner. If you want financing, the closest regional director meets with you in person. Then, an executive committee reviews a formal report that the director prepares.

After you are accepted as a franchisee and begin training, you are evaluated again; if you do not meet their requirements, you can be asked to leave because Jackson Hewitt executives do *not* sign your franchise agreement until you pass muster during training. As a result of this very thorough screening, the company is turning down one-third of its applicants before they reach training and another fifth during training.

Only then can you open your doors and start hiring your part-time employees on Jackson Hewitt's practically "idiotproof" expert automated system. In fact, this expert system holds the secret to your success: With it, you can hire relatively low-paid, inexperienced people who basically are trained to follow a fill-in-the-blanks tax return presented to them on screen. Your market consists of middle- and low-income wage earners, many, if not most of whom expect tax refunds. You earn income by charging fees that vary with the amount of time you spend to prepare the return and by the return's complexity. You also receive a small fee for setting up refund anticipation loans. In short, you generate high customer volumes. Fortunately, the franchise has relatively low start-up costs.

How Much It Costs

Jackson Hewitt charges a $15,000 franchise fee with total estimated start-up costs of about $28,000. The table shows a range of possible costs:

Category	Low End	High End
Franchise fee	$15,000	$15,000
Initial advertising	3,000	5,000
Equipment and signs (a)	1,500	2,000
Training travel	250	1,400
Lease deposits/improvements	1,900	2,500
Insurance	500	750
Miscellaneous (b)	1,000	1,500
Working capital (c)	3,500	4,000
Total	$26,650	$32,150

a. Leases for fax machines, computer, signage.
b. Business phone deposits, licenses, professional fees, and so on.
c. Office operating costs for the first two or three months of operation.

Royalty and Advertising Fees and Financing

You pay several fees, including a 12 percent royalty and a 6 percent advertising fee. If you have an accounting practice with existing tax return clients, you must also pay a $5-per-client fee to exempt them from the royalty payment. And when you are in business, you must pay Jackson Hewitt $2 for each electronic return, somewhat less than 3 percent of the average price per return to the client. The fees might seem fairly high, but Jackson Hewitt does provide all the electronic systems and processing for all your returns, so you receive fair value for its services.

To reduce your initial cash investment sharply, you can finance your equipment leases and a significant portion of your start-up cost. If you qualify, you can lease up to $25,000 worth of equipment and finance your initial cash requirements above $15,000. You may also finance up to $10,000 of advertising costs that Jackson Hewitt incurs on your behalf. For the last two loans, you pay 11 percent interest, and you must pay back the start-up cash loan by the end of February of your first tax season and the advertising loan by the end of February of your second tax season.

You may even be able to borrow up to $50,000 for three years from a bank through a Jackson Hewitt program to finance everything; the interest rate equals the prime rate plus 2.5 percent. So, with enough equity, you could open your doors without spending any of your own money, but remember, that path creates the serious danger of overextending your personal financial resources. You could forfeit any profits for the first three years and in essence work for the financiers and Jackson Hewitt, not for yourself and your family.

What You Get

In return for your fees and costs, you receive the following benefits, which may be the best in the industry:

- *Exclusive territory.* You receive an exclusive territory with about 50,000 people determined by zip codes or census tracts; make sure you locate your office in the middle of many relatively young middle- and low-income families because they make up your primary market. You also receive the right of first refusal to operate a Jackson Hewitt center at any local branch of a national account. For example, Jackson Hewitt has placed its offices in Montgomery Ward department stores around the country. You can operate those offices, or let the company put a corporate office in the store if it is in your territory.

- *Training.* You receive five days of headquarters training in managing and marketing the business. Then, as you set up your office, a field consultant helps you for two days to learn how to process tax returns.

- *Support.* You receive a very strong two-tiered support program, the anchor of which is the regional director. At the second tier is a field consultant who works with 12 to 15 franchisees within a four-hour drive. You receive intensified support during the three-week rush during January tax season. You can call a toll-free hotline to ask tax questions of a staff of 16 experts. And a computer support group has 30 staff members. In short, when you need help, you can get it.

- *National marketing.* Jackson Hewitt has a very aggressive national advertising and public relations campaign that benefits everyone.

In sum, you receive the training and support you need to grow rapidly.

How Much Can You Make?

Although Jackson Hewitt does not make earnings claims, the executives did say that the average tax return fee is $69. In addition, with a $300 minimum refund, most of your customers want the 24-hour refund anticipation loans (a notable company advantage; most competitors take three days) and you charge fees ranging from $27 to $31, of which you keep $10. You pay your preparers $5 or so an hour plus bonuses, and it takes them about two hours to prepare a return. Subtract the 18 percent royalty fee (about $13), $15 to pay the preparers (including a bonus), $2 for the electronic filing fee, and you have a gross profit of about $39 per return before your overhead expenses. Depending on the overhead variables and financing, you can net about $15 per return, or about 25 percent before taxes.

If you build the business rapidly, you should hire four to five employees and do more than 500 returns during the January rush and double that during the rest of the season. Your net income would range between $2,000 and $3,000 per month during your first season. You would recoup your initial investment, and begin to show significant ROIs during your second and third tax seasons, especially if you expanded your staff so they could multiply the volume of returns. In sum, Jackson Hewitt is the most exciting and forward-looking tax preparation franchise.

Rainbow International

Rainbow International
Carpet Dyeing & Cleaning Company
1010 North University Parks Drive
P. O. Box 3146
Waco, TX 76707
(800) 583-9100
(817) 756-2122

Rainbow International is the flagship of The Dwyer Group, the franchise conglomerate assembled during the late 1980s and early 1990s by entrepreneur Don Dwyer. Other franchises in this growing group include two other franchises in this book, WorldWide Refinishing and Mr. Rooter; a well-established business services franchise, General Business Services; and four small, but growing, franchises that Dwyer has acquired since 1990: Environmental Air Services, which offers indoor air quality and clean-up services; Aire Serv, a heating and air conditioning conversion franchise; Kitchen Magic, which sells cabinet refinishing, refacing, or replacement services; and Mesa Systems, a software consulting franchise.

But Rainbow remains the largest fixture in Dwyer's firmament. It usually ranks among the five best in its industry segment, carpet, upholstery, and drapery cleaning. However, in contrast to most of its competitors, Rainbow emphasizes dyeing, tinting, and coloring carpets with steam cleaning, carpet shampooing, carpet repair, fire and water damage restoration, flood damage restoration, odor control, drapery cleaning, and furniture cleaning and dyeing as auxiliary services. By late 1993, Rainbow's Dwyer reported that the company had 675 U.S. and 475 foreign franchisees, for a total of 1,150 worldwide. These totals look smaller than earlier reports, but the company changed how it counts its franchisees. It used to report the total number of franchise territories sold; now, the new number represents the actual number of franchisee owners in operation.

Two Franchise Types

Since 1990, Rainbow has added a new type of franchise: a regional director who invests in the rights to an undeveloped area of about 500,000 population. The director then recruits five individual franchisees and trains, supervises, and helps each of these five to develop his or her territory. In effect, Rainbow's regional director works the way this book defines an area representative: He sells and services the local franchisees, but he does *not* sign franchise contracts or act as a subfranchisor.

Becoming a regional director requires a $50,000 franchise fee, about $6,500 for an equipment package, between $5,000 and $15,000 for a van with decals, and $6,000 or more for additional start-up expenses, for a total initial investment ranging from $67,500 to $76,500. In return, a director receives a 2 percent royalty on all gross sales by individual franchisees in his area until he has five individuals, then it doubles to 4 percent. He also receives a 5 percent rebate on the franchisees' chemical purchases.

Dwyer said that Rainbow seeks as regional directors individuals with strong sales and management experience. Existing successful franchisees can also move up to this level to create more profit opportunities.

How Much Does an Individual Franchise Cost

Rainbow charges what has become an average franchise fee for a cleaning service—$15,000 minimum. It has not changed since 1990. The fee is based on a charge of $300 for every 1,000 population in an exclusive territory with at least 50,000 population. Unlike most franchisors, Rainbow will finance up to 74 percent of the fee for a weekly payment of at least $50 at 12 percent interest. The first payment does not begin until two months after you have opened your business.

As I say repeatedly, be careful about how much financing and debt you take on as you begin. Although financing significantly lowers your up-front costs, it may raise your monthly operating expenses for several years. You may pay a franchisor hundreds of dollars a month on the loan, a leasing company for your equipment, and a second leasing company for your van. You could end up working for your lenders for several years before you make a profit for yourself!

Total Start-up Expenses

Rainbow estimates that your total up-front expenditures will equal the numbers in the first column; I include a more liberal estimate, if you pay cash or incur other expenses estimate the following:

Category	Company	Author
Franchise down payment	$ 4,000	$15,000
Equipment package (a)	6,500	6,500
Van down payment (b)	1,000	15,000
Training travel	1,500	2,000
Working capital	2,500	2,500
Insurance	2,000	2,000
Utility deposits (c)	0	500
Initial advertising (d)	0	1,000
Total	$17,500	$44,500

a. Required purchase from Rainbow.
b. Low end represents van lease deposit and first month's payment; high end represents purchase price.
c. Rainbow would advise you to work from home; I add a figure if you want to rent a small office.
d. Rainbow incorporates this into its working capital category; I prefer to separate it because working capital will include any wages for helpers, business licenses, and myriad other small-business start-up costs.

The $44,500 figure is definitely high, but you can safely estimate start-up costs, including the fee down payment, in the $20,000 range before you start earning a breakeven income.

The only other fee is a 7 percent weekly royalty on gross sales. Rainbow does not charge an advertising fee.

What You Get

Rainbow has strengthened its support system to help its local franchisees compete against its major competitors in various markets. You receive the following rights and types of support:

- *Territory.* As noted, a minimum of 50,000 population to which you can add for $300 per 1,000 population. However, note that Rainbow expects you to grow and maintain a gross sales volume of at least $800 per week for each truck in a multitruck operation and at least $1,000 per week in a single-truck operation.

- *Term.* The agreement lasts 10 years with the right to renew for one additional 10-year term at no cost.

- *Training.* You receive one week of training of classroom and on-the-job training at its Waco headquarters. If you buy a territory with a regional director, the director will also train you and help you plan your start-up.

- *Marketing.* In addition to the usual marketing program and materials, you are assigned a marketing director who acts as your direct contact to help you grow your business.

- *Ongoing support.* Rainbow offers these services:

Fourteen-hour-per-day technical hotline.

Two hundred training meetings per year companywide.

National account sales that generate contracts and referrals from major chains.

Monthly newsletters and bulletins.

- *New services.* Rainbow also develops a steady stream of new services, backed by inexpensive equipment packages, such as a ceiling cleaning service first offered in 1993.

- *Research and development department.* It develops new safe, environmentally friendly chemicals.

- *Daily positive reinforcement.* As important as the material support, Dwyer insisted, is the emotional and psychological support that Rainbow provides. He said, "We have daily incentives and awards for our franchisees, and they join new clubs as they attain new levels. They can win trips and prizes, but more important, we do something every day to make them feel good about their effort."

Perhaps best of all, Rainbow has realized that to increase profits, it must help its franchisees replace labor with technology, that is, higher-quality, more powerful, quicker, longer-lasting equipment that does the same job in less time with fewer people. For example, during 1994, Dwyer emphasized, Rainbow will introduce no-residue cleaning with new procedures and powerful new equipment that removes all cleaning and dyeing residues from a carpet. This step fulfills customer demands, yet saves the franchisee time and money.

All these services add up to an effective support program.

How Much Can You Make?

Although Rainbow used to publish a pro forma income projection, it no longer does so. In the past, it has been reported that a company-owned operation grossed about $400,000 with a net profit in the 20 to 25 percent range. Yet, you will find it hard to identify a typical Rainbow franchise. Dwyer said that franchisees range from part-timers content to gross less than $20,000 a year to aggressive businesspeople with multitruck operations who earn net incomes in the $100,000 to $200,000 range. Remember, too, that the single-truck minimum quota implies a minimum desired gross income of $50,000 a year with net pretax profits in the 30 percent range. To recoup your investment, you need to double that within two years. In short, you can make of a Rainbow International franchise what you want. If you want to build quick and high ROIs, you need to expand into a multitruck operation as soon as your financial resources and market development allow.

DYNAMARK SECURITY CENTERS, INC.

Dynamark Security Centers, Inc.
19833 Leitersburg Pike
Hagerstown, MD 21742
(800) 342-4243
(301) 797-2124

Since 1990, Dynamark has continued to strengthen its position as the leading residential and commercial security franchise. By the end of 1993, it had more than 130 franchises. It offers a professional and potentially highly profitable system of designing, marketing, installing, servicing, and monitoring security and fire systems. Dynamark does not manufacture any equipment, but sells the products of dozens of leading manufacturers through its warehouse, the largest single warehouse for security products in the United States. Dynamark integrates the many pieces of a complete security system for each customer to meet his or her needs, yet build the franchisee's profits.

As a franchisee, you buy the products at wholesale prices from Dynamark and resell them as security systems to the home or business owner. Then, you sell a monthly subscription service for which Dynamark's corporate headquarters monitors the alarm system in each customer's home or business. And you service the systems if something happens to them.

I like this business because it offers so many continuous income streams: (1) you sell and install the systems, earning markups on equipment and installation charges, (2) you receive subscription payments each month for the monitoring system, and (3) you sell annual service contracts. You make money coming and going.

This industry continues to go through consolidation as the some 13,000 independent security businesses find it more and more difficult to keep with the major competitors, such as ADT and Dynamark. ADT, the largest competitor, has some 400,000 accounts, and Dynamark, the largest franchise, has more than 42,000 accounts. Most of the rest are scattered among the thousands of small, local firms. Nevertheless, Dynamark continues to hold its market share and gradually increase it.

During the early 1990s, the competition intensified—and the total potential market expanded dramatically—when ADT introduced a seemingly inexpensive system to appeal to lower middle-class customers. Dynamark responded with its own low-end system and its executives noted that their new system gives far more protection, such as fire alarms, than the ADT system at slightly higher cost. As important, franchisees can now reach a very large new market of middle-class households and not just the established market of affluent households.

Since the number of small commercial businesses and single-family residences continues to grow about 3 to 5 percent a year, the long-term market potential continues to be excellent.

In fact, recent market research estimates show that only 15 percent of all U.S. households are protected by a home security system; Dynamark estimates that between 60 and 70 percent of all households could benefit from a system, so less than 25 percent (one quarter) of the market has been tapped, leaving significant room for growth.

How Much It Costs

Since 1990, in a positive step, Dynamark has reduced its fee from $25,000 to $15,000 for new franchisees and just $5,000 for conversions from existing local security system dealers. In return, you receive an exclusive 100,000-population territory.

Dynamark has also introduced a financing program through which you can borrow the funds for up to 75 percent of your franchise fee and initial inventory costs; if you are qualified, you can pay $5,000 down and borrow $15,000 for 51 months through a national franchise financing company. By late 1993, the monthly payments were $424, but that would vary according to the going interest rate.

Beyond the fee, the additional, estimated total start-up costs are relatively low. The following table applies only to new franchisees because conversions will have few expenses other than training, signage, and inventory.

Category	Low End	High End
Franchise fee	$15,000	$15,000
Inventory/marketing	5,000	5,000
Rent (a)	0	800
Deposits (b)	0	1,000
Insurance (c)	800	1,200
Travel training	500	1,500
Licenses, permits	250	500
Professional fees (d)	250	500
Working capital (e)	18,000	18,000
Total	$39,800	$43,500

a. You can work from home at first or rent a small office.
b. Includes telephone and similar deposits.
c. Down payments for comprehensive business insurance and other required policies.
d. Legal and accounting fees for reviewing the agreement and setting up your business.
e. Everything else you need to spend, including payments to installers, preopening costs, office equipment, and as Dynamark stresses, 6 to 12 months of living expenses. If you have a working spouse, you may reduce this total substantially. Conversions can easily change over for less than $10,000.

Helpful No-Royalty Arrangement

Dynamark has made several beneficial changes in its royalty arrangements since 1990. First, you pay *no* royalty during the first

12 months. After that, you pay royalties *only* if you do not meet minimum performance (product purchase) requirements. The performance quota totals monthly product purchases of $1,000 for every 50,000 people in your territory, or usually $2,000 a month. However, note that the average system has a wholesale cost between $600 and $700, so you need to sell and install three or four comprehensive systems a month to exceed the requirement.

If you do not meet the quota, then you have to pay a $100-per-month royalty for every 50,000 of population, or about $200 a month for the usual territory. This is a significant and helpful change since 1990 when the company charged a percentage royalty.

In another good change, the company's advertising fee does not take effect for the first six months, and even then, it equals only 1 percent of your monthly gross volume. In addition, through a Franchise Advisory Council, the company's franchisees manage how they spend ad fees placed in this separate fund. This group, elected by the franchisees, is very active and even rebates funds to all franchisees for local, approved advertising.

Furthermore, you must buy all your equipment from Dynamark or approved suppliers, and these costs will amount to 90 percent or more of your ongoing expenses. And you must connect every installation to the DynaWatch® central monitoring station system. These product and service sales make up most of Dynamark's income, but with no percentage royalties, franchisees seem content to buy products from the company at competitive prices.

What You Get

Dynamark offers a very dynamic marketing program that appeals to customers in market segments from lower middle-class households in troubled neighborhoods to affluent homeowners to small retail businesses and small industrial-warehouse operations. Its proven program generates leads with referrals from existing customers and through low-cost advertising media. Other important elements of its program include the following:

- *Agreement term.* Dynamark has again increased its initial term from five to 10 years (after it increased it from three to five in the late 1980s) with the opportunity for a 10-year renewal. This giving you a better chance to build long-term equity.

- *Training.* The company has expanded its training program dramatically since 1990. It now encompasses 18 weeks of at-home work, headquarters training, and in-field training. You receive an orientation week of training at headquarters and then continuous follow-up. The company has a very strong training program based on videos, demonstrations, manuals, and in-field work.

- *Cause-related sponsorships/marketing.* Acting as a socially responsible corporate citizen, Dynamark sponsors the Child Seekers® program to help raise funds for the National Center for Missing Children. Its local franchisees go to fairs and schools to fingerprint and photograph children, sponsor sports tournaments to raise funds, and engage in other fund-raising efforts. The company also sponsors the U.S. Olympic Bobsled Team and has gained international publicity for its efforts to boost it.

- *Advertising programs.* Dynamark continually updates its advertising, promotion, and public relations programs and provides sales kits for on-site demonstrations, the way you make most of your sales.

- *New product research.* Dynamark has developed several new product and service offerings to help you expand your sales: closed-circuit television security, intercom systems, central vacuum systems, in-home theater systems, and card access systems. Working with the manufacturers, Dynamark seeks to offer the highest-quality products at competitive prices, stated company executives.

- *Other support programs.* You receive weekly phone calls and regular on-site visits from company reps, a national training school for installers, an annual convention, and regional meetings.

- *Payment plans.* Dynamark also makes leasing and credit card plans available to franchisees' customers to make the sales easier.

How Much Can You Make?

The secrets to the remarkable profit potential in this franchise are the multiple revenue streams:

- *Installations.* You make significant gross profits in the 40 to 70 percent range on systems installation, so you net between $400 and $550 on the average system.

- *Subscriptions.* Here is the beauty of the system: On average, you charge $20 per month for the monitoring service, yet you pay Dynamark only $5.00 to $5.50 for the service, and you keep the remaining $14.50 or $15.00 per month. Dynamark's best franchisees build up to 1,000 or more accounts within three years, so they bring in $15,000 a month just on monitoring fees—that cost them nothing.

- *Service contracts.* You also sell annual service contracts that cost $150 to $200, and about half your customers buy those. And you charge the other half $45 to $75 an hour for service calls.

Thus, you should be able to build your system sales and your monitoring accounts fairly quickly during the first several years. On average, you should sell 10 to 20 accounts per month, so after three years, you would have between 350 and 700 accounts, spinning off $5,250 to $10,500 per month, less a few percent for billing charges.

One warning: Not everyone will buy the monitoring service, although the system is not that useful without it, and you can expect some normal turnover of 10 to 15 percent per year from relocations, deaths, and the like. So, you need to sell that many more systems each year just to stay even with the previous year.

Furthermore, Dynamark encourages you to increase your volume by marketing to builders. You want them to buy security systems to add to their new homes; you sell a builder dozens or hundreds of systems for all the homes in a new development. You hire installers to prewire the home for the system. And you can also sell the builder central vacuum systems, stereo/theater systems, and more. In turn, builders can offer these built-in, prewired, prepiped systems as value-added amenities to their home buyers—at a higher price and profit, of course. Security systems, indeed, should act as significant selling features in homes of the future.

At the low end of the market, Dynamark offers its SAFE (Security Affordable For Everyone) unit to compete with ADT. Priced at $399, SAFE includes far more than ADT's $299 system. It gives three window/door contacts, a smoke detector, a motion detector, and central unit monitoring. ADT's low-end system offers only two contacts and a motion detector, but no smoke detector or central monitoring. Of course, the monitoring fee is where you realize the long-term profit.

Dynamark executives noted that the SAFE product makes local franchisees major players in that lower middle-class segment, but its pricing still allows them to make a profit.

Huge Long-Term Equity

As good as the ongoing revenue streams is Dynamark's potential for long-term equity buildup. Dynamark values your accounts at $500 each. If you have 1,000 accounts, that means you have $500,000 in equity in a business that costs less than $45,000 to begin.

For example, Dynamark's top franchisee for 1993, Ted Pindell, a minority businessperson, had built his territory to 1,500 accounts since 1989. So, he was receiving a minimum monthly income of $22,500 from his monitoring revenues, and had built an equity of $750,000. Interestingly, Dynamark had helped finance his franchise purchase, so his total start-up costs were minimal.

Of course, not everyone will do as well, but the opportunity for truly remarkable ROIs is available through Dynamark.

COMPUTERTOTS

COMPUTERTOTS
10132 Colvin Run Road
P.O. Box 340
Great Falls, VA 22066
(703) 759-2556

I had the privilege of writing one of the first stories about COMPUTERTOTS when founders Karen Marshall and Mary Rogers began their franchise in 1989. Even then, I liked the founders, their company, and their concept of computer training for young people. Since then, I have worked with them in a regional franchise association in the Washington, DC, area, and they have also impressed me with their very professional, highly ethical, and very honest approach to both franchising and their business.

Not incidentally, I believe, they have made COMPUTERTOTS into the top-rated franchise in the United States according to one major national survey, one of the best home-based franchises, and one of the best franchises for women. During 1993, it doubled in size to some 135 franchises, but the founders reined in that rapid growth. They now plan to add 36 per year during the mid-1990s as their major territories become saturated and they open new markets.

A COMPUTERTOTS franchisee offers half-hour computer training to various age groups in child care or after-school programs. You do not own any facilities; rather, you (or your trained teachers) go to the centers, schools, libraries, community centers, and so on to offer the classes. COMPUTERTOTS has also expanded the age groups to whom it offers classes and now even offers some adult classes to help expand its market base and revenue streams for its franchisees.

You teach computer training based on computer education curricula that the company has designed with commercially prepared software. You must obtain these curricula from the company. You charge the parents of the students fees that range from $28 to $40 per month for one-half-hour-long class per week. You obtain students by selling the service first to the child care center operators or facility managers and second to the parents. Fortunately, the child care center owners are often looking for new services to provide more child development activities for their students, so selling them is often fairly easy.

With average start-up costs below $30,000 and significant returns on your cash investment, COMPUTERTOTS offers an excellent opportunity for anyone interested in building a business that helps children and their parents learn valuable computer skills.

How Much It Costs

COMPUTERTOTS offers three franchise "models":

- *Manager Model with a $23,900 franchise fee.* You primarily sell your services; hire, train, and supervise teachers; and manage the operation. For this, you receive a major territory, usually a large city or significant portion of a major metropolitan area. However, except for resales, many major territories are sold out, the founders said.

- *Educator Model with an $18,900 fee.* This model gives you a small-city territory or a small suburban area. You act as salesperson, teacher, and manager and hire part-time teachers as you grow. You should have a teaching background.

- *Mini-Education Model with a $15,900 fee.* This applies to a small-town or rural-area territory. You also need a teaching background for this model.

Other Start-up Costs

You can run a COMPUTERTOTS from home and keep your overhead costs very low. In the best case, you may be able to start this franchise for less than $5,000 above the franchise fee, or you could spend up to $25,000 more. The following table lists the low and high ranges for start-up costs:

Category	Low End	High End
Franchise fee	$15,900	$23,900
Computer equipment (a)	3,275	4,420
Office machines (b)	1,100	1,100
Training travel	600	1,500
Insurance	445	1,650
Business telephone	600	1,000
Incentives to operators (c)	0	2,000
Office supplies	200	500
Teacher salaries (d)	1,000	2,000
Licenses and fees (e)	250	600
Commercial office (f)	0	5,800
Working capital (g)	2,000	3,000
Total (h)	$24,570	$47,470

a. For portable computers, monitors, and printers for small classes of four students each.
b. For home answering machine and personal copier.
c. You may have to pay some operators an incentive to allow you to give your classes in their facilities, but not always, and the amount varies. You may be able to arrange a commission or percentage for each student who enrolls to encourage the operator to promote your classes.
d. Most often, you pay teacher salaries after you receive payment for the classes, but this amount serves as additional working capital.
e. Includes licenses and permits and fees to attorney or accountant to review the UFOC.
f. If you work at home, you do not pay any of this, but the $5,800 is a high-end estimate for starting a small office.
g. For minimum monthly franchise royalty, marketing materials, and other supplies.
h. Note that these totals do *not* include any money for living expenses, so your spouse or partner must bring in that amount during the first 12 to 18 months of your business's development.

Royalty and Advertising Fees and Quotas

You must also pay a 6 percent royalty on gross revenues, or a $250-per-month minimum royalty for existing programs, perhaps more as you choose to offer more programs. The advertising fee equals 1 percent of gross sales to a national fund managed by a franchisee advisory council.

Most important, you must meet minimum annual gross sales quotas, as the following table shows:

Model:	Manager	Educator	Mini-Educator
Year 1	$20,000	$10,000	$ 8,000
Year 2	35,000	15,000	12,000
Year 3	50,000	20,000	18,000
Year 4	65,000	25,000	23,000
Year 5	80,000	30,000	28,000

These quotas provide incentives for you to build your business, but they are minimums if you expect to increase your net income to mid- to upper five-figure levels.

What You Get

- *Exclusive territory.* Each franchise model has its own territory rights:

  Manager Model. Large city or large suburb with at least 100 to 170 day care centers with 20 students or more each.

  Educator Model. Small city or small suburb with between 60 to 100 day care centers with 20 or more students each.

  Mini-Educator Model. Small town or rural area with less than 60 day care centers with 20 or more students each.

The actual boundaries are determined by zip code, county lines, or geographical features.

- *Training.* You receive five and a half days' training at COM-PUTERTOTS suburban Washington, DC, headquarters in all aspects of the business: teaching the lessons, marketing the business, recruiting teachers, and managing your growth. You must also attend a regional or national conference and its training seminars at least once a year.

- *Marketing program.* You receive an initial marketing program and materials and the corporate parent ECW helps design your marketing program to "jump start" your effort.

- *Purchasing assistance.* You use DOS 386Sx or Macintosh LCIII computers, monitors, and printers because the educational software for the age groups that you teach is simple and easy. This keeps your costs low, too.

- *Courseware package.* More importantly, you receive the educational software you need to begin offering your courses to children ages 3 to 5, the primary COMPUTERTOTS market. You can add more courseware to appeal to different markets, including "computer explorers," that is, children ages 6 and older, and special programs such as summer computer camps, specialty site classes, and "Mommy (or Daddy) and Me" classes for young children and their parents to learn computer skills together.

Through the specialty sites program, you offer classes through YMCA/YWCAs, Boy and Girl Scouts, park and recreation departments, Head Start centers, after-school programs, and community centers, among others.

- *Expert knowledge.* Best of all, you work with Rogers and Marshall, two true pioneers in the business of computer-based learning for children, and learn from them how to turn what seems like a school course into a thriving business.

- *Ten-year term.* You receive a 10-year agreement term and the right to renew for a payment equal to 5 percent of the then-current franchise fee.

- *Very low termination rate.* Since it began, COMPUTERTOTS has terminated only three franchises. This is an excellent record for a firm that has grown as rapidly as it has. As important, it also has had no lawsuits against it from its franchisees.

How Much Can You Make?

Of course, COMPUTERTOTS appeals to many people who enjoy working with children or teaching, but who know little about building a business. However, your goal must be to build a business based on a valuable service: In the future, children's success both in their schools and in their work will depend on how well they understand useful computers, and not just play computer games. Since you fill a serious void the schools and parents are not filling now, you need to place an appropriate value on that service and receive income for it.

You can do very well with this franchise. For example, Ann Brown of Cottage City, Maryland, grossed more than $180,000 during 1992, according to a magazine report. She nets a very high five-figure income doing what she loves to do.

You build these revenues by charging $28 to $35 per child per month for one weekly half-hour class, or about $7 to $8.75 per hour per child. Each class has four children for a gross income of $56 to $70 per hour. Unless you teach the class yourself—which you will do less and less as you grow your business—you pay a teacher $15 to $18 an hour. You might have to pay a per-child fee or commission to a day care center owner, but often you do not. To be conservative, add $1.50 per child, or $12 per hour. Subtract other operating expenses of about 21 percent and your "contribution"—as the company calls it—to yourself as owner totals about 30 percent of total revenues.

If you work from home, as COMPUTERTOTS advises, you can expect to net 30 percent before taxes and depreciation. Your income depends directly on how many day care centers, YMCA/YWCAs, Head Start centers, and the like you can convince to offer your classes. Then, you and the center managers must encourage the parents to pay for the service, but you have a crucial selling point: on-site computer training that will give children a step up on their peers as they compete in school and in life.

In sum, I'm glad that I gave Rogers, Marshall, and COMPUT-ERTOTS a helping hand on their way to the top. They put a woman's twist on one of my favorite principles: Nice women do finish first, especially when they are as knowledgeable, professional, and enthusiastic as the founders of COMPUTERTOTS.

If you want to build a business that serves a serious need for young people and their futures, COMPUTERTOTS is one of the very best choices to explore. As Wayne, Pennsylvania, franchisee Alan Oppenheimer put it, "The bottom line is that customers love COMPUTERTOTS." And you should love the profits that it can bring you.

7

Franchises with Fees from $16,000 to $20,000

THE MAIDS INTERNATIONAL

The Maids International
4820 Dodge Street
Omaha, NE 68132
(402) 558-5555
(800) THE-MAID (843-6243)

The Maids International seeks to attract buyers with management experience who want to expand their territories. By late 1993, the company had 240 territories sold in 34 states and all nine Canadian provinces, four fewer states than in 1990. It had a total of 80 owners and 95 offices, and as you will see in detail shortly, more than 62 percent of all owners had gross incomes above $100,000 a year.

Although a few major metropolitan areas have been saturated, most areas have many territories available.

The company uses a four-person cleaning system because its time and motion studies show that that size team provides the fastest, yet most thorough, service.

In this very competitive industry, The Maids has added two services to help you increase your revenues: (1) a $39 "Maid Lite" limited-area cleaning service and (2) a very popular full-service laundry and dry cleaning delivery service. These attract very profitable add-on sales from current customers and attract new customers. It has also updated and reduced the prices for its line of cleaning chemicals and has made available a very sophisticated computer program that manages the entire operation, including labor scheduling, route planning, pricing, payroll, and the like.

How Much It Costs

The Maids' franchise fee for your first territory is $17,500, an increase of 10.1 percent since 1990, but you can add more territories for just $12,500 each. The fee includes a territory based on customer demographics, not population. This distinction is critical to your success because you receive enough targeted households that can afford your service to build a substantial business.

The Typical Customer

The Maids' market research shows that its typical customer is a married working woman between the ages of 35 and 54 whose husband also works. The primary wage earner—or both—is employed as a professional or a manager. Most live in homes they have owned for at least four years. Some 85 percent of The Maids' customers are women who don't have time to clean. In short, look for affluent suburban areas or urban neighborhoods with professional couples who do not want to spend their leisure time cleaning the house.

New Royalty Structure

In addition, The Maids has changed its royalty structure since 1990, but retains a declining scale. Now based on annual gross volume, the royalty equals 7 percent up to the first $500,000 of revenue and 5.5 percent above that amount.

You must also pay a 4 percent advertising fee (double that in 1990) into a national fund administered by a nine-person advisory council. Eighty percent of this fee is reimbursed to the franchise owner, and the company strongly urges you to spend at least $1,000 a month on local advertising because you attract customers through four advertising media: (1) direct response mailings, your best; (2) Yellow Pages, second best; (3) newspaper coupons, third best; and finally, (4) radio, door hangers, and, in large metro areas, cable television.

You may also buy cleaning chemicals and equipment from the company, but you are not required to do so.

Total start-up costs range from about $34,000 to $49,000, depending on what you include. The following table discusses the possible range:

Category	Low End	High End
Franchise fee	$17,500	$17,500
Advertising	6,000	12,000
Auto leases (a)	1,400	1,800
Computer system (b)	1,500	3,000
Insurance deposits	500	1,500
Initial labor, training	700	1,200
Phone, utility deposits	200	500
Training travel	500	1,500
Legal/accounting fees	250	500
Signage	100	800
Office lease deposit (c)	0	1,000
Office furniture	0	2,000
Manager salary (d)	0	1,400
Working capital	2,500	5,000
Total	$31,150	$49,700

a. The Maids offers an excellent long-term lease with the required colors and logo already on the car.

b. If you have hardware, you only pay for software.

c. Most new franchisees start in a small office and keep their monthly rent in the $300- to $500-per-month range.

d. If you hire a manager to operate the business, you must expect to pay a salary until your business produces cash flow.

However, The Maids encourages you to grow rapidly, adding new crews as quickly as the market and your ability to find quality employees allow. The executives noted that you need a crew cleaning at least 30 houses a week to begin to make a profit. One four-person crew can clean five to seven houses a day, so you should be profitable when your first crew reaches its maximum capacity, but you should develop a second and a third crew before that happens so you can continue to expand.

You can also add new territories for less than half the cost of opening your first territory, so you want to develop your first territory and acquire adjacent territories as soon as you can.

What You Get

In return for your fee, you receive the exclusive territory and enough equipment and materials to outfit two crews. You also receive the following services and support:

- *Training.* It has one of the most extensive programs in the industry, with six weeks of at-home training, one week of training at corporate headquarters, 13 days of hands-on training with an established franchisee, and four months of posttraining support. President Dan Bishop said that a staff person walks the new franchisee through all aspects of the operation during those four months. You also receive at least one field visit each year.

- *Computer system.* The new state-of-the-art system does practically everything but hire and fire the employees and clean the houses. As noted, it streamlines scheduling and route planning, does payroll and bookkeeping, and provides a variety of important reports.

- *Insurance programs.* The company has assembled the most comprehensive package of insurance protection, including general business liability, auto theft and vandalism, third-party liability, employee honesty bonding, extended property damage, lost key liability protection, commercial umbrella, and other coverage.

- *Advertising and marketing program.* The executives take pride in their precisely targeted campaigns that specialize in direct response advertising. More than 25 percent of your customers come from these mailings. The company also offers a very worthwhile cooperative ad program that helps you pay your media costs.

In short, you receive a comprehensive program designed to help you succeed and expand as quickly as your skills and resources will allow.

How Much Can You Make?

Company executives insisted that The Maids does not make earnings claims; however, clearly, you can gross very significant revenues with The Maids. A recent company publication showed the following numbers had exceeded $100,000 in annual gross revenues:

$100,000 to $199,999	27 franchisees
$200,000 to $299,999	11 franchisees
$300,000 to $399,999	7 franchisees
$400,000 to $499,999	1 franchise
$600,000 to $699,999	1 franchise
$700,000 to $799,999	2 franchisees
$800,000 to $999,999	1 franchise
More than $1 million	1 franchise

Remarkably, the most successful franchisee is in Pittsburgh, which is usually considered a relatively inexpensive place to live. The franchisee nets about 20 percent after tax and operates four offices and dozens of crews.

The other highly successful franchisees report net after-tax profits in the 20 to 25 percent range. Of the some 80 owners, 51, or 62 percent, gross more than $100,000. You make these significant profits cleaning one house at a time by charging on average $72 per cleaning per house. The four-person crew should clean an average three-bedroom, two-bath house in less than an hour or between five and seven houses a day for an average daily gross income between $360 and $504, or annual gross based on 50 weeks a year of $90,000 to $126,000. If you manage the crew yourself, you should have a pretax income of between $25,000 and $37,750 per year per crew.

Your ROI on your initial investment should exceed 100 percent by the end of your second year, or by the time you have had a second crew in the field for a year. Clearly, you want to build a multiple-territory franchise because they net $150,000 and more per year.

In short, The Maids provides among the most comprehensive and sophisticated support in the industry. But to whom much is given, much is required. Company executives said that they are very selective in whom they allow to become franchisees and do what they have to do to protect the system's reputation.

MR. ROOTER

Mr. Rooter Corporation
1010 North University Parks Drive
Waco, TX 76707
(800) 583-8003
(817) 755-0055

Since 1989, when Mr. Rooter was purchased by Don Dwyer, founder of Rainbow International, Inc., the company has grown rapidly to a total of more than 200 franchisees (by early 1994) in 38 states. Mr. Rooter, a plumbing, sewer, drain, pipe and septic tank cleaning service, plans to add six new franchisees a month for the foreseeable future, said company executives.

Mr. Rooter has made a very significant shift from small "Mom and Pop" owner-operators to business managers and conversions of existing plumbing services. It has also boosted the professional image of this industry, often looked down upon as a messy, blue-collar rip-off. President Robert Tunmire stated that from the clean appearance of the van to the surgical boots that the workers wear when they enter a home, everything that Mr. Rooter, its franchisees, and their employees do enhances this new, more professional image. This creates a significant marketing advantage in the intense competition for customers.

Mr. Rooter also continues as one of the many pieces in Dwyer's puzzle to assemble a franchise conglomerate with 10,000 franchises in a worldwide service industry empire by 1996.

With a Mr. Rooter franchise, you buy the cleaning equipment from Mr. Rooter, learn its marketing procedures and operations, and provide plumbing and drain cleaning services. Tunmire noted that Mr. Rooter has shifted its focus from drain cleaning to complete plumbing services because the available market for both exceeds the size of the market for drain cleaning alone by many times. At present, almost 80 percent of the company's franchisees are licensed plumbers; if you are not one, you must hire one so you can do business in your area.

Mr. Rooter continues to face tough competition from both national brand names with decades-old reputations and a new franchise from the United Kingdom as well as a plethora of local plumbers and drain cleaning services. However, Mr. Rooter continues to offer an inexpensive and very profitable opportunity if you want either to get your hands dirty or to build a business providing these lucrative services.

How Much It Costs

Since 1990, Mr. Rooter's franchise fee has increased 75 percent, from $10,000 to $17,500, for a territory with 100,000 population. You can add more population for $175 per 1,000 people. Tunmire said that most franchisees buy territories based on Yellow Pages coverage and demographics, so the average population per territory exceeds 150,000 people and the average fee equals $30,000. Make sure that your territory includes mostly affluent or middle-class households that can afford your services and many restaurants and commercial establishments, for they usually need plumbing service more frequently than office buildings. Be sure to analyze the demographics before you buy, but hundreds of territories remain available.

Mr. Rooter may finance up to half your franchise fee if you have good credit and meet its criteria. The company charges 12-percent-per-year interest with minimum weekly payments.

You pay a declining scale royalty on annual gross sales:

- 6.0 percent on the first $299,999 of gross revenues;

- 5.5 percent on revenues between $300,000 and $499,999;

- 5.0 percent on $500,000 to $999,999;

- 4.0 percent on $1 million to $1,499,999; and

- 3.0 percent on $1.5 million or more.

This represents a dramatic and beneficial change since 1990 when the rate was a flat 6 percent or a $30-per-week minimum. You must still contribute a 2 percent advertising fee and buy a minimum-sized Yellow Pages ad. The company reserves the right to establish regional cooperative ad groups, but had not done so by the end of 1993 and did not plan to do so during 1994.

Total Start-up Costs

Mr. Rooters gives a range of estimated start-up costs—in addition to the fee—of from $10,695 to $37,795, but Tunmire stated that the average franchisee spent about $30,000 for a total initial investment of $60,000. You may finance half the fee and lease some of the equipment to reduce your cash requirements to $30,000 or so. If you don't already own a plumbing service, Mr. Rooter recommends that you start from home and ask your spouse to act as office manager. Then, you can avoid renting industrial-warehouse space. Here are low and high ranges of start-up costs:

Category	Low End	High End
Franchise fee	$17,500	$30,000
Equipment (a)	2,000	7,000
Computer system (b)	3,295	3,295
Motor vehicle (c)	0	16,000
Inventory (d)	500	1,000
Security deposits (e)	200	500
Training travel (f)	1,000	1,500
Miscellaneous (g)	500	1,000
Working capital (h)	5,000	10,000
Total	$29,995	$70,295

a. Author's estimate at high end is for about 150,000 population.
b. Enough equipment for one truck.
c. If you own a truck or van, you spend nothing. If you need to buy a vehicle, the purchase price would be about $16,000, but your down payments would be about $1,000 to $3,000. If you lease a vehicle, your payments may not exceed $1,000 for two payments.
d. Many franchisees already own services, so they may not face these costs.
e. Business telephone line deposits and installation costs, which vary with area.
f. Your travel expenses to and from training are additional.
g. Usual start-up expenses for a home-based business.
h. Low end for existing businesses to hire additional workers; high end for those who must have living expenses for the first three to six months.

What You Get

The franchise agreement lasts 10 years, with an option to renew for an additional 10 years without paying another fee. For your fee, you receive an exclusive territory of at least 100,000—usually many more—people. You can exercise an option to buy adjacent territories. In one benefit, Mr. Rooter does not require you to meet minimum business volumes or pay any minimum royalties to maintain your exclusive territory. This allows you to stay in business even when you struggle, and the company has learned that most franchisees will succeed so the executives do not need this protection clause in their agreements.

You receive a basic franchise equipment package so you can equip one truck. You also receive five days of training at corporate headquarters or another franchisee's location. You may also be required to attend the company's annual convention. You may bring two additional people to the training session, but you must pay for their travel expenses and salaries for employees.

This training involves only business management and marketing training, not the technical side, because Mr. Rooter wants the franchisees to build the business and establish the brand name in your area, not clean drains. You also must take in-field regional training seminars for one and a half days each year.

Mr. Rooter also provides a grand opening promotional and marketing package of advertising and direct mail materials. After you begin, Mr. Rooter provides a toll-free telephone hotline for technical questions and a monthly newsletter. A director of marketing delivers new materials regularly, and regional managers and field directors visit and offer advice as you need it.

How Much Can You Make

As with any franchise, the amount you earn depends on your willingness to do the work. However, the company reported that systemwide revenues had soared from $3 million during 1990 to more than $14 million during 1993, a 467 percent surge in three years.

Tunmire attributed this dramatic growth to four reasons: (1) rapidly growing brand-name recognition through local and national advertising, (2) its professional approach to the industry, (3) a major shift from drain cleaning to complete plumbing services, and (4) a major shift from owner-operators to manager-owners who build the business and hire employees to do the work.

Although the vast majority of franchisees are two years old or younger, Tunmire asserted that average franchisee gross revenues exceeded $120,000 per year. Tunmire added that he has sold hundreds of franchises and that he has found that, at first, new franchisees find a "comfort level" close to the amount they earned at their last job. Only during the second and subsequent years do their incomes begin to rise 25 to 50 percent per year or more as they seek to reach a new comfort level.

From a business viewpoint, you charge $60 to $100 or more per hour for plumbing services and $80 to $125 per job to clean out a residential septic tank, much more for commercial jobs. To reach the average gross revenues with an average fee of $100, you would need to do only 1,200 jobs a year, four to five per day. If you hire a plumber's helper and share the work, or have the helper do the jobs, you can expect to have a net pretax profit margin in the 30 to 40 percent range. That margin will fall as you add trucks and employees, but your gross revenues should increase and your net profits soar.

You can increase your first-year net profits by financing part of the franchise fee, but be sure you do not borrow too much money; if you do, you may pay all your profits to Mr. Rooter and the banks. In sum, after two to three years, if you concentrate on growing the business, you could have 100 percent annual ROIs on your cash investment. You would also build equity in a national franchise with a protected territory; as you build your customer roster, they recognize the brand name and add value to your business.

For example, Mike Stone, the Mr. Rooter franchisee in Palm Springs, California, used to own his own plumbing service, but he found he could not sell it because it had no name recognition or customer loyalty. In 1990, he bought a Mr. Rooter franchise, and by 1992, he had built it into a six-truck operation with his partner, Scott Wheelock, with equity far exceeding his initial investment and subsequent expenses to build his fleet. In short, to multiply your ROI in Mr. Rooter, you need to build your fleet and market the business.

COPIES NOW

Copies Now
Sir Speedy, Inc.
23131 Verdugo Drive
Laguna Hills, CA 92653
(800) 854-3321
(714) 472-0330

Copies Now, a subsidiary of the well-known Sir Speedy quick printing franchise, is perhaps the last best hope to enter the printing industry for an investment of less than $100,000. A Copies Now center provides retail photocopying, document preparation, graphics, and binding services for offices and businesses. Of course, the copying service business is very competitive, especially in downtown areas and major suburban centers, but the demand for photocopying and related services is so great that you can build significant profits very quickly.

Vice President Dave Collins explained that Copies Now centers are located close to their customers, preferably on the street level of a major office building in a downtown area with dozens of similar buildings, or a suburban area within an area clustered with office buildings. For example, he said that one of the top five franchisees was in the New York City suburb of Bound Brook, New Jersey, but prospered with an aggressive outside sales effort and proximity to a major interstate highway. Its trucks picked up and delivered materials for clients up and down that highway. On the other hand, the leading franchise—with a volume of $1.3 million—is in downtown Washington, DC, near the White House.

Simply, if you provide good customer service and quality work, you can build a significant business with a Copies Now center.

By late 1993, Copies Now had almost 90 franchises in operation, a number that usually stays constant because so many successful Copies Now franchises convert to Sir Speedy printing centers.

How Much It Costs

Copies Now has a very reasonable $17,500 franchise fee with additional start-up costs ranging from about $70,000 to about $80,000, far less than any quick printing operation. Equally interesting, Copies Now has strong incentives to grow or become a Sir Speedy franchise:

- A very low $7,500 fee to open a new center in a new territory;

- A minuscule $1,000 fee to open a satellite center within your existing territory; and

- No fee to convert a Copies Now center to a Sir Speedy franchise.

So, the company wants you to grow in any way you can. The following table illustrates the start-up cost range:

Category	Low End	High End
Franchise fee	$17,500	$17,500
Equipment package (a)	34,500	34,500
High-speed copier (b)	0	0
Working capital (c)	30,000	35,000
Total (d)	$82,000	$87,000

a. Total Copies Now equipment package for turnkey operation, including signage, build-out improvements, and so on. Company provides a $5,711 build-out allowance package.
b. Must have a high-speed copier, but under a deal with Kodak, you can use its copier for six months rent free.
c. Includes lease deposits for average 1,000-square-foot store, utility deposits, several months' operating expenses, insurance deposits, and so on; rents will vary according to location—urban or suburban—and geographic region.
d. Collins said that the average start-up falls closer to the low end of the range.

Royalty and Required Payments

Copies Now charges a very low 4 percent weekly royalty on gross sales for the first 12 months to help new franchises generate cash flow but increases that fee to 6 percent for the rest of the agreement. It also levies a 2 percent advertising fee that goes into a separate ad fund.

You must also have a Yellow Pages ad that will cost between $500 and $6,000 a year, the company estimates. And if the company forms regional advertising cooperatives, you must join and pay the agreed-upon fee, which may range from $50 to $400 a month.

Through an authorized leasing agent, you may reduce your start-up cash by leasing the equipment package with *no* outside collateral. You use the equipment as its own collateral. The lease term is for five years at about 11 percent running interest. A typical monthly payment equals about $800.

What You Get

Although the total start-up cost is relatively low, you receive a very generous package:

- *Territory.* You receive a protected territory that may range from as large as a two-mile radius around a suburban territory to as small as an "address-only" franchise for a downtown location. Collins emphasized that the territory is usually defined by blocks in downtown areas and zip codes for suburban industrial areas. The company does a thorough market survey of these factors: business licenses, mail deliveries, area business development, business types and climate, competition, site availability, vendor proximity, and distance from and impact on other Copies Now franchisees.

- *Twenty-year term.* You receive a very generous 20-year agreement with a right to renew for free.

- *Self-termination.* Equally generous is your right to terminate the agreement with 30 days' notice if you meet certain conditions spelled out in the offering circular. Regardless of the conditions, this provision is unusually open, but it does avoid any cause for conflict. In fact, during 1991, 1992, and 1993, 15 franchises were terminated, but that is misleading because some of those converted to Sir Speedy centers. And the most successful store was sold in early 1993 for a huge profit, so the Copies Now failure rate is far below average.

- *Start-up assistance.* The company helps you find a site, negotiate a lease, and build out the center.

- *Start-up equipment and supplies.* With the exception of the high-speed copier, you receive all equipment, supplies, signage, paper inventory, pressroom supplies, window and wall graphics, and so on that you need to open your doors.

- *Training.* In a rare benefit, the company pays the transportation and room (but not food) costs for you and one other person during your 10 days' training at its California headquarters.

- *Grand opening support.* A support representative spends five days with you during your grand opening week to set up and operate the center, hire and train employees, and help establish operating procedures.

- *Grand opening marketing program.* You also receive a grand opening marketing awareness program that includes a data base mailing list of targeted business customers in the territory and help with designing and executing a direct mail marketing program and setting up a telemarketing program.

Even better, the company sends a promotions professional to work with you for three days to distribute materials to your customers. The company pays for your postage costs for your first 12 mailings to a total of 1,300 businesses during your first six months in business.

Best of all, Copies Now gives you $5,000 for your initial advertising and promotional programs.

- *Continuing support.* In addition, the company pays for your first 12 months' accounting and bookkeeping services with the company-approved firm. You also have toll-free telephone support from six "expediter lines," annual or more frequent visits from its business management consultants, and a monthly mailer filled with marketing and promotional materials, a newsletter, and a catalog of supplies.

The company has state and regional associations of Sir Speedy and Copies Now franchisees, an annual convention, and regional roundtables at 14 to 17 different locations each year. It also has a strong franchisee advisory council that meets three times a year to review all new marketing materials.

In short, for its very reasonable franchise fee, Copies Now provides one of the most comprehensive support packages that I have ever seen, especially in the printing industry.

How Much Can You Make?

Collins stated unequivocally that your success as a Copies Now franchisee depends directly on how much marketing you do. He insisted that you must go out and grow the business with sales calls on potential customers. The only constraint on your revenue potential is your own "comfort zone," that level of income and effort at which you feel satisfied.

However, if you are ambitious, you can easily and inexpensively add a small satellite office to take in work that you then deliver to your main operation for service. With a satellite, you can maximize the efficiency of your main store's operations. Or you can open a new store in a new territory adjacent to your existing one, or you can convert to a Sir Speedy printing center. Collins emphasized that if you want to grow, you will find it very easy to do.

Copies Now does not make earnings claims, but some reports showed that the average Copies Now center grosses about $250,000 a year. The Bound Brook, New Jersey, location grosses about $750,000; the largest center grosses more than $1 million; a location in the Chrysler Building in Manhattan grosses more than $300,000, and the owner never makes sales calls. But the most successful locations have up to six large copiers working constantly because the owner or a salesperson constantly generates new business.

Yet, after you subtract low labor costs, low overhead costs, equipment rents, and leases, you can easily net 20 to 30 percent before taxes. In conclusion, Copies Now is an excellent, relatively inexpensive way that can either prosper by itself or give you an inexpensive entry into the even more lucrative quick printing business through the back door. Your choice depends on your ambitions and preference, but Copies Now's very comprehensive and sophisticated support programs mean that you can trust that they truly want you to succeed.

MONEY MAILER, INC.

Money Mailer, Inc.
14271 Corporate Drive
Garden Grove, CA 92643
(714) 265-4100

For this edition, I was very leery about including a direct mail advertising franchise because several others have not done well during the early 1990s. But Money Mailer's continued strong growth and the personal reports of several regional subfranchisors and local franchisees convinced me that Money Mailer is a genuine long-term opportunity.

As a Money Mailer franchisee, you sell half-page-sized coupon advertisements to local businesses, such as pizza shops, cleaning services, fast-food restaurants, home improvement contractors, doctors and dentists, real estate brokers—any business or professional practice with a neighborhood or local customer base. Every two months or so, you package together all the ads you have sold, and using Money Mailer's printing and mailing services, you mail the coupons to at least 40,000 households in your area. You earn income by charging between $350 and $400 per advertising insert.

During 1993, Money Mailer's more than 300 franchisees in about 400 territories distributed bimonthly mailers to a total of more than 80 million households in the United States. Money Mailer reaches one-third of the 44 million homes that are defined as "mailable domiciles." A mailable domicile, stated company executives, is one likely to have the income and demographics to buy the products and services that Money Mailer clients advertise. The total value of Money Mailer coupons represented $54 million worth of retail sales during 1993.

Money Mailer franchisees produce these results because they deliver verifiable, trackable results for their clients. The owner of a pizza shop or cleaning service or packaging store can count the number of coupons that customers bring in, which kinds of promotions or discounts work best, and how much extra income and profit he or she generates. In fact, the owner of a Mail Boxes Etc.

franchise whom I know told me that he receives 50 percent more returns from his Money Mailer coupons than any other direct mail coupon he has tested. These and similar measurable results boosted the direct mail industry by 218 percent during the 1980s, far greater than the sales increases for any other advertising medium, including radio and television.

Money Mailer sold more than 130 local franchises during 1993 and plans to add some 200 more during 1994. With these impressive statistics, Money Mailer plans to maximize its growth in 1997 when the U.S. territories will be saturated. It may well do so because it has been rated the best direct mail franchise every year for the past eight years by key ranking services.

How It Works

You buy your Money Mailer franchise from regional owners (also known as subfranchisors) who are responsible for training you in the field and supporting you from your start-up throughout the term of your agreement. However, subfranchising in general worries me because the quality of your local, individual support depends directly on the quality of your subfranchisor's marketing, training, and support acumen. Despite corporate executives' best intention to sell territories only to quality "subs," they, too, make mistakes that both of you pay for. So, be sure to investigate the subfranchisor's performance with other franchisees in your region before you buy this franchise. I do know two Money Mailer subfranchisors, one in Connecticut and one in Illinois, and both were considered top performers.

At present, Money Mailer has 45 regional owners in 40 states and Quebec, Canada. A region has at least 500,000 mailable homes, divided into 50 zones. An individual franchise buys the rights to at least four zones or a minimum of 40,000 households for a base franchise fee. Although you can buy up to six zones, Money Mailer managers prefer that you start with four and develop their potential before you grow to six or more. At present, the most zones any one franchisee controls totals 12; the largest region has about 300 zones.

The Money Mailer Business Cycle, as the company calls it, works like this. First, you sell ads to the local merchant. Then, you pay the regional office a fee to design and layout the ads. Next, the region transmits the ads to the corporate printing and mailing facility. The company mails the completed ads in envelopes to each household around the country. Consumers find coupons they want to use and redeem them at their local merchants' store or service. The merchants then buy more ads from you in a circle that can become very profitable.

How Much It Costs

The Money Mailer franchise fee varies from a low of $18,000 to a high of $24,000, with an average of $22,000. You negotiate the territory with the regional subfranchisor, doing your best to exclude low-income or nonmailable households from your territory. Every time you send out a mailing, you also pay your region "sub" a regional development fee equal to a minimum of $400 per zone or $40 for each advertisement you insert. For each mailing, you also must pay Money Mailer, Inc., for the fixed costs of envelopes, postage, affixing your labels, and inserting, which total about $1,800 per zone ($90 per ad for printing and $18 per ad for inserting over a total number of 18). If you do not use Money Mailer to print and mail your ads, you must pay a "national development fee" equal to $194 per zone (during 1993). This fee is adjusted each year according to the rise in the Consumer Price Index for the Los Angeles area. However, 99 percent of its franchises use Money Mailer production services to save time and money.

In short, company executives stated that excluding your own operating expenses, you do not break even until you sell at least 10 ads ($3,500 to $4,000) per mailing, but every ad above that number generates profit.

Although it would seem that Money Mailer makes a significant profit from these charges, company executives stated categorically that they do not do so. They said that they earn their profits by retaining the right to include up to nine coupon inserts in your mailing. They sell national accounts, such as Sears, MasterCard, and so on, who want to reach millions of households at relatively low cost.

You also must pay for your training travel costs and buy a fax machine. You should have a business telephone, although most new franchisees start from home. You must also have general liability insurance. The following table shows these estimated start-up costs.

Category	Low End	High End
Franchise fee	$18,000	$24,000
Rent, deposits, phone (a)	1,000	2,600
Training (b)	2,000	4,000
Insurance	350	500
Computer system	1,000	5,000
Fax machine	400	1,500
Working capital (c)	5,000	10,000
Total	$27,750	$47,600

a. Low end represents work-at-home expenses for phone deposits, office furniture, and so on; high end represents office lease, security deposits, phone deposits, and office start-up expenses.
b. Transportation and room and board for both headquarters and regional training sessions.
c. Business operating and living expenses for at least the first six months. It should take about three to four months to complete your first mailing.

What You Get

In return for your franchise fee, you receive a territory of at least 40,000—four zones—qualified mailable homes and the right to use the regional and national design and production services. But far more important, when you buy a new franchise territory, you receive a first mailing free to 20,000 homes (at least half of your territory) to help you earn income from the beginning. You also receive the following training and support:

- *Five-year term.* You receive an initial five-year term and the right to renew for additional terms for a small fee.

- *Training.* You receive five days at corporate headquarters to learn all the basics of selling the ads and marketing the business in your area. You work with the regional sub for at least another five days in your daily activities. And you can always call on the regional sub to help you.

- *Design support.* The regional sub provides all graphic design and layout support to create the ads.

- *Ongoing support.* The regional sub also provides ongoing sales and marketing support.

- *Office facilities.* Most franchisees work from home and use their regional sub's office to make calls, use the fax machine, have meetings, and use a photocopier. It reduces their costs and puts them in close contact with their support staff.

The company provides national marketing programs and promotes the system through the national media and its national account sales program. Of course, it also produces and mails all the ads and mailers.

How Much Can You Make?

Direct mail sales is a very competitive and intense activity. You face competition from other national franchises and national companies with their own sales forces as well as local efforts. This competition drives down your per ad price to your customers. During 1993, as the economy began to emerge from the recession, the average franchisee sold 18 ads per mailing for about $375 each, or a gross income of $6,750 and a gross margin of about $3,000. Furthermore, the average franchise does between six and eight mailings a year for a gross margin between $18,000 and $24,000. Therefore, if you own a four-zone territory, you could achieve a gross margin between $72,000 and $96,000 per year.

However, note that these averages reflect dozens of franchises less than two years old. Your income directly relates to your time in business, your persistence, and your patience building the business. Franchisees in business two years or more average higher piece counts and average sales prices per mailing for a gross margin of about $5,000 per mailing, or $40,000 a year per zone.

However, you can boost this income by "cross-selling" ads, that is, you share space with other franchisees in your region; If a neighboring franchisee has a client who wants to cover more geographic territory, he pays you a fee, usually $250, to allow his client to run his ad in your envelope. You split the costs: You pay for the printing ($95 or so) and the neighbor pays for the design service. You earn a substantial net profit of more than $140 for owning the mailing area.

More important in the long run, everyone in the region has a chance to piggy-back the same kind of advertisers in their envelopes and cross-sell with everyone else. For example, suppose a regional McDonald's cooperative advertising group wants to insert coupons in your envelope, but you do not cover all the same territory that the McDonald's co-op covers. You could lose the sale or offer the "piggyback" service and work with your neighbors to boost everyone's profits.

These numbers show that succeeding in direct mail ad sales is difficult, but the long-term payoff of developing major cross-selling opportunities could make it worth the effort. In fact, Money Mailer reports relatively low failure rates, about 6 percent per year, far below average for this industry. Company executives stated that about half of that number are new franchisees, and some are mutual terminations because the franchisees do not want to do the work any longer. The 6 percent does not include resales or those who chose not to renew. In sum, in this tough industry, Money Mailer is the best available franchise.

BLIMPIE SUBS AND SALADS

Blimpie Subs and Salads
1775 The Exchange, Suite 215
Atlanta, GA 30339
(800) 447-6256
(404) 984-2707

Blimpie Subs and Salads is one of the fastest-growing and lowest-cost submarine sandwich and salad franchises. By early

1994, it had almost 700 stores, with plans to have 1,000 open by the end of its 1995 fiscal year. It is promoting its rapid growth with 81 "subfranchisors" and placing new stores in nontraditional sites, such as Blimpie franchises inside convenience stores, on university campuses, in airports, and some 15 other unusual locations.

Blimpie has grown very rapidly since the mid-1980s, more than 60 percent, and it bases its concept on a simple, noncooking system that does not require any restaurant experience. It supports its franchisees with five weeks of training and a dynamic national and regional marketing program.

As important, it is in a market for sub and salad shops that has grown 60 percent during the last three years, many times faster than hamburgers and three times faster than pizza. President Anthony Conza asserted that this type of shop offers a wide variety that its competition cannot match.

However, this rapid growth has its perils: It cannot continue forever. Further, the "subfranchising" growth method has its perils. So far, Blimpie appears to have avoided the worst problems that can face a system based on "subfranchisors," actually, area representatives as this book defines the term. These area reps buy large territories, but in return, they must usually follow fast growth plans to saturate their markets within three to five years.

Note that Blimpie calls these area reps "subfranchisors" or "area developers," but according to their functions, they fit this book's definition of area representatives. They provide training and support for the local franchisee; however, the local franchisee signs the agreement with the company and pays his franchise fee and weekly royalties to the company, which in turn pays the area representative. The company even signs and owns the lease for the local store so it does not lose the location if the individual franchisee does not do well with the store.

This explanation aside, Blimpie has taken these actions to avoid the problems. First, Conza encouraged the creation of a five-member, elected National Franchisee Advisory Council (NFAC) that now meets quarterly at different locations around the country.

Unlike some FACs that are limited to advertising issues, the Blimpie FAC can—and does—discuss any issue. Conza reported that the company and its franchisees share the same goals: to increase market penetration and to increase the sales volume and profit margins of each store. He insisted that forcing corporate decisions down franchisees' throats was not acceptable any more in the franchise industry.

Second, Conza understands the advantages and disadvantages of subfranchisors. He stated that this method has two main disadvantages: (1) The company must give an area rep half of the royalties, so it reduces its revenues, and (2) his area reps must be as good as the franchisor—and they sometimes do not live up to those expectations.

However, Conza said that Blimpie uses the system because of these advantages: (1) The company can immediately achieve a strong market presence in many areas at the same time and create a compounding effect that benefits everyone; (2) good area reps provide hands-on, local training and marketing assistance to the individual franchisees who can earn more income more quickly; and (3) the company can provide more support for the area reps than it could provide to the individuals.

I provided this detailed discussion of the area rep situation because several major franchisors have created very difficult situations with poorly conceived, high-pressure subfranchise systems in which the regional subfranchisor signs franchise agreements with the individual and receives both fees and royalty payments. Poor-quality subfranchisors have wreaked havoc on these systems.

In short, Blimpie has worked out the ingredients of a fast-growth system that appears to work best for all levels.

With a Blimpie Subs and Salads store, you run a fast-food operation that emphasizes quality products. Of course, you compete with major competitors across the country, but Blimpie has been rated the second best of these for many years. It has also developed a continuous stream of innovative marketing ideas, such as community charity programs, a children's promotion, a national marketing and advertising campaign to build brand recognition, an incentive plan to improve customer service, and a value-priced menu.

How Much It Costs

The average start-up cost for a Blimpie franchise equals about $90,000, and with good equity and credit, you can lease most of the equipment to reduce your cash requirements. The franchise fee is a very reasonable $18,000. The table shows a detailed breakdown:

Category	Low End	High End
Franchise fee	$18,000	$18,000
Equipment/fixtures (a)	32,000	42,000
Construction (b)	20,000	60,000
Insurance deposits (c)	4,150	12,300
Inventory	2,500	5,000
Opening advertising	2,000	2,000
Working capital (d)	3,000	10,000
Uniforms	270	270
Lease security (e)	1,000	10,000
Total (f)	$ 82,920	$159,570

a. Includes Blimpie required equipment package, but much of this may be leased.
b. High end is very high and would be for raw space in expensive metropolitan areas in large stores. Average stores in existing space cost much less to build out.
c. Covers wide range of required policies, including workers' compensation, business liability, business interruption, plate glass, and so on.
d. Covers several months' operating expenses, but a Blimpie generates cash flow quickly.
e. For stores ranging in size from 600 square feet to 4,000 square feet with the average about 1,800 square feet.
f. The high end is very high for this book, but Conza assured me that the average was $90,000, well within my parameters.

Royalties and Fees

In addition, you must pay a 6 percent weekly royalty and a 3 percent advertising fee. That's it, no hidden charges. You do have to buy certain company-approved products and supplies and use company-approved equipment and signage to make sure every unit conforms to its standards.

What You Get

In return, you receive a turnkey fast-food sub and salad restaurant:

- *Territory.* You receive a nonexclusive territory, but Conza said that the company was well aware of the encroachment problems that its competitors had experienced and did not plan to build close enough to existing locations to dilute their revenues.

- *Training.* You and your employees will receive a total of five weeks' training at various locations, including one week's training at its marketing and training location in Atlanta. You also must do 80 hours of work in an existing Blimpie restaurant either in Atlanta or near your location. And Blimpie trains your employees before you open and works with you during your grand opening week.

- *Twenty-year term.* In one of the longest terms in franchising, Blimpie gives a 20-year agreement with the right for automatic five-year renewals at no cost, an important benefit.

- *Marketing support.* Blimpie understands very well that the heart of its success comes from marketing, advertising, promotion, and new product development. It has a very aggressive and innovative department that constantly feeds the system new ideas.

- *Low termination rate.* A very important reason Blimpie is in this book is its relatively low termination rate for its market segment. Conza reported that during fiscal 1992, 39 franchises, or about 6 percent, closed, but many were older stores whose leases had expired. Only a handful were terminated for failure to pay royalties or similar causes.

How Much Can You Make?

Conza reported that the average national store volume totaled $239,000 a year during fiscal 1993. That figure included dozens of new stores that were less than one year old. So, the average gross revenues for stores two or three years or more old probably exceed $300,000. Conza did not make any net profit claims, but industry averages show that sub and salad restaurants can earn net profits in the 20 to 25 percent range.

If you find a good location with most of the interior construction already done, you should be able to open an average-sized store for less than $90,000. You may also be able to negotiate delayed rents and landlord payments for construction in certain areas and reduce your start-up costs even more. If you lease your equipment, you may be able to save an additional $20,000 to $30,000 in cash. With these and similar negotiated advantages, you could open your first Blimpie for $50,000 cash and earn very high ROIs on that cash investment by the third year, according to my estimates based on known industry averages.

In conclusion, as long as Blimpie avoids the perils of fast growth through area representatives, you cannot find a better sub sandwich and salad franchise.

SERVPRO Industries, Inc.

SERVPRO Industries, Inc.
575 Airport Blvd.
Gallatin, TN 37066
(800) 826-9586
(615) 451-0200

SERVPRO remains one of the largest and most well-established cleaning franchises, with more than 865 franchises (including distributors) in operation during 1993. It has been consistently rated among the five best carpet cleaning and disaster restoration services for many years. It has been offering franchises for 25 years and has franchises in all 50 states.

SERVPRO emphasizes marketing your services to insurance company adjusters for water and fire damage restoration, retail stores, real estate and property management firms, commercial and institutional building managers, and homeowners.

How Much It Costs

SERVPRO offers a regular franchise sold and administered through a two-level distributor organization. The basic SERVPRO cleaning franchise costs $36,000 (a 13 percent increase since 1990) and includes one complete equipment and supplies package. Of that total, some $18,800 is attributed to the franchise fee and the rest for the equipment package and training.

If you pay cash, you receive a 5 percent discount ($1,800), or you can finance the purchase price with $15,000 cash down with an estimated 13.5 percent interest rate, a term of 72 months, and a $427 monthly payment (in late 1993).

As you grow and add teams and vans, you can finance other equipment packages from cash flow. However, as I have warned earlier, be very cautious about all this financing. It does reduce your up-front costs, but it puts very heavy pressure on you to succeed quickly just so you can pay your debt to the company.

General and Director Distributors

SERVPRO also licenses experienced, successful franchisees to sell franchises and acts as trainers and support for new or existing franchisees in their territories. General distributor rights, which includes an area with about 150,000 people or six regular territories, cost $36,000; director distributor rights to a territory with about 750,000 people or some 30 territories cost $150,000. Under various discount plans, you can reduce that amount somewhat. General and director distributors are also expected to purchase and maintain a 45-day supply of chemicals, parts, and so on that franchisees normally use in their territories.

General and director distributors receive income in three main ways:

● They share the royalties that franchisees pay, up to 60 percent of all royalties paid to SERVPRO.

● They receive directors' and trainers' commissions on product and equipment sales to their franchisees.

- They are paid to sell franchises and train new franchisees.

However, they act like area representatives; they do *not* sign contracts or own the subfranchise rights. They only sell franchises and train and support franchisees.

On the other hand, regular franchisees are required to buy chemical, supplies, and business forms from SERVPRO; those purchases will equal between 5 and 6 percent of your total annual operating costs. SERVPRO cannot force you to buy the chemicals, and it has developed an extensive list of approved suppliers during its 25-year history.

Total Start-up Costs

Your total start-up costs will fall into a broad range, primarily determined by how much you finance and whether you buy a new van or lease a used one. The table that follows describes this range:

Category	Low End	High End
Franchise fee (a)	$15,000	$33,200
Van lease/purchase (b)	1,000	16,000
Van painting	400	800
Office furniture/supplies (c)	300	900
Insurance	500	1,500
Business licenses	0	200
Telephone deposit	50	250
Equipment sales tax	0	1,350
Working capital (d)	2,500	5,000
Total (e)	$19,750	$59,200

a. From down payment with financing to cash payment with discount. Includes complete equipment and materials package, the list for which takes up 20 pages in the agreement. The franchise fee portion totals about $18,000.
b. The company advises you to buy or lease a used van to keep your overhead down. The low end covers a lease deposit and first month's payment; the high end represents a new van purchase price.
c. The company advises that you begin from home until you have reached a volume large enough to support an office comfortably. Be sure to check local zoning

laws to make sure you can park your van in your driveway, or you may have to find another parking area.

d. This includes several months' salaries for anyone who helps you and any funds for living expenses. Increase this amount if you or your spouse do not have additional incomes to pay basic living expenses.

e. Company executives commented that the average start-up cost tended to fall in the lower end of the range.

Sliding Royalty Structure

In addition to a $100-per-month minimum royalty, regular franchisees pay a sliding scale royalty based on gross monthly volume, as shown in the following table:

Gross Income	Amount/Percentage (%)
$0 to $5,999	$45 + 10.0%
$6,000 to $9,999	$65 + 9.0%
$10,000 to $14,999	$85 + 8.0%
$15,000 to $19,999	$95 + 7.5%
$20,000 to $34,999	$115 + 7.0%
$35,000 to $49,999	$2,450 + 6.5% of excess over $34,999
$50,000 to $74,999	$3,425 + 6.0% of excess over $49,999
$75,000 to $99,999	$4,925 + 5.5% of excess over $74,999
$100,000 and over	$6,300 + 5.0% of excess over $99,999

SERVPRO wants you to make more as you earn more. And in one benefit, SERVPRO does not charge an advertising fee.

What You Get

In return for these fees and payments, you receive the following services:

- *Nonexclusive territory.* A territory usually consists of an area with a population of between 25,000 and 100,000, with the average between 75,000 and 100,000, a beneficial increase since 1990. Although the territory is not exclusive, SERVPRO has a strict policy of avoiding encroachment, company executives stated, and only on very rare occasion has this occurred, they noted.

SERVPRO emphasizes the insurance company and retail store markets, so it has special limits that restrict how widely you can solicit this business outside your own boundaries. Usually, if you contract with a chain of stores to do their cleaning, you can pay other franchisees a commission for permission to work in their areas.

- *Expanded training program.* With a new $1 million training facility, SERVPRO has dramatically improved its training program with

  A 40-module home-study course before you attend headquarters training;

  Twelve days' training at the new center;

  Five days' setup training in your territory with your area's general or director distributor or company trainer; and

  Certification course that lasts all of your first year and works like a correspondence course to teach you all aspects of building the business.

- *Paid transportation.* SERVPRO also pays for the round-trip transportation costs for a franchisee and a spouse and gives you a $600 allowance for room and board.

- *Continuous support.* SERVPRO offers a very thorough support program at all three levels:

  Meetings. You attend national conventions (with a 10 percent royalty rebate that helps pay your trip costs), regional meetings, area meetings three times a year, and an annual statewide meeting.

  Business reviews. You do a general business review for yourself three times a year, and you have an annual face-to-face review with your director distributor or a corporate manager.

  Personal visits. You receive personal visits from your director distributor at least twice a year (a total of three).

- *In-house advertising agency that develops marketing materials.*

- *Catastrophic loss team.* In a unique program, SERVPRO has organized teams of company employees who can respond within hours to an urgent call from a franchisee who needs help coping with a major disaster. The need for these "quick response" teams developed during the severe floods and fires of 1993 when individual franchisees became overwhelmed by the demand for their services, but had few ways to quickly expand their teams to fill their customers' very pressing needs.

- *National account program.* The company sells national insurance companies and commercial firms, but does not charge any fees for this service.

- *Adjuster training.* The company also trains insurance adjusters in their work at the new training facility; this also acquaints them with SERVPRO and subtly encourages them to work with you.

- *Five-year agreement.* The company gives a five-year agreement with low-cost, unlimited renewals ($250 each) as long as you remain in good standing.

- *Termination at any time.* One of the vital reasons SERVPRO is in this book is that it allows mutual termination at any time and franchisee termination with 120 days' notice. Both constitute liberal policies. Moreover, the company reports a low to average termination rate, with 111 in the three years between September 30, 1990, and September 30, 1993. This represents an average of some 35 per year, less than 5 percent of the total number of 744 individual franchises. Of that total, the company terminated 58 for nonpayment of debts or abandonment and 53 were by mutual agreement.

In short, you receive a very complete package of equipment, training, and support services that will help you succeed.

How Much Can You Make?

SERVPRO does not make any earnings claims, but you can make this into a very, very profitable business. You can expect net profit margins in these ranges: 30 percent if you have gross revenues between $25,000 and $250,000, 25 percent if your revenues range from $250,001 to $500,000, and 20 percent if your revenues exceed $500,000. Note that the net pretax income increases from the low to middle five figures to more than $100,000. It also appears that the new training program is boosting new franchisees' gross revenues very substantially, with reported averages between $150,000 and $200,000 by the end of their first year. In short, you can earn back your cash investment very quickly and build a very high ROI.

How well you do depends on your goals. You can stay with one van and one full-time employee working with you and earn a middle-class income, or you can build a fleet of trucks and earn a very affluent income. The most profitable franchisee has eight trucks, acts as a director distributor, has 15 employees, and grosses more than $1 million a year.

In conclusion, SERVPRO is a well-established company that has a deliberate policy to grow steadily and introduce new programs constantly to help strengthen its franchisees.

CEILING DOCTOR, INC.

Ceiling Doctor
5151 Beltline Road
Suite 950
Dallas, TX 75240
(800) 992-6299
(214) 702-8046

Since 1990, Ceiling Doctor has become a worldwide franchise with master franchise agreements for more than 25 European countries, Japan, Mexico, and the United States. It has grown slowly in the United States from 15 franchises in 1990 to 35, but it has 26 in Canada, 40 in Japan, 6 in Mexico, and 12 in Europe. President Kaaydah Forest, one of the most professional women franchisors that I know, said that the company has a solid U.S. core group, all earning significant profits, and a new U.S. master franchisee that should provide the financial base for far more rapid growth.

Since the late 1980s, Ceiling Doctor has consistently been rated one of the best franchises for women and a leader in both franchising and the acoustic tile cleaning industry. It specializes in environmentally safe cleaning of acoustic tiles, ceiling materials, and interior and exterior walls. You concentrate on commercial buildings and institutions, especially grocery stores, hospitals, factories, shopping malls, office buildings, and the like. Your marketing advantage consists of a major price break: It costs about 20 cents per foot to clean a tile ceiling, but it costs $1 to $2 per square foot to replace it. Property managers save time and dollars cleaning rather than replacing.

How Much It Costs

Ceiling Doctor has reduced its franchise fee from $20,500 to $19,500, including a required equipment and supply package, training, operations manuals, and support. Forest noted that of the total, $10,500 covers the licensing and training, while the rest pays for the equipment and materials package. Some competitors do not include the equipment and materials in their franchise fees. However, Ceiling Doctor has reduced the size of its average territory from 500,000 people to 250,000 people. Forest explained that the company's experience has shown that franchisees can build a substantial business in that area, but have a difficult time growing their businesses beyond that area. Ceiling Doctor also discontinued a troublesome formula through which it raised or lowered the fee depending on population.

You must also lease a van and use the company's logo, name signage, and decals on it. Fortunately, you can work from home and use your own telephone line, saving thousands of dollars in start-up costs. Even if you rent an office, you can rent a small 200- to 300-square-foot one at a low monthly rent. Here are low- and high-end estimates of Ceiling Doctor's very low total initial investment:

Category	Low End	High End
Franchise fee	$19,500	$19,500
Van lease	500	1,000
Office lease	0	600
Prepaid insurance	500	1,000
Training travel	500	1,000
Miscellaneous	100	500
Working capital (a)	2,500	5,000
Total (b)	$23,600	$29,600

a. To cover initial operating expenses, including marketing, hiring part-time help, and so on and living expenses.
b. The company estimates lower totals, but does not include travel costs or living expenses in its estimates.

Royalty Fees and Required Purchases

Ceiling Doctor has increased its royalty from 6 percent to 8 percent and charges a 2 percent advertising fee for both local and national marketing campaigns in trade journals for commercial building managers. And you must spend about 3 percent of your gross revenues on Yellow Pages and other local ads. One good point: Ceiling Doctor does not require you to pay royalties on the value of discount coupons and programs like some companies do.

After you pay for the initial equipment and materials package, you must buy the company's chemicals and cleaning units, but these supplies should cost only about 4 percent of your gross annual revenues. In fact, Forest stated that the company has reduced its chemical prices and improved its cleaning methods to make the franchisees' operations less expensive (lower labor costs) and more profitable.

However, it no longer offers a financing program primarily because most prospects did not want or need one.

What You Get

Ceiling Doctor provides a comprehensive program, including unique, safe chemicals. With growing concern about indoor pollution and toxic chemicals, using safe chemicals makes you a responsible vendor to your customers.

Further, at the request of its franchisees, Forest said, the company has changed its training program to seven days and five evenings. It includes intense classroom and on-site, hands-on training at the company-owned operation in Dallas.

Forest also continues to emphasize a close relationship with her franchisees and a "buddy system" in which experienced franchisees work with new ones. Field consultants or company executives speak with you at least once a week. They visit at least twice a year or more, if you need help. It has an advisory council, holds an annual convention, publishes a newsletter, and encourages a suggestion program.

You also receive a zealously protected territory set up by city or county boundaries and zip codes. Be sure that you pick territories with numerous potential customers: shopping malls, health care institutions, grocery stores, office buildings, and so on.

In fact, the company has a new national accounts program that has gained contracts with the Disney Stores, Kroger stores, and Target stores, to name just several. You have the right to market to those stores in your area.

The franchise term is only five years, but you can renew for up to nine additional terms for a fee equal to 2 percent of your gross annual revenues. This does give you the chance to build substantial equity.

How Much Can You Make?

Ceiling Doctor does not publish any earnings claims, but you can easily earn gross margins equal to 70 to 80 percent if you work from home. Your costs include 10 percent royalty and advertising fees, 4 percent materials, and 6 to 15 percent labor.

To help you increase your profits, Ceiling Doctor, as noted, has not only reduced its chemical costs and improved its cleaning methods, but also begun national insurance, printing, and promotion programs that have reduced franchisee costs sharply. Further, Ceiling Doctor earns no markups or profit on these auxiliary products and services.

Although the company still has a performance quota in its offering circular, Forest said that the company has never had to enforce it because every franchise exceeds it. A Part I quota requires $75,000 in minimum gross annual revenues, while a Part II quota requires just $25,000. The quota varies with territory size and potential customer demographics.

By your third year, you should earn gross incomes between $150,000 and $200,000 with net pretax incomes between $75,000 and $100,000, depending on how well you control your expenses.

Of course, the company wants you to expand your business rapidly, so it seeks people with business management, sales, or administrative backgrounds who can communicate well with their customers—building, maintenance, and property managers.

For a very low start-up cost, you can quickly earn annual returns in the hundreds of percent and a substantial middle five-figure income while you build long-term equity in a thriving industry.

RE/MAX INTERNATIONAL, INC.

RE/MAX International, Inc.
5445 DTC Parkway
Suite 1200
Englewood, CO 80111
(800) 525-7452
(303) 770-5531

Frankly, I became convinced RE/MAX was a winner when in early 1990, Chairman David Liniger predicted that home mortgage interest rates would probably fall to 6 percent. Almost everyone scoffed at his prediction at the time because interest rates were poised about 10 percent and the recession had not hit its stride. But from my own reading of the situation—the Baby Bust and a severe recession that my business had begun to experience—I thought

Liniger was right. As time has shown, Liniger has been more accurate than almost all others.

Further, Liniger and his executives have built a phenomenally successful franchise on a simple concept: open real estate offices that employ only the best available salespeople and let them keep 100 percent of their commissions. Since 1973, this concept has grown from a few offices to more than 2,000 franchised offices, more than 300 more sold but not yet open, more than 34,000 agents, and more than $75.5 billion worth of systemwide transactions during 1992. During 1993, the company sold more than 300 more franchises with projections of adding hundreds more during 1994. President Robert Fisher asserted that during late 1993, the company was on its hottest growth streak ever. This rapid expansion bodes extremely well for both future RE/MAX franchisees and the real estate market of the mid- and late 1990s.

With this success, you may ask, "What's left for me?" Fisher advised that the answer depends on where you are and where you want to live. The East Coast offers the greatest opportunity because it has more population and more density, RE/MAX has the fewest offices there, and the real estate market there will recover the most slowly. The "heartland" Midwest, Canada, and Mexico also offer significant potential. Furthermore, RE/MAX International has announced plans to expand into 21 European countries and is exploring other opportunities for global growth.

During 1992, the agents grossed more than $2.26 billion in commissions and closed more than 652,000 transactions.

The RE/MAX System is simple: Each RE/MAX sales associate shares the cost of office overhead and pays for personal advertising, telephone, and similar expenses.

The franchise owner earns a profit by charging the agents monthly management fees. Nonetheless, the agents keep 95 to 100 percent of their commissions compared to far lower commission structures in more traditional offices. This powerful incentive—the Maximum Commission Concept, as RE/MAX calls it—attracts aggressive, experienced, productive agents. For example, RE/MAX sales associates averaged $79,224 in gross commissions during 1992 (based on associates with the company for the full calendar year).

Brokers like this franchise because they receive a projectable monthly income based on the number of sales associates paying management fees. They don't have to waste time training novices or poor performers.

Clearly, RE/MAX is the best franchise for the most successful and ambitious brokers and associates. To encourage this rapid growth, RE/MAX relies on a very extensive master subfranchisor system with most regions independently owned and operated. Through this system, RE/MAX has expanded into all 50 states and all Canadian provinces and is growing quickly in Mexico and the Caribbean. Each subfranchisor receives certain franchise fee payments from the franchises that he or she has sold and sends a portion to international headquarters. In turn, the company provides a wide variety of systems and services.

How Much It Costs

A RE/MAX franchise fee is $20,000 for a territory with about 15,000 people, except for some smaller-population territories where the fee ranges from $15,000 to $17,500. In return, the owner receives a commitment that RE/MAX will not open another office within a given area (most commonly within a one-mile driving radius of the office). The total start-up cost for an average office ranges from $60,000 to $100,000 although costs can be higher or lower depending on many factors, including location and office size. First, you must rent an office that can accommodate rapid growth; RE/MAX executives suggested renting enough space to hold 20 people. They asserted that brokers in urban areas would be unwise to remain small. Second, they recommend that you should lease your office furniture to keep your cash expenses down, but you will need a substantial telephone system, signage, extensive start-up advertising budget, salaries for secretarial help, and other common office opening expenses. The following table illustrates the range of start-up costs:

Category	Low End	High End
Franchise fee	$15,000	$20,000
Insurance (a)	2,000	10,000
Legal expenses	500	2,000
Training travel	800	2,000
Broker license	125	500
Realtor association	200	1,200
Signage	750	1,750
Fax machine	500	2,500
Computer system	2,500	7,500
Secretary	1,200	2,000
Fees to franchisor	450	525
Office opening (b)	30,000	50,000
Total	$54,025	$99,975

a. Potentially high figure depending on how many agents you have and the cost of errors and omissions insurance in your market.
b. Costs for a minimum 1,200-square-foot office with furniture, telephone systems, a full-time secretary, and appropriate equipment.

Furthermore, RE/MAX requires you to grow quickly; you must have at least seven top-producing agents on board within the first year and expand to at least 15 by the end of the second year and 20 by the end of the third. You will spend much of your time during your first two years identifying and recruiting the best agents.

Complex Fee Schedule

In the RE/MAX System, management income is based on a fee schedule. The broker-owner receives a management fee from each sales associate. The owner then sends a portion of that fee, usually 20 percent, to the regional office. The region in turn sends a portion (also usually 20 percent) of the fee received from all the offices in that region to RE/MAX International. The company also charges certain other fees, most of which the franchisee collects from his or her sales agents. Note that these fees had increased between 10 and 30 percent between 1989 and 1993.

- *Management fee.* The franchisee usually pays the regional sub-franchisor a minimum of $100 per month for each sales agent, or one-fifth (20 percent) of the management fee that the sales agent pays. During 1993, RE/MAX suggested that this monthly fee should total $500.

- *Annual dues.* The sales associates pay $300 per year in annual dues to RE/MAX International. During the first year that a sales associate joins an office, many broker-owners charge an initiation fee and often will send the associate's annual dues to RE/MAX International from this initiation fee. The broker-owner retains the balance of the initiation fee.

- *Advertising fee.* Each associate must also pay—through you to the regional subfranchisor—a monthly advertising fee that varies from $50 to $100 per month. This amount is used exclusively for regional advertising programs that benefit you and them.

- *Institutional advertising development fund.* Each sales associate contributes $5 per month (which the broker-owner collects) to RE/MAX International. The company uses these funds to develop advertising campaigns available to all regions, raise money for charity, and advertise the local franchise offices.

- *Renewal fee.* Each agreement lasts for a fairly short five years. To renew the franchise, you must pay a fee equal to 50 percent of the then-current fee if you are in compliance with the current agreement.

What You Get

Primarily, you get the benefit of perhaps the most dynamic real estate organization in North America and the concept of filling an office with the best and brightest real estate agents in your area. You also benefit from the cumulative impact of the enormous RE/MAX marketing and promotion effort that has created one of the most recognized corporate logos in North America, the RE/MAX Hot Air Balloon. RE/MAX offices and regions everywhere promote this logo with "For Sale" signs, advertising, and constant appearances of the real thing—a fleet of some 80 individually owned red-over-white-over-blue balloons.

You also receive five days of training at corporate headquarters, learning how to recruit top agents and how to manage a RE/MAX office. In addition, you receive a wide variety of benefits, including advanced education seminars, publications, awards and recognition programs, a referral system, an approved supplier list, and an annual international convention.

You also receive direct advice and support from the regional subfranchisor through his or her professional support staff. Regional offices have a variety of services from communication to marketing programs. Throughout the system, subfranchisors and broker-owners focus on recruiting and retaining top-producing agents.

Further, Fisher noted that RE/MAX plans to add more services that can generate new revenue sources for local franchisees. These services may include, for example, mortgage banking and title insurance.

You also receive multiple ways to communicate with either corporate, regional, or other local franchisees with an electronic mail network and a CD ROM–based directory of all sales agents. Through these, you can share referrals and cooperate on relocation efforts. Local subfranchisors constantly communicate with fax bulletins, phone calls, and monthly broker meetings. These meetings, Fisher added, push the local franchisees to understand their customers—their own sales associates—and to encourage these agents by giving what they want most: ways to make more sales.

How Much Can You Make?

You earn income by charging your sales associates monthly fees and making each associate pay a proportional share of your overhead expenses, including salaries for secretaries and/or office managers. In a typical office, you would charge the sales associate $500 per month as a management fee; you would keep $400 and send $100 to the regional office. Sales associates share office expenses, including salaries for secretaries and/or office managers. Once you have recruited enough associates to pay for your office expenses, you earn income or gross "profit" from management fees. So, the larger the office—a direct result of how well you recruit and retain agents—the greater the income stream. If the broker-owner charges the typical fee, a 20-agent office will generate a base of $8,000 a month in net management fees.

RE/MAX publications give an idea of how well the best operations do. For example, the huge 97-associate RE/MAX Southeast office did a total sales volume of $312 million during 1992, or more than $3.2 million per agent. Eighteen of the top 25 real estate offices in the country—measured in terms of transactions per agent—were RE/MAX offices. These offices had between 21 and 110 agents, or between $8,400 and $44,000 per month net management fees for their owners.

Of course, if you are also a broker or agent, you earn income by making your own sales or by investing in real estate to earn even higher investment returns.

In sum, RE/MAX continues as the most exciting opportunity in real estate franchising.

HOMES AND LAND PUBLISHING CORPORATION

Homes and Land Publishing Corporation
1600 Capital Circle, S.W.
Tallahassee, FL 32310
(904) 574-2111

Although Homes and Land Publishing remains the largest real estate advertising publication franchise in the United States, its total number of franchises fell during the recession from about 300 to about 250 by the end of 1993. Simply, the very sharp recession in real estate during the early 1990s took its toll on a portion of the franchisees. However, company executives emphasized that a significant percentage of the apparent terminations were not, in fact, failures. They said that many were "paper terminations" of existing franchisees who had planned to expand into second and third territories, but who never did so. These still-active franchisees never fulfilled their expansion contracts, and the company terminated them so it could sell those fallow territories to new franchisees.

From this perspective, the drop in numbers since 1990 looks much better and reflects an average failure rate in the 5-percent-per-year range. Yet, like so many other franchises that boomed during the 1980s, Homes and Land has also scaled back its rapid growth.

For the hardworking person with direct sales experience, Homes and Land—with its sister franchise Rental Guide, discussed later in this chapter—remains an excellent opportunity. Homes and Land is a real estate advertising sales and magazine distribution service franchise. You sell advertising for homes and property to local real estate agents and brokers, take pictures of the featured homes, and prepare the ad copy. You pay Homes and Land to publish the magazine, and then you distribute your copies throughout your territory. You put them on countertop or free-standing racks anywhere you can obtain permission to put the racks. So, you are constantly cruising your territory calling on agents to sell ads and filling your racks. To succeed with this business, it appears that you must enjoy being constantly on the move and have excellent face-to-face selling skills. In short, this is a very difficult, time-consuming business in a very competitive industry, but you can also make large profits if you are good at it or you can expand rapidly enough to hire a staff and divide the onerous tasks.

For example, H&L's most successful "associate publishers," as franchisees are called, have salespeople and distribution employees whom they manage.

The competition is intense not only from other franchises, but also from regional publishers and sometimes, area boards of real estate. For example, in October 1993, the board in Baltimore, Maryland, began its own publication and planned to do its best to exclude the competition from its members' offices. This would sharply reduce the available distribution points for competing publications.

In any case, by the end of 1993, the company stated that its franchisees were distributing 3.3 million magazines per month (10 percent more than in 1990) through various points, such as racks in front of real estate offices, grocery stores, convenience stores, and shopping centers' anchor stores; through the real estate agents; or by direct mail to home buyers.

Homes and Land also offers a second franchise called Home Guide for smaller markets through which you sell ads for a lower-cost magazine printed on a less expensive book stock paper; H&L franchisees can add the Home Guide as a way to reach a broader market of lower-cost homes and the agents who sell those. You can buy a Home Guide franchise separately and grow into a Homes and Land, or vice versa, but H&L executives advise beginning with a Homes and Land because you can earn more income more quickly.

How Much It Costs

These cost figures are given for both Homes and Land and Home Guide. Homes and Land has increased its start-up cost estimates sharply to account for working capital and living expenses; it has also increased its franchise fee from $15,000 to $20,000 for H&L. The fee for Home Guide totals only $1,500.

When you want to add more territory, you pay reduced fees: $16,000 for Homes and Land and $1,200 for an additional Home Guide. If you convert from a Home Guide to a Homes and Land, you pay $18,500, the difference between their initial fees. But, best of all, if you want to add a Home Guide to a Homes and Land franchise, the cost is a nominal $1.00.

The secret to this business is to keep your start-up costs as low as possible. You can—and should—work from home; after all, you'll spend so much time on the road, you will hardly use an office. You will need a telephone, an answering machine, a fax machine, a copier, a car phone, and a hand-held camera (unless you subcontract the photos). If you have most of these or can arrange to share a fax and a copier, you can save thousands of dollars. Here are the separate estimates for H&L and Home Guide taken from both the UFOC and my own estimates:

Category	Homes and Land		Home Guide	
	Low End	High End	Low End	High End
Franchise Fee	$20,000	$20,000	$1,500	$1,500
Equipment (a)	500	5,000	500	3,000
Leasehold Improvement (b)	0	500	0	500
Insurance (c)	250	500	250	500
Advance Pay (d)	2,400	8,000	1,200	5,000
Training (e)	100	250	100	250
Working Capital (f)	25,000	50,000	10,000	40,000
Total	$45,850	$76,250	$12,350	$45,750

a. If you don't own a fax, a phone, or copier, then you could spend this much, but you can also lease them to reduce your start-up costs or arrange to use existing ones or share the cost with someone else.
b. Only if you need to do anything to rented office space, but you would be unwise to start from an office unless you have tens of thousands in working capital dollars.
c. Standard comprehensive business liability coverage.
d. Covers the initial deposit for your first issue. H&L charges $100 for each black and white page and $200 for color; Home Guide requires full advance payment of the estimated publication costs.
e. As a benefit, the company gives you $75 per day to cover lodging and meals; this figure covers miscellaneous expenses.
f. You *must* have enough money on hand to cover 6 to 12 months of living expenses or have a partner/spouse who earns enough income to cover the family's living expenses.

Other Fees and Payments

In addition to these start-up costs, you must pay the company both a royalty and magazine printing costs. Your printing costs decline as the size of your publication grows, meaning that you make higher gross profit margins. Homes and Land's costs for its color digest magazine for the West Region as of July 1, 1993, declined from a high of $185.08 per page for the minimum 16-page magazine with a total of 8,000 copies printed to $146.33 for a 128-page publication with the same number of copies. The price also declines as you increase circulation. The net result is that the more copies you print and the more pages you sell, the more your per-page costs fall. These prices may have changed since mid-1993, so be sure to read the offering circular carefully.

However, the company charges competitive printing rates; otherwise, its franchisees would be a very unhappy group. In any case, the cost for printing and production will equal 85 to 90 percent of your monthly expenses.

You also pay a royalty that varies from 10.5 percent for each color page to 16 percent for a black and white page for Homes and Land, but only a flat $15 per page for Home Guide.

What You Get

Homes and Land's best advantage—the magazine *Homes & Land*—is the company itself and its national coverage and name recognition. It does offer a higher-quality product than its competitors. For your fee, you receive the following:

- *Territory.* You receive an exclusive territory usually based on city or county boundaries. You do best in suburban or residential urban areas with a steady or growing number of real estate transactions. To find the best, survey your area's boards of realtors to determine the number of agents and brokers and the number of transactions. Homes and Land needs a population base of at least 50,000 to 70,000, according to company executives.

- *Training.* Five days of training in sales, management, marketing, layout, and photography at corporate headquarters.

- *Start-up field support.* A company rep works with you as you begin selling your first issue and searching for distribution points.

- *Advertising package.* You receive a complete package of business stationery, 10 floor racks, 40 table model racks, 10 outdoor racks, and a supply of sales brochures, cards, calendars, media kits, samples, "thank you cookies," and so forth.

  Under a lease/purchase plan, you can also lease racks from the company for $60 for used models and $125 for new ones.

- *HomeLine service.* This toll-free hotline gives any caller two free copies of *H&L*. The company receives 10,000 to 12,000 calls per month. And the company inserts more than one million mail-in reply cards in *H&L* magazines every month to generate requests for free copies. This makes you a referral service for your customers—real estate agents who buy your ads.

- *Continuous support.* You receive ongoing marketing and promotional programs, telephone or on-site technical assistance, magazine layout supplies, a newsletter for your clients, and regional and national meetings through a franchisee-elected advisory council.

- *Homes & Land electronic magazine.* This service provides listings via facsimile and through on-line data base services. Callers to HomeLine can request a fax of key data from listings in a magazine of their choice. If you are a subscriber, you can access the data base through providers such as Prodigy. This "electronic magazine" lists on screen information such as community, bedrooms, baths, house style, price, and so forth.

How Much Can You Make?

The company does not publish any estimated earnings claims for Homes and Land or Home Guide. Note, however, that it does publish some figures for Rental Guide, so see those figures in that section. Homes and Land does report in its literature that most of its franchisees work full time—probably more than 40 hours a week at first to build the business.

To earn income, you charge advertising fees per page. You charge more per inch for ads smaller than a page and less for ads larger than a page. You also give discounts based on the number of insertions, that is, the number of times per year that the customer buys an ad. However, you charge much higher rates as you increase your circulation. With Homes and Land's advice and a review of the fees that the local competition charges, you will develop a rate card that describes your fees and discount structure.

In any case, you must begin with a 12-page minimum magazine (16 pages for the *Digest*) and a circulation of at least 8,000. If you charge $300 per page, your expenses will include $185 for printing, so your gross profit would be $115 or $1,840 before delivery and your own operating expenses. Again, your income goes up as you sell more pages and increase your circulation and distribution. For example, if you triple your circulation to 25,000 copies, you can almost triple your rates or gross income, but your printing costs increase only from $185 to $273, about 50 percent. So your gross profit could more than double.

The company reports that the average *H&L* issue has a distribution in the 11,000- to 15,000-copy range, with none lower than 6,000 and some as high as 50,000 per issue.

Note, too, that the larger franchisees save their time for sales and marketing and hire photographers, distributors, and office workers to do the mundane tasks. A few hire additional commission salespeople.

By the end of the first year, you should be netting about $25,000 per year and $40,000 by the end of the second year based on net profit margins in the 30 to 40 percent range. Two factors determine your success: (1) previous successful direct sales experience and (2) the health of the local real estate market. Be prepared for a difficult time during real estate downturns like the one that occurred between 1990 and 1993, but be equally prepared to prosper during real estate upturns, such as the one that should take place during the mid- and late 1990s. If you live in an average or active real estate market and have excellent selling skills, you can achieve an affluent annual income working from your home.

RENTAL GUIDE

Homes and Land Publishing Corporation
1600 Capital Circle, S.W.
Tallahassee, FL 32310
(904) 574-2111

Rental Guide is a sister publication franchise for *Homes & Land* magazine that probably offers more long-term opportunity than Homes and Land for several reasons. First, as of late 1993, only 30 Rental Guide franchises had been granted, one-eighth the number of Homes and Land territories. Second, your market—apartment managers and owners—has a more consistent and more urgent need to advertise their available rentals. Third, they tend to buy larger ads because they need to promote their apartments' amenities to attract renters, so you earn more revenues per page.

However, Rental Guide has several drawbacks that mean you need more working capital to survive your first year. Company executives stated that the Rental Guide requires larger initial print runs, you have larger territories to cover, and you need to hire salespeople. Furthermore, property managers sometimes pay more slowly than real estate brokers and may spread payments for one issue over several months, reducing your cash flow. Your minimum territory must include at least 75 major apartment complexes with at least 50 units so you can sell enough ads to make your effort profitable. Your operating expenses, particularly your auto expenses, will be somewhat higher than those with a *Homes & Land* magazine.

The Rental Guide offering circular also reported many terminations, but all these were additional territories that current franchisees had not used, so the company took them back so it could sell them to new franchisees. In short, all Rental Guide franchisees were still in business.

Like Homes and Land, you sell advertising space in a high-quality magazine that you publish and distribute at least three times a year. You distribute them in racks you place in apartment offices, grocery stores, strip shopping centers, and so forth. You earn income by negotiating prices for the ads and build cash flow by giving discounts for multiple insertions. Each *Rental Guide* issue must have at least 16 pages with a press run of at least 15,000 copies.

How Much It Costs

Rental Guide also has a $20,000 franchise fee and a range of start-up costs similar to and somewhat higher than range of the Homes and Land start-up costs, as the following table shows:

Category	Low End	High End
Franchise fee	$20,000	$20,000
Equipment (a)	1,500	3,000
Liability insurance	250	500
Advance payment (b)	3,000	6,000
Training travel (c)	100	500
Leasehold improvements (d)	0	500
Working capital (e)	25,000	50,000
Total	$49,850	$80,500

a. Costs for fax machine, telephone, answering machine, copier, car phone, and so on. Share equipment to cut start-up costs.
b. Partial payment for printing each issue must be made in advance.
c. In a benefit, the company pays you $75 per day to attend training at headquarters; these figures represent personal expenses beyond that amount.
d. Work from home and save any costs of fixing up an office.
e. You face miscellaneous selling and production costs of up to $1,000 per issue. More important, you need six to eight months' living expenses and operating costs before you begin to break even.

Other Fees and Royalty

In addition, you must pay Homes and Land to print the publication and a royalty based on the suggested retail advertising rate. The royalty totals 10.5 percent for color pages and 16 percent for black and white.

The minimum per page cost for a color page totals about $200, so with a minimum of 16 pages, your initial advance payment will be about $3,200.

Fortunately, you do not make any other payments to the company, unless you buy materials and supplies from it.

What You Get

In return for your fee, you receive the following:

- *Exclusive territory.* You receive a much larger territory than the one for a *Homes & Land* magazine, but you need it. It should include at least 75 major apartment complexes. The company determines the area by growth patterns, county/city lines, apartment association service area, competing publications' areas, population, and so on.

- *Training.* You receive five days of training at headquarters and additional days of in-field production and sales training to help you sell and produce your first issue. You may also receive ongoing training with computer-based systems for three more days at headquarters, in a region, or in your local area.

- *Five-year term.* You receive a five-year term that you can renew at nominal cost, a significant advantage for both Homes and Land publishing franchises compared to most franchises.

- *Brand name.* You receive the benefit of the company's national brand name.

- *Distribution materials and supplies.* You receive 25 wire floor distribution racks, 30 customized outdoor street racks, and accompanying supplies.

- *Marketing materials and programs.* You receive a large supply of marketing materials from direct mail brochures and letters to media kits to stickers, and so on. The company also does the same national HomeLine and HomeMail marketing efforts for Rental Guide that it does for its other magazines.

- *Consultation.* Company executives are always available by phone to consult with you on distribution and marketing situations.

How Much Can You Make?

Fortunately, the company publishes pro forma income statements for Rental Guide. The offering circular explains that Rental Guides have been operating from one to five years in markets as diverse as Seattle, San Diego, and Columbus, Georgia. Population densities vary from as few as 38,000 people to as many as 4 million. Population size does not appear to affect circulation or issues; the most significant factor is the number of potential advertisers, that is, apartment and condo managers with empty apartments.

By late 1993, of the total number of franchisees, 17 were published three or more times a year with 10 of those published quarterly. The average number of pages per issue ranged from the minimum of 16 to as high as 216 pages with a median of 32 pages. More than one-third of the franchises print more than 40 pages per issue. Further, the number of copies varies from as few as 6,000 per issue to as many as 204,000 with the median amount 25,000. Nine franchisees print 35,000 or more copies per issue.

Equally important, production costs paid to Homes and Land total about 46.4 percent of retail sales, that is, gross revenues, but 10 franchisees had costs below 45 percent.

From these numbers, the company offers three pro formas that give "achievable" gross profits before operating expenses. Each pro forma reflects different sets of circumstances and factors:

Large-Market Pro Forma

Population: 400,000 or more
Rental properties: 150 or more with at least 50 units each
Print run: 60,000 copies per issue
Pages per issue: 56
Page sale price: $895.38 (suggested retail price; many franchisees must discount this)
Page production/delivery cost: $372.24 (franchisor's rate sheet)
Projected annual sales: $300,875
Production cost: $125,073
Gross profit: $175,802 (58.4 percent)

Medium-Market Pro Forma

Population: 250,000 to 400,000
Rental properties: 90 to 150
Number of issues: 4 times a year
Print run: 40,000 copies per issue
Pages per issue: 40
Page sale price: $733
Page production/delivery: $326.81
Projected annual sales: $117,373
Production costs: $52,290
Gross profit: $65,083 (55.5 percent)

Small-Market Pro Forma

Population: 100,000 to 250,000
Rental properties: 75 to 90
Number of issues: 3 times a year
Pages per issue: 28
Page sale price: $653
Page production/delivery: $325.98
Projected annual sales: $54,825
Production costs: $27,382
Gross profit: $27,443 (50.1 percent)

In short, you must work hard to grow as quickly as possible to begin to earn substantial ROIs on your investment. If you have significant direct selling experience and you want to build your own business, Rental Guide offers substantial opportunity in the advertising publication industry.

8

Franchises with Fees Above $20,000

AMERISPEC, INC.

AmeriSpec Home Inspection Service
1855 West Katella Avenue
Suite 330
Orange, CA 92667
(714) 744-8360
(800) 426-2270

AmeriSpec's President Tom Carroll not only has a highly profitable, low-cost franchise, but also shows deep genuine personal concern for his franchise "family." Many franchisors talk about their franchises as "families," but treat their families like Cinderella's sisters treated her—constantly taking advantage of them and ignoring their basic needs. To the contrary, Carroll has gone out of his way to take what he calls a "pro-active approach" to franchise relations. AmeriSpec has a very active and open Franchisee Advisory Council that has the power to approve new programs and manage its advertising fund. Carroll surveys his franchisees three times a year to discover their concerns—and acts on them by modifying the company's operations. Furthermore, the company's executives must call some franchisees every week to discuss their operations. The company has restructured its support programs to allow for more expansion, yet stay close to the existing franchisees. In sum, Carroll's concern for his franchisees stands heads above that concern most franchisors express.

As important, AmeriSpec Home Inspection Service is a rapidly growing franchise in a recession-resistant market. By early 1994, it had 180 operating franchisees with plans to add 50 more per year during the next several years. Its maximum growth potential totals between 500 and 600 franchises in the United States.

As an AmeriSpec franchisee, you do basic home inspections for home sellers and home buyers to identify any potential problems that may require professional repairs (plumbing, heating, termite infestations, structural damage, water damage, and so on). You charge between $300 and $400 per inspection to earn income.

This industry has boomed since the early 1980s, more than quintupling the number of inspections from 10 percent of all homes to about 60 percent. Yet, with legal liability problems hanging over the real estate industry's heads, the National Association of Realtors is lobbying for state disclosure laws to require all homes to be inspected. Eventually, Carroll predicts, all homes will be inspected, so your market has plenty of room for growth during the 1990s and beyond.

At present, AmeriSpec franchisees have about a 3 to 4 percent market share as they conduct some 80,000 inspections a month in a market of about 3.5 million sales of existing homes each year. All home inspection franchises hold less than a 7 percent market share, so the potential for market consolidation remains significant. Note that these figures show that AmeriSpec is the largest home inspection franchise by far.

As important, although anyone can now set up shop as a home inspector, certified professionals are becoming more important to consumers. And at present, the industry is very disorganized, with several franchises and thousands of independents, the latter often no more than glorified general contractors looking for ways to expand their businesses. As the industry matures and becomes more regulated, the demand for trained professionals will grow and the market for systematic franchisees will grow with it.

Contrary to popular thought, your primary customers are not home buyers; rather, they are the top-producing real estate agents in your area who sell 80 percent of the homes. To sell your services to them requires patience, persistence, and a strong marketing program based on presentations and personal selling skills. It is simple but difficult because the agents and brokers are suspicious—they've heard it all before—often irascible, very busy, and unlikely to accept you until you show that your service surpasses those that the competition offers.

Helping you persuade these tough customers is AmeriSpec's most significant advantage. It sponsors very sophisticated marketing programs based on computerized data bases to reach the agent/brokers and generates referrals for your franchise. It also promotes national fire protection awareness and home security programs to develop name recognition and build the company's—and your—image as a socially responsible organization.

In short, AmeriSpec offers significant advantages over competing home inspection franchises.

How Much It Costs

AmeriSpec has a two-tier franchise fee, offers significant discounts for cash payments, and gives veterans a significant discount. It also partially finances the franchise fee, in certain circumstances. First, for an urban territory, the normal fee equals $20,900; if you pay cash, you receive a $3,000 discount for $17,900. If you are a veteran, the fee equals $18,810, a 10 percent discount, or $16,110 if you pay cash. This fee gives you a territory with 3,000 real estate transactions per year. The company will finance $10,450 or half the fee at 12 percent interest for 24 months ($9,405 for the military).

Second, for a rural territory with at least 1,500 real estate transactions, the fee is $9,950. You cannot finance this fee.

The total start-up costs range from a low of $23,600, assuming you are a military veteran who pays cash, to a high of $34,500, but this does not include working capital for at least two months' operating and living expenses, so add $5,000 to $10,000 to the company's estimates. The following table shows the division:

Category	Low End	High End
Franchise fee (a)	$16,110	$20,900
Computer system (b)	300	3,500
Office rental (c)	750	1,200
Initial deposits (d)	2,000	3,000
Opening promotions (e)	1,500	2,050
Furniture/equipment (f)	500	1,000
Errors/omissions insurance (g)	2,384	2,850
Working capital (h)	5,000	10,000
Total	$28,544	$44,500

a. Low end represents cash discount for veterans. If a rural franchise, the fee will equal $9,950 with most other costs about the same.
b. Low end represents first month's lease; high end represents complete system purchase cost.
c. AmeriSpec requires you to open an office, and these costs cover two months' rent.
d. This covers business telephone, bank, regular business liability insurance and similar deposits, and any bonds or required license fees.
e. For grand opening advertising and promotion costs.
f. Pays for office furniture and equipment, such as a fax machine, and so on.
g. You must have this insurance to protect you from mistakes and oversights in your work.
h. This is supposed to cover training travel expenses, two months' operating expenses, initial inspector fees or salaries, and two months' living expenses, if needed.

You pay AmeriSpec a 7 percent or $250-per-month minimum royalty, but the minimum does not begin until 90 days after you open your doors. You also pay a 3 percent or $125-per-month minimum advertising fee. In the rural territory, the minimum ad fee is reduced to $65 per month, but the standard royalty still applies. The ad fees are put into an ad fund that the franchisee advisory council helps administer. That's all you pay to AmeriSpec under normal conditions.

What You Get

In return for your fee, you receive the following benefits:

- *Exclusive territory.* Your area derives from boundaries that include 3,000 real estate transactions per year based on court and local realtor records. A rural territory consists of an area with 1,500 transactions.

- *Training.* You take 10 business days of training at company headquarters, one week in marketing and management and a second week in how to conduct inspections. After that, you can attend the company's Management Institute for any of six advanced courses each year. You also receive an "initial service visit" as you begin from a field support rep. The company also holds numerous regional training seminars and devotes most of its annual national convention to marketing, operations, and technical seminars.

- *National charity/promotion programs.* The company has sponsored two nationwide efforts to raise consumer awareness: (1) During 1991 and 1992, it created "Operation Cease Fire" and gave away thousands of free fire extinguishers during National Fire Prevention Week, and (2) during 1993, it gave away free First Aid kits.

- *Marketing programs.* One of AmeriSpec's key advantages is its sophisticated marketing and promotion programs that keep your business's name in front of your prospects. They include a series of ten color 9 × 7 postcard mailings, one each month, to 40,000 potential customers across the country. Each large postcard gives a homeowner's tip about an important system, for example, heating, air conditioning, hot water, and so on, and has the address and phone number of the local franchisee imprinted on it.

- *Property Inspection Management System.* PIMS is the data base that the company uses to identify your sources for leads and that acts as the key marketing tool.

- *AmeriSpec Information System.* This "bulletin board" lets you communicate electronically with other franchisees and company executives. You can ask questions, seek help, or swap information on how to do business.

- *Relocation Business Division.* This national account effort generates home inspection leads for corporate relocations for you.

- *AmeriSpec ProTek+.* This is a one-year home protection plan for homeowners who want a warranty against defects in the homes they buy. This cannot be offered in all areas because of state laws.

- *Franchise relations programs.* As I said at the beginning of this discussion, AmeriSpec truly does offer one of the most comprehensive and caring franchise relations programs in all of franchising. Carroll and his staff do take your concerns seriously and respond to them.

- *New Market Development.* The company also develops new services that you can offer to increase your revenues. In early 1994, it planned to introduce minor repair services that franchisees could add at low cost to both them and the homeowner and perform as an added service while they were inspecting the home.

- *New technology applications.* AmeriSpec has developed a laptop computer system that automates its superior inspection process. Using the computers to do the inspections will reduce inspectors' fees or salaries and save them a significant amount of their time to do more inspections. This, in turn, sharply reduces your expenses and boosts your net profits. And AmeriSpec continues to explore similar ideas to decrease franchisee overhead and boost net profit margins.

In short, AmeriSpec knows that to keep its franchisees happy, it must pay close attention to their concerns, respond with new marketing and operations programs, and find ways to reduce their costs and increase their profits. It does that far better than most franchisors.

How Much Can You Make?

AmeriSpec has been very forthcoming about how much income one can generate and what it takes to do so. Carroll said that, all things equal, growing this business is a function of two factors: (1)

time in business—to overcome the suspicion and skepticism of real estate brokers—and (2) your aggressiveness in establishing relationships with and giving presentations to real estate agents in your market. If you do not want to pursue the agents and constantly create opportunities to present your service to them, avoid this franchise.

In fact, most franchisees come from management or marketing backgrounds. They find it best to hire or train inspectors quickly and spend their time developing and maintaining relationships with agents.

To earn money, you charge $300 to $400 for each inspection, less in competitive areas and much more (as much as $900) for inspections of mansion or estate properties. The average is $350. Carroll said that the average should be $450 to $500, but the untrained competition keeps the price down.

Carroll said that systemwide, the average franchise inspects 55 houses per month, for an average monthly income of $19,250. He also noted that first-year franchisees should expand to between 30 and 35 inspections per month ($10,500); second-year franchisees should do 40 to 50 per month ($14,000); and third- to fifth-year franchisees should average 80 to 100 per month ($28,000). The best franchisee, about six years old, averages more than 300 inspections per month, or $50,000.

Your expenses include 10 percent to AmeriSpec (royalty and ad fee) and 25 to 30 percent ($60–62 average) for the independent inspector's fee or employee's salary. After operating expenses, you should net $75 pretax from each inspection, or a pretax profit of $4,125 per month by the third year, if you are an average franchisee. For example, *USA Today* reported that AmeriSpec franchisee Jim Chadderdon paid about $50,000 for an existing franchise, increased its volume 400 percent in nine months, and made first-year sales of $150,000. He planned to increase his gross sales to $225,000 to $250,000 by the end of his second year—that franchise's fourth year in business. And he anticipated netting a six-figure income.

Even the average franchisee's income represents a cash ROI of between 150 percent and 300 percent each year after the third year. Clearly, in a growing real estate market, AmeriSpec represents an opportunity to profit from any boom in existing home sales, but the only drawback might be a decline in the number of inspections during a real estate recession. However, during the severe recession in the early 1990s, AmeriSpec lost only nine franchisees during the three-year downturn. Three were caused by failure to pay royalties, and six were mutual terminations. Seven more were sold to buyers like Chadderdon. In short, AmeriSpec's strong support programs helped its franchisees stay afloat and grow during the worst real estate recession in decades. If it keeps up its strong relationship with its franchisees, the system should continue to prosper throughout the 1990s.

PROFUSION SYSTEMS, INC.

ProFusion Systems, Inc.
2851 South Parker Road
Suite 650
Aurora, CO 80014
(800) 777-FUSE (3783)
(303) 337-1949

During the past decade, ProFusion Systems has turned the fly-by-night vinyl repair business into a professional quality—and customer-oriented—industry. Its franchisees primarily use a permanent, unnoticeable method of repairing vinyl, leather, velour, and Naugahyde®, but in the early 1990s, the company dramatically expanded its market with new methods of repairing laminates, marble, porcelain, and hard and soft plastics. It also remains the only franchise in this category with a 100 percent money-back guarantee on every repair.

Confirming its leading position, ProFusion has been rated the best in its category by all leading franchise ratings services, including *Entrepreneur* and *Entrepreneurial Woman* magazines. I have known about ProFusion and its dynamic young chairman, Bill Gabbard, almost since its inception, and although it had a difficult time during 1990 and 1991, it has bounced back more robust than ever.

Backed with a serious ongoing research program, ProFusion offers an excellent low-cost, high-profit opportunity. It has doubled the number of franchisees since 1990 with more than 300 by the end of 1993.

Thanks to a very successful national accounts program, it has also opened 18 company locations in major cities because, Gabbard explained, major corporations and government agencies needed service in areas where ProFusion did not yet have franchisees. This growth began with a major Air Force contract to repair custom-built engine covers for fighter jets and AWAC radar planes; these covers, which ProFusion developed, weigh one-tenth as much as the old covers and cost one-tenth the price, yet keep out sand and salt. This performance helped impress other national accounts, but these accounts also mean that the company must deliver the service regardless of location.

Along these lines, you can expect 85 percent or more of your business to come from commercial accounts. You would benefit from the national accounts that needed service in your area, but primarily, you would market to a wide variety of commercial customers: restaurant chains, hotel-motels, schools, hospitals, airports, nursing homes, military installations, fleet owners, auto dealers, public vehicle maintenance departments, and dozens more. The company lists 66 types of potential prospects.

Furthermore, the company appears to have a very strong appeal for husband-and-wife or family teams. More than half of the franchises are owned either by women alone or by married couple teams. Because the work is easy and light, both men and women can do it, but usually, both owners market and manage the service and farm out the actual work to employees or independent contractor technicians. One very successful franchisee does this: The wife sells large accounts, the husband sells Mom and Pop accounts and manages five technicians, and a second female salesperson sells to public and nonprofit organizations.

The company recommends that you plan to grow rapidly and have four to five technicians in the field within the first year. Although you can begin working from home, you should open a retail location within one year. In fact, Gabbard noted that a retail location can increase gross incomes by more than half very quickly, and the company encourages people who buy large territories to open a retail location immediately to attract more business.

How Much It Costs

ProFusion has not raised its total franchise fee since 1989; it remains at $20,500 ($10,500 for training and equipment and $10,000 for the franchise license and the exclusive territory with between 70,000 and 100,000 population). You can add population in groups of 100,000 for an additional $5,000 fee per group. The territories follow county or city boundaries or zip codes within major metro areas.

Fortunately, the company has begun to finance 50 percent of the franchise fee at an interest rate of two percentage points over the bank prime rate for up to 36 months.

You also pay a 6 percent royalty or a minimum monthly fee of $40 for each 100,000 population in your territory. You also pay a 1 percent advertising fee managed by an advisory council for the direct benefit of the franchisees.

Additional start-up costs are very low, especially if you start in your home; they range from as low as $4,000 to about $8,500 if you open a retail location. You can place a retail location in industrial-warehouse space, but you will have to pay rent, buy or lease office furniture and equipment, and expect a spouse to manage the office or hire an assistant. The following table discusses these costs in detail.

Category	Low End	High End
Franchise fee (a)	$20,500	$30,500
Liability insurance	400	1,000
Telephone deposits	200	400
Office supplies	100	300
Auto expenses	100	200
Repair supplies	200	300
Initial commissions (b)	200	1,000
Working capital (c)	3,000	5,000
Subtotal (d)	$24,700	$38,700

Rent deposits (e)	500	1,000
Leasehold improvements (f)	4,500	6,500
Utility deposits	250	500
Business licenses	100	500
Grand opening expenses (g)	500	2,000
Subtotal	$5,850	$10,500
Total	$30,550	$49,200

a. From a minimum territory to one with some 300,000 people.

b. Paid to technicians before you earn substantial income.

c. Needed to pay expenses until you break even and/or to pay personal expenses until you can afford to take a salary.

d. Subtotal for at-home start-up.

e. Deposits to rent warehouse space to open a retail location.

f. Cost of improving bare space and buying signs. Much less if you can negotiate build-out payments by the landlord in your lease.

g. Varies with how much you plan to spend on initial advertising and marketing campaign.

So, you can expect your total start-up costs to range from about $30,000 to $50,000, and you can finance half the fee, reducing your cash outlay by at least $10,000. If you are like most ProFusion franchisees, you should plan to pay for your retail location and improvements out of cash flow as your business grows.

What You Get

In return for your investment, you receive the following:

- *Exclusive territory.* As noted, at least 70,000 to 100,000 of population, but most franchisees either buy more territory at the beginning or add it quickly for $5,000 per 100,000.

- *Training.* Nine days, including technical repairs, but emphasizing marketing and management to help you build your business. Then, you spend five more days at a company site with a trainer.

- *Start-up visit.* An experienced sales trainer spends four days (one more day than before) to help you begin to make sales calls, sign contracts, and work with local managers of national account locations.

- *National accounts.* You benefit from the established accounts that you can service in your area.

- *New processes.* Although you start the business with vinyl and similar repairs, you can sell add-on services with the new processes to repair laminates. For example, if you had a contract to repair 25 chairs in a bar, you could offer to repair the dings and burns on its plastic-coated tables, too. You can take the approach, "While we're here, let us fix that table for you at low cost." It usually works, takes very little time, and boosts your profit margin.

- *Ongoing research.* Its consulting lab, Hauser Laboratories, pursues a thorough research program.

How Much Can You Make?

You earn very high profit margins because the cost of materials is very low, about 21 cents per repair, yet you charge an average retail price of $45 per chair, or 20 percent of the replacement cost. For a major job, such as repairing hundreds of hotel or restaurant chain chairs, your price may fall as low as $7–$10 per chair, but your volume more than makes up for the lower price.

The company estimates that you will spend your gross income in these percentages:

- 6 percent on royalties;

- 5 percent on required advertising and direct marketing expenses;

- 7–9 percent on required materials purchases;

- 15 percent on sales commissions (you pocket this if you do the selling);

- 20 percent commissions to independent contractors—much lower if you hire technicians; and

- 20 percent overhead expenses if you rent an office—much less if you work from home.

Your net profit should range from a low of 25 percent to a high of 45 percent. Note that more and more franchisees are hiring technicians to ensure a reliable labor supply, but pay them $10–15 per hour plus percentage incentives on each job.

You charge customers for your services based on several factors: (1) replacement cost, (2) number of repairs in the job or contract, and (3) account expansion potential. Your gross income should grow quickly. Franchises have stated in published reports gross incomes ranging from $8,000 a month to more than $40,000 a month. After two years, if you emphasize building your large account business, you should net $40,000 to $75,000 a year before taxes.

In short, this franchise appears to just have hit its growth stride. Even with 288 territories awarded and 32 countries sold, its system can accommodate hundreds more in the United States and North America. And its ever-widening range of services will allow aggressive franchisees to expand their markets.

PADGETT BUSINESS SERVICES USA, INC.

Padgett Business Services
160 Hawthorne Park
Athens, GA 30606
(800) 323-7292

Padgett Business Services has been ranked among the leading business service franchises by several national rating services for many years. Its franchisees offer bookkeeping, income tax preparation, business counseling, data processing, and similar services to small businesses and self-employed professionals in their areas. The company has a very high percentage of female office owners—28 percent—and many more husband-and-wife teams. By late 1993, it had 168 U.S. franchisees with 71 more in Canada. It seeks to encourage "controllable growth" of 30 to 40 franchises per year. Padgett is in this book because it has a clean record without any litigation with its franchisees and it has a relatively low failure/termination rate compared to others in this service sector.

How Much It Costs

Padgett Business Services charges a total of $34,500, of which $22,000 is the franchise fee and $12,500 is a separate training fee. It charges a 9 percent monthly royalty on gross receipts from your service fees or a monthly minimum that increases during your first 15 months in business. The minimum royalty increases in this manner:

Months in Business	Minimum Royalty
First three months (0–3)	$50 per month
Second three months (4–6)	100 per month
Third three months (7–9)	150 per month
Fourth three months (10–12)	175 per month
Fifth three months (13–15)	250 per month
Months 16 and up	300 per month

However, you must pay 9 percent whenever your receipts exceed these minimums. In a benefit, the company does not charge any advertising fees.

You can finance up to $20,000 of the initial $22,000 for five years at a fixed interest rate through a well-known franchise financing firm.

Total start-up costs range from as low as $52,000 to about $62,000, including the franchise and training fees:

Category	Low End	High End
Franchise fee	$22,000	$22,000
Training fee	12,500	12,500
Insurance (a)	800	1,000

Training travel	1,000	2,000
Marketing start-up	3,000	4,000
Personal computer	2,000	3,000
Lease deposits, etc. (b)	750	3,000
Miscellaneous	1,000	1,000
Working capital (c)	9,000	13,700
Total	$52,050	$62,200

a. Required liability insurance, workers' compensation, and so on.
b. Most start at home, but this category covers lease deposits and office start-up expenses if you rent a small office.
c. For office operating expenses for up to several months and perhaps living expenses if your spouse does not earn income.

You must include in that working capital figure amounts for required copier and fax machine, filing cabinets, and similar office equipment and furniture.

What You Get

In return, you receive a very thorough training program, a very liberal 20-year agreement so you can build long-term equity, a nonexclusive but protected territory, proprietary software, and a complete office management and marketing package.

- *Territory.* You receive a territory with at least 3,000 target small to medium-sized businesses, including some types of professional offices. The boundaries are fixed by zip codes. "Nonexclusive" means that the company will not locate another office in that territory; however, you can solicit business outside its boundaries, and other franchisees can do the same in your territory. After a year in business, you can expand to a second territory for a $5,000 fee if you open a satellite office.

- *Training.* You receive a total of four weeks of training, including two at headquarters. The first week concerns operations, and the second teaches marketing to develop clients.

You spend the third week with an existing franchisee to get hands-on training in systems and marketing.

Finally, during the fourth week, a franchisee trainer will spend five days in your own territory helping you set up your operation and make calls on client prospects.

- *Agreement term.* The agreement lasts 20 years and gives an option to renew for additional 20-year periods with a small fee equal to 5 percent of the then-current franchise fee.

- *Ongoing support.* The company offers extensive training courses throughout the year, gives unlimited toll-free telephone support in all technical areas, provides tax updates and tips in its monthly newsletter, and holds annual marketing seminar and tax update training.

- *Low termination rate.* The company reported 13 terminations during 1992, a rate of about 10 percent, but during 1990 and 1991, only seven others failed, so it appears that the 1992 failures happened because of the recession's bite. During 1993, the company reported only five failures, a low 3 percent rate, with strong growth of new franchisees in the system. Some of the failure rate can also be attributed to franchisee choice, reducing the rate of terminations for default or failure to pay royalties to a very low percentage.

Company executives insisted that since Padgett offers only intangible services and brand-name recognition, it must emphasize strong support to keep its franchisees happy. Its lack of litigation and its low failure rate signify that its franchisees prefer to stick with the system.

How Much Can You Make?

Padgett Business Services does not make earnings claims, but you can expect 75 percent of your income to come from monthly and quarterly accounting and bookkeeping services that you provide for small to medium-sized businesses in your area. The other 25 percent comes from tax return preparation fees during the winter tax season.

Your income will vary according to how aggressively and how well you market your businesses through your local chambers of commerce and business groups. The Padgett monthly newsletters consistently indicate that the most successful franchisees are those that participate best in their business and community affairs to provide service and to establish name recognition.

You can estimate your income potential like this: For your tax return services, you can charge $200 to $1,000 or more for each return for a self-employed professional and similar or higher fees for small businesses. The fees for monthly accounting and bookkeeping will vary widely, depending on the type of work you perform, so I find it difficult to generalize in this area.

However, if you do 50 to 100 tax returns per season—with an assistant—you should gross at least $15,000 to $30,000 or more. With the 75–25 rule, that means you should gross at least $50,000 to $100,000 or more. I would believe that it would be safe to assume that these represent minimum gross receipts. More experienced franchisees should gross in the $200,000 to $300,000 range with part-time assistants during the tax season and a full-time bookkeeper during the year. Or, as many do, couples work together with one performing much of the numbers work while the other manages and markets the business. At that level, you would net a high five-figure to low six-figure income before taxes.

In short, this business should begin to produce significant returns by the end of the third year.

K & N MOBILE DISTRIBUTION SYSTEMS

K & N Mobile Distribution Systems
4909 Rondo Drive
Fort Worth, TX 76106
(800) 433-2170

K & N Mobile Distribution Systems offers an essential service to manufacturers, service and repair centers, truck shops, and similar businesses. That service is delivering thousands of small, but vital electrical components to assemblers and repair workers when they need them. These customer firms use these components to repair and maintain their machines, manufacture their products, or provide their services to their own customers.

You drive a "mobile showroom" that carries the inventory from location to location for the on-the-spot sales and service. You have to compete with established wholesale distributors, electrical supply companies, and similar operations.

In this industry, however, K & N is a 22-year-old, well-established company, especially in the Southwest. It has been franchising the concept since 1987, and by late 1993, had 23 franchises in operation. Although the market is affected by recessions somewhat, it does resist recessions because you serve every industry that requires electrical components, and different industries go through recessions in different ways at different times. Furthermore, the two major products you sell—connectors and fasteners—make up huge multibillion-dollar industries that remain strong through recessions and grow rapidly during economic upturns.

K & N offers several distinct advantages compared to similar franchises that qualified it for this book:

- *Money-back guarantee.* If you are dissatisfied with the franchise after six months, K & N will give you back your entire franchise fee and pay you either what you paid or the fair market price for your remaining inventory, marketing materials, and so on. Note that K & N is prohibited by state regulations from offering this guarantee in 18 states. Ask the company whether your state allows the refund.

- *Operating analysts.* Unlike the vast majority of franchises, K & N provides a thorough analysis of actual operating results so you can study very closely how much current franchisees are making and estimate how well you can expect to do.

- *Fragmented market.* The overall market is growing steadily as the demand for electrical and electronic equipment continues to grow. Franchises tend to succeed best in fragmented markets to which they can bring professional distribution and customer service. K & N achieves this.

- *Automated systems.* An on-board computer eliminates most of the accounting, bookkeeping, and inventory hassle; you do automatic invoicing and inventory control, and you communicate with the K & N warehouse by computer every night. Company executives asserted that this system alone reduces the work hours and expands the leisure hours of their franchisees by 50 percent or more.

How Much It Costs

K & N charges a $23,500 franchise fee and a regular 13 percent royalty. The royalty may seem high, but it covers the cost of the automated billing, inventory management, and related systems. If you buy an existing company operation, you must pay an additional 9 percent royalty on sales to *existing* customers for five years. You pay the regular royalty for new customers that you develop.

You must also spend at least $1,000 on grand opening advertising and 1 percent of gross sales per quarter on continuous advertising and marketing efforts.

The total start-up costs, including the fee, ranges from about $46,000 to $107,000; the high figure applies only if you buy the fully equipped, special truck, but no one does, so that reduces the maximum start-up cost by almost $27,000. Instead, you lease the truck and make monthly payments. The following table shows these estimates in detail:

Category	Low End	High End
Franchise fee	$23,500	$23,500
Inventory (a)	13,000	15,000
Working capital (b)	5,400	23,000
Insurance (c)	2,000	3,000
Training travel	0	4,000
Grand opening advertising	1,000	2,000
Office supplies/equipment (d)	350	9,500
Vehicles (e)	650	26,800
Total	$45,900	$106,800

a. Company-recommended amounts on preloaded and outfitted truck.
b. Covers operating expenses for the first year and includes salaries, vehicle maintenance, and so on. This is a very generous estimate for business expenses, but it is wise to include a figure for your own salary or living expenses.
c. Includes required auto and comprehensive business policies.
d. Most people manage the business from their trucks and a small at-home office. The high end includes cost for office space and the like.
e. Low end represents a month's lease payments; high end represents purchase price of fully outfitted truck.

Minimum Performance Quotas

In addition, the company sets increasing minimum gross sales requirements that you must meet to maintain your exclusive territory rights. Fortunately, K & N's earnings reports show that you should not find it difficult to exceed the early quotas:

First 12 months	$50,000
Second 12 months	100,000
Third through fifth 12 months	110 percent of preceding years' requirement.

Note that the latter does *not* apply to actual performance; rather, it applies to the quota whether you fulfill it or not.

To encourage you to meet these performance standards, the company also requires you to meet minimum sales and marketing requirements. You must make at least 15 personal sales visits and 40 telephone calls to prospects each week to generate new business and call or visit in person at least 80 percent of your existing customers at least once a month. In short, you have to work hard to build the business.

What You Get

In return for your money and your labor, you receive the following:

- *Area of primary responsibility.* As long as you meet the minimums, you have the right to an exclusive territory with 100,000 or more of population. It is also determined by demographics and zoning regulations—whether you can park your truck at your house. Be sure to look for territories with fewer people and more small electrical businesses, manufacturers, repair shops, and so on that need your products.

- *Five-year term*. You can also renew for three additional five-year terms for free.

- *Training*. You receive at least 10 days and up to 15 days of training at corporate headquarters and working from company locations in Fort Worth.

- *Start-up support*. A company representative will work with you for three days during your first two months in business to help you approach customers and learn the operations.

- *Ongoing support*. Most importantly, you obtain most of your products at very competitive prices through K & N's warehouse. You also receive ongoing training at least twice a year for up to four days, and you may have to attend monthly or quarterly meetings to discuss new products and operations.

- *Company culture*. K & N is dedicated to your success, and its very liberal guarantees show that it firmly believes in fair dealing and support for its franchisees.

Area Development Agreements

You can also arrange an area development agreement through which you put additional trucks on the road in new territories. You pay a declining scale franchise fee for each additional territory that goes from $21,000 for the second to $13,500 for the fifth and each subsequent territory. Start-up costs remain about the same because of the cost of the truck and initial inventory, hiring and training territory reps, and marketing the new territory. You do best to build one territory for six months to a year before you acquire or develop more territories, but to build long-term equity, you must build a multiple-truck operation in more than one territory.

How Much Can You Make?

K & N publishes very thorough analyses of actual average operating results. However, these results are from newly established company-owned territories with new salespeople, a situation that approximates that of a new franchisee. These averages represent results from 16 new territories in years 1 and 2 and 12 new territories in year 3 in territories that are about the same size as a franchise territory:

Year 1 = $94,200   Year 2 = $161,000   Year 3 = $224,700

These figures represent results in the years 1990, 1991, and 1992, the most recent for which data were available.

Company executives report high net profit margins ranging from 25 percent to 40 percent with averages well above 30 percent. In that case, assuming average performance, you reach breakeven early in your second year, and begin to show substantial returns by the end of your third year.

However, the company does not make actual earnings claims and warns that earnings represent averages of both franchise- and company-owned territories. It also warns that most of the franchise territories had been developed by the company before they were sold, so the results for new franchisees may be different. Regardless of these disclaimers—which I agree are appropriate—you can earn 100 percent or higher net pretax profits each year on your original cash investment.

In sum, K & N offers one of the best little-known, but high-profit mobile franchises.

MAIL BOXES ETC.

Mail Boxes Etc.
6060 Cornerstone Court West
San Diego, CA 92121
(800) 456-0414
(619) 455-8800

Mail Boxes Etc. (MBE) continues as one of the most rapidly growing franchises in the United States as it surpassed 2,000 centers in June 1993. It will triple in size in less than six years, spurred by a very aggressive regional and area development plan. MBE projected reaching its 1995 goal of 2,500 franchises worldwide by early 1994, almost one year early.

However, this rapid growth does not mean that the opportunity is exhausted. MBE President Tony DeSio said that the company plans to have a total of 5,000 U.S. centers and 5,000 more around the world. You still have time in some areas to catch a ride on this rising star.

MBE is also a leader in encouraging women to own franchises. Twenty percent of its area developers and regional owners are women, some 41 percent of all franchisees are married partners, and 30 percent are individual women owners.

Of course, MBE has been consistently rated as one of the best franchises among all the magazines and services for at least five years. The only chink in its armor occurred during the recent recession, when some franchisees found that they could not achieve their profit projections from the late 1980s. Clearly, although this business can do very well during business upturns, it can flatten out or even decline during recessions because fewer people ship packages as gifts. However, MBE experienced an average 17 percent same-store sales growth during 1991 and 1992. Although MBE remains a top opportunity, you need to consider it with realistic growth projections.

A Timely Idea

MBE's concept has boomed because it offers a convenient and diversified alternative to the retail services that the U.S. Postal Service offers. The USPS's shows its vulnerability by the tremendous growth of competitors such as United Parcel Service and Federal Express. MBE plans to become the UPS or Federal Express of the retail postal service industry. MBE franchises offer more timely, better quality, more complete, and more varied services in convenient locations that are open longer hours than the post office. They are like the "7-11" of postal and business services.

In fact, the original services—packing and shipping, mail box rentals, and so on—have become almost secondary to the services it offers small businesses: faxes, mailing, copying, packaging materials, overnight delivery, office supplies, and so on. These services cost very little; for example, sending a fax costs only a few cents worth of paper, yet you charge on average $1.50 a page to send—and receive. You also charge from $3.00 to $5.00 to hand a package to an overnight delivery service. That's almost pure profit, except for the cost of a form and labor.

Note that MBE prefers and encourages UPS deliveries for two reasons: First, UPS is the largest and most efficient company that offers a complete range of domestic and international ground and air deliveries, and, second, UPS bought a very large portion of MBE's stock in 1990.

DeSio also emphasized that MBE continues to widen its products and services to increase your profit centers. In late 1993, for example, the company was testing using MBE centers for airline ticketing. You could order and/or pick up your airline ticket at a local MBE office instead of going to a travel agent's office, waiting in line at the airport, or waiting for the mail to arrive.

More meaningful in the short run, MBE centers were becoming "depots" or drop-off points from which consumers can send equipment to large manufacturers for repairs or replacements. A consumer just takes a broken computer or VCR to her local MBE office, the center ships it to the manufacturer's repair depot that ships a repaired or replaced PC or VCR back to the center, and the consumer picks up the product.

DeSio said that the major mail order and direct marketing companies are considering a hold-for-pick-up system because they and their customers lose so much merchandise left on doorsteps at homes or small businesses. In the future, if you order something from a catalog, you may have to go by a MBE center to pick it up on your way to or from work.

Last, but not least, DeSio said that major companies who have hundreds or thousands of employees on the road (field reps, salespeople, and so on) or who have thousands of "telecommuting" employees are turning MBE centers into "home offices." DeSio noted that the major companies want their employees to use MBE centers for all their office services: packing and shipping, copying, faxing, and so on. These companies save enormous amounts of money on unnecessary equipment purchases, and it increases productivity because the employees can stay on the road instead of returning home to send faxes, type up reports, or do other time-wasting office activities.

You will offer all these highly profitable services from a typical 1,200-square-foot center located in a strip shopping center. You will do both the mundane—packing, shipping, selling stamps and stationery, making keys—and the unusual—"home office" and repair depot services.

How Much It Costs

At present, the MBE franchise fee equals $24,950, a $2,000 boost from 1993, and a $5,000 jump since 1990, showing how prices rise when demand outstrips supply.

Total start-up costs have also increased to between $85,000 and $90,000, including a minimum of $15,000 for working capital. This does not include an amount for living expenses. Among these expenses, MBE has also increased its training fee from $1,300 to $1,500 and added a $500 design fee for giving you a store layout. Note that most franchises include both training and design in their franchise fee. Here are the company's low and high start-up cost estimates (I have added working capital, travel training, and living expenses); be warned that De Sio emphasized that his estimate of $85,000 to $100,000, including working capital, tended to be the average and that the actual amount of working capital will depend on how aggressively you promote your business.

Category	Low End	High End
Franchise fee (a)	$24,950	$24,950
Training fee	1,500	1,500
Design fee	500	500
Leasehold improvements (b)	14,700	37,000
Supplies and inventory (c)	6,625	16,550
Deposits (d)	900	3,600
Prepaid business expenses (e)	2,705	8,830
Travel training	1,000	2,000

Working capital (f)	5,000	15,000
Living expenses	2,000	5,000
Total	$59,880	$114,930

a. If you wish to convert an existing, similar store, you can negotiate a much lower franchise fee. And, if you want to buy multiple territories, you can pay lower franchise fees: $19,500 for the second store and $16,500 for third and subsequent stores.
b. Varies widely depending on whether you use conventional or modular construction techniques, how much build-out the space needs, and so on.
c. Includes retail office and packaging supplies inventory, equipment and store operation supplies, and sales tax on leased or bought equipment.
d. Includes deposits for telephones, utilities, one month's lease.
e. Includes first month's rent, insurance premiums, license fees, leased equipment deposits (15 percent), prepaid postal caller service, and the like.
f. Includes salaries for workers, operating expenses, and so on for up to three months.

Note that these numbers do *not* include the purchase price of your important equipment, such as cash register, computer system, passport camera, fax machine, copiers, and so on, only the lease down payments.

Royalty Fees

MBE charges a 5 percent royalty on gross sales, except for postal and delivery service income; you pay the royalty on gross profits. You also pay a 2 percent marketing fee into a national ad fund; half of that fund promotes the company as a whole, and the other half promotes regional and area franchise growth.

You must also belong to an area advertising co-op and pay whatever amount that the group agrees each member should pay up to $250 a month, and pay a one-time initiation fee of up to $1,000 for membership and administrative costs. You should also spend a percentage of your monthly revenues to promote yourself.

The most effective local ad medium appeared to be direct mail coupons that brought in new customers and encouraged repeat business from regular customers. You may also participate in national promotions, for example, October as Customer Appreciation Month, during which you charge sharply discounted prices to generate more volume year round.

What You Get

In return for your fees and costs, MBE offers a very broad and deep program, although some franchisees complained that some of their regional or area franchisees who manage field support did not provide adequate service, but pressured them to increase sales. These area franchisees can do very well from franchise sales and royalty fees; they receive 40 percent of the franchise fee and half of the ongoing royalties. For example, in the Washington, DC, area, one area developer owned 3 stores and had sold 25 others. She had a three-person staff to do marketing and franchise support, and within her area were several of the consistently most profitable stores among all MBE centers.

However, MBE does offer these benefits that no other competitor in its market can:

- *Market presence.* MBE has become the 900-pound gorilla in the packing and shipping and small-business-services markets. Its market share has soared, probably to 40 to 50 percent of all industry revenues.

- *A ten-year agreement term renewable for additional ten-year terms with payment of 25 percent of the then-current franchise fee.*

- *Start-up assistance.* Lease negotiation, site selection, store layout, construction management (for a fee equal to 10 percent of construction costs, not to exceed $2,000), and so on.

- *MBE University.* You receive 10 days of thorough training at the company's training facility called MBE University and five days of in-store training at an area developer's existing location. MBEU training for you costs $1,500, and you have to pay $300 for each additional person you bring.

- *Comprehensive marketing campaigns.*

- *Volume purchasing discounts.*

- *Continuing support.* This mostly comes from your area developer, but the national company concentrates on developing new products and services with national accounts and major manufacturers. Headquarters also provides quarterly marketing campaigns that the local and/or regional association decides whether or not to use.

How Much Can You Make?

MBE does not make any earnings claims; however, you can estimate your projected gross revenues fairly well by using the company's financial statements. In fiscal year 1993, the latest year for which figures were available, the company reported $13.3 million in royalty revenue from individual franchises, more than double the $5.8 million from fiscal 1992. From that, you can extrapolate that systemwide sales, subject to royalty payments, exceeded $266 million from about 1,750 operational centers during fiscal 1993, including start-ups. By dividing the revenues by the number of franchises, you can "guesstimate" average gross revenues of about $152,000. This is low, but remember that it includes several hundred new stores in the United States and foreign countries. Stores that are two years old or more report that, on average, they have revenues subject to royalty of about $200,000 a year.

Here's how you build revenues by offering a plethora of packaging and small-business services:

- *Parcel/overnight shipping.* You receive fees ranging from $2.00 to $5.00 to prepare and give to the major shippers parcels and overnight packages. You also receive fees from the shippers for acting as their agent.

- *Business services.* You can charge $2.00 to $3.00 per page for faxes, or offer discounts to $1 per page if the customer buys a 20-fax, 40-fax, or 60-fax grouping. You also charge $2.00 to $3.50 per page for typing/word processing services.

- *Mail box rentals.* Rentals costs $10 to $25 per month or more, and each center has up to 250 mailboxes. If you rent half at the median price of $17.50, you would receive $2,187.50 per month.

- *Supplies and convenience items.* You charge high markups on mailers, envelopes, packing boxes, office supplies, and so on.

- *Other profit centers.* You can add other profit centers—repair depot, electronic income tax returns, and so on—and earn high fees for little or no cost.

In short, with an MBE center, you accumulate revenues with thousands of small sales, each of which has a significant gross profit ranging from 50 percent to the hundreds of percent. You do face inventory costs, space leases, equipment leases, and labor costs, so you can expect to net between 25 and 30 percent per year, or between $60,000 and $70,000 in an average store.

Clearly, MBE is a long-term growth opportunity with significant ROIs coming when you lease the equipment, open additional centers, and market your most profitable services.

Important Note

Despite its rapid growth, MBE reports a 5 percent failure rate that is determined by dividing the number of store closures by the total number of stores opened. Its offering circular noted a significant amount of turnover during the three years between late 1989 and late 1992, the latest year for figures. It reported that 290 franchises had been sold or transferred, with most of those in California (80), Florida (33), Arizona (21), and Massachusetts (16). Note that those states were hit hard by the recession or natural disasters.

Furthermore, the UFOC reported 78 MBE-initiated terminations, broken down as follows:

- Thirty-seven for nonpayment of royalties;

- Twenty-three abandoned by the franchisees;

- Eleven voluntarily terminated by franchisee; and

- Seventeen various other reasons, such as eminent domain proceedings, failure to open the store, and failure to comply with system standards.

During that three years, MBE grew from about 850 franchises to about 1,600 franchises, so the termination rate is definitely below average. And even the stores that changed hands did not close; other buyers were found, or area developers kept them open until they could find new buyers or other franchisees bought them.

As important, note that an MBE center is very location- and customer service-driven. I have seen this in my area. One MBE was simply around the corner in a strip center that faced a major highway and across the street from a major competitor facing the same highway and down the highway from two other major competitors that also had highway frontage. The state opened a new interstate highway that relieved congestion on the major highway, and three of the four package/mail services centers failed. But the MBE one failed first because no one could see it from the highway.

On the other hand, another MBE owner had two stores, one again around a corner from a major artery in a tiny strip center with terrible parking, and the other in the student union of a major university. The store in the strip center was consistently the best performer in its region because it attracted not only undergraduates, but graduate students, professors, and local small-business people. Customers flocked there to fax resumes to potential employers, ship packages to foreign countries, make copies of their class papers, and so on. The one at the student union did well, too, but it did not attract off-campus traffic. The moral of my story: With an MBE, location is everything!

MBE executives asked me to add that in addition to location, customer service plays a critical role in the overall success rate. I agree wholeheartedly; the successful store I have mentioned here provides excellent customer service. The one with a poor location also had mediocre service, so both factors played a part in that failure.

THE LITTLE GYM INTERNATIONAL, INC.

The Little Gym International, Inc.
150 Lake Street South
Suite 210
Kirkland, WA 98033
(206) 889-4588

Little Gym Chairman W. Berry Fowler proves the reverse proverb: Nice guys do finish first. During the past two years, I have interviewed and worked with Fowler and his staff many times: In my 17 years in this industry, I have never met a more pleasant, more professional, or more dedicated individual.

Beyond that, Fowler first succeeded when he founded Sylvan Learning Centers in 1978 and built it into one of the leading franchises of the 1980s. After he sold Sylvan in 1987, he "semiretired" for several years, but now, he is back with a franchise concept that promises to be even bigger, better, and more lucrative than Sylvan's one-on-one tutoring approach. Called The Little Gym, the franchise is a unique total child development program that combines upbeat music, enjoyable movement, and positive motivation to teach fitness to and build self-esteem in children.

The Little Gym addresses a critical need among modern children, most of whom spend an average of six hours a day in front of the television and do very little, if any, exercise either in school or at home. In short, every study shows dramatically that our children are fatter, unhealthier, and less fit than ever before. Worse, modern kids face families wracked by divorce, addiction, and overworked or uncaring parents and schools filled with drugs, violence, and social problems. Consequently, many, if not most, kids receive less attention and emotional support and are exposed to more negative influences than ever before. So, perhaps more important in the long run, The Little Gym emphasizes children's self-esteem and positive image in ways that, one hopes, will help them overcome their negative surroundings.

Although Fowler only became involved in 1992, The Little Gym fitness and motivation concept and program had been proved in the crucible of experience for 17 years in the Seattle area.

Robin Wes, a child development guru, opened the first Little Gym in the mid-1970s and had grown the idea to five company and franchised locations when Fowler found out about it.

Fowler's introduction to The Little Gym and his professional response exemplifies how remarkable this franchise is. Fowler was spending a few months in Seattle in 1991, and his wife and he needed to find something for their young daughter to do during the day. His wife found The Little Gym and enrolled their daughter. Fowler said that his daughter clamored for him to come with her to see how much fun it was. He finally found time to go with her and saw a room filled with children having a marvelous time, yet learning very positive messages about themselves and others. He met Robin Wes, and found that Wes had a small franchise but few resources to expand it. Fowler quickly saw the enormous potential for combining his experience and resources with Wes's unique program.

Exploding Business Opportunity

Yet, Fowler and his group are not starry-eyed do-gooders; far from that, they are consummate businesspeople who believe that you can do good and do well at the same time. They demonstrate a very deeply held attitude and belief that true prosperity derives from true service.

And with the failure of the schools to address the critical development issues facing a new generation of children—and perhaps to even make them much worse—Fowler and The Little Gym have created a prime business opportunity that has soared into national prominence during 1993. During its first 12 months in business, The Little Gym franchised 50 territories. And with his strong financial resources, Fowler put into place a support staff large enough to add 100 more franchises per year. He also made an agreement to open 185 centers in Japan by the year 2000. In short, The Little Gym offers a true ground-floor opportunity to participate in one of the hottest franchises in one of the most promising markets during the 1990s.

I know that all this sounds hyperbolic, and I normally temper my enthusiasm for any new franchise, but The Little Gym's predecessor franchises (like Gymboree) and the social situation in American families and schools proved to me that a huge market for these fitness and motivation services has tremendous potential both to do good and to generate significant revenues. And Fowler's background and resources and The Little Gym's multiple revenue streams, adaptability to the market, and high-powered advertising and public relations proved that the company was ready to quickly dominate this business.

The Little Gym works like this: You rent space in a strip shopping center or higher-quality, low-rise office park in or near middle-class neighborhoods within easy driving distance of hundreds of children. Being within driving distance of child care centers also opens up a significant revenue source, one that an early franchisee suggested—The Little Gym on Wheels, a van with which you take equipment to child care centers so you can offer classes to their children. The same service is also in high demand from preschools, parks and recreation departments, and public school systems.

At the center, you offer classes throughout the day and on Saturday mornings. If you have a large nearby preschool population, you also offer morning classes. Your primary program is a once-a-week class for each child at a cost of about $35 to $40 per month. You hire and train instructors, often college students studying or graduates with degrees in early childhood development, and pay them by the class.

You add to your revenue streams by setting up "The Little Gym Pro Shop" in your location and selling music tapes and videos and apparel and fitness accessories specially designed for The Little Gym with its logo prominently displayed on each item. All these products are "kiddie-size" and fashionable, for example, fanny packs, exercise clothing, gym and tote bags, back packs, and water bottles.

To keep your space busy—a quiet room means no income— you offer Parents Survival Night on Friday and Saturday nights. You "baby sit" the kids while the parents go out by themselves, and you charge $5 to $6 an hour for an evening of games, music, and movement.

Even more profitable, birthday parties generate significant revenues because you charge $125 to $150 per party. Several parties each week can add $2,000 per month to your gross income. Specialty camps (e.g., cheerleaders' training), swimming programs, sports development programs, and The Little Gym's special type of karate classes also add to your revenue streams.

Simply, Fowler means to do his best to fulfill the company's mission statement: "To promote the healthy and successful physical and mental development of the children of the world, and thereby help our franchisees achieve their business and personal goals."

How Much It Costs

Equally surprising about The Little Gym, it has relatively low start-up costs, ranging from about $55,000 to about $75,000, more than half of which are the $27,500 franchise fee and a required $10,500 kit of exercise and gym equipment and supplies.

The Little Gym has also launched a second franchise called "The Little Gym On Wheels" for smaller, more rural territories. This area typically has about half the population of the larger one and aims to reach the market in small cities and towns. You can open a center in the smaller territory, but it is optional and depends on the demand in your area. Although centers in smaller areas will probably be smaller than a regular one, you could open a larger one because the space costs per square foot are so much lower in those areas. One or more vans can service 300 to 600 children *and* sponsor birthday parties and other programs, so the revenue streams will be similar.

The following tables show a range of start-up costs for both franchises, but Fowler noted that the average cost for a complete center was in the $50,000 to $60,000 range and about $33,000 for a "Wheels" franchise.

The cost varies according to how many services you can afford to offer at the beginning. If you operate a full center, you may do best to begin your mobile operation after your center has been running for a few months, so you can fund the lease payments from your cash flow. The following table gives low and high start-up cost ranges.

LITTLE GYM CENTER

Category	Low End	High End
Franchise fee	$27,500	$27,500
Start-up kit/inventory	10,500	10,500
Equipment/fixtures (a)	3,000	7,500
Furnishings/supplies	3,000	5,000
Security deposits (b)	2,500	4,000
Training travel	1,800	3,000
Start-up expenses (c)	3,200	4,500
Working capital (d)	5,000	15,000
Total	$56,500	$77,000

a. Includes leasehold improvements for space, but you can negotiate these costs with your landlord and reduce them significantly.
b. Includes space lease deposits, business telephone deposits, and deposits on required insurance policies.
c. Start-up advertising program, training costs for instructors, and all the expenses for opening an office.
d. Operating expenses; if a spouse/partner covers your family's living expenses, you can probably reduce this amount. The Little Gym quickly generates cash flow.

THE LITTLE GYM ON WHEELS

Category	Low End	High End
Franchise fee	$17,500	$17,500
Equipment	3,000	3,000
Van lease	1,000	1,250
Advertising	500	1,000
Training travel	1,500	2,000
Van decals	1,500	1,500
Home office	500	1,000
Miscellaneous	500	1,000
Working capital	6,000	6,000
Total	$32,000	$34,250

Note that salaries are not included in these figures since most owners manage the business at first, so if you intend to hire managers and a staff, you will need to add more working capital.

Royalties and Fees

You must also pay an 8 percent monthly royalty and a 1 percent advertising fee. In addition, you must spend the greater of either $700 per month or 4 percent of gross revenues on local advertising campaigns. You buy Little Gym accessories through the company or approved suppliers at wholesale prices and sell them at retail. These make up your only payments to the company.

In short, compared to some very inexpensive programs, The Little Gym may seem expensive, but what you receive and what you can earn far surpass those programs. Furthermore, Fowler deliberately designed the franchise to attract businesspeople with management and/or marketing experience and to give them a substantial business with multiple revenue streams and profit centers through which they could build equity and long-term investment returns.

What You Get

First and foremost, you receive Fowler's exceptional successful experience as a franchisor serving children's needs and Wes's 18 years of experience developing The Little Gym's child development program. Furthermore, you receive a very substantial franchise program with a professional support staff—Fowler brought with him all his top executives at Sylvan Learning—that most new franchises simply cannot match.

- *Territory.* You receive an exclusive territory with up to 100,000 of population based on the number of children between toddler age and 12 years old and socioeconomic factors.

- *Ten-year term.* The franchise agreement lasts 10 years, and even better, you can renew for additional 10-year terms at no cost.

- *Training.* You receive a comprehensive ten-day training program at The Little Gym College of Fun & Fitness, a dedicated training facility.

- *Support.* You have ready access to The Little Gym's 20-person support staff. You will receive regular visits from field reps.

- *Marketing campaigns.* The Little Gym already has in place a major national marketing campaign to promote the brand name and make it as well known as Sylvan Learning Centers. That benefits you because you will be recognized as a professional operation from the beginning. It also provides a complete start-up advertising and public relations package for you and develops new marketing campaigns depending on the season—summer, beginning of school, holidays, and so on.

- *A successful concept.* Most importantly, The Little Gym concept has been proven for 18 years, and the kids and their parents almost always give it rave reviews. I can say that the music Wes has written makes you—even jaded teenagers and middle-aged adults—want to get up and dance and have fun. And the messages that the music delivers not only promote self-esteem, but also encourage children to learn to appreciate differences among their peers and get along well with everyone.

How Much Can You Make?

Of course, many great concepts have fallen by the wayside because their inventors did not know how to help people make money from them. Fowler began the concept with several revenue streams, and by listening to his franchisees, added several more during 1993. Here's how you make money with The Little Gym:

- *Monthly class fees.* As noted, you charge $35 to $40 per month for weekly classes. The Little Gym expects you to rent a center through which you can easily work with 300 to 500 children per week in classes of about 12 to 18 kids. That would mean minimum monthly revenues of $10,500.

- *The Little Gym Pro Shop.* The company expects you to add at least 10 percent to your gross revenues each year with accessory sales through your shop.

- *Parents Survival Night.* You can charge $5 to $6 an hour for a two- to three-hour session every Friday and Saturday night for as many kids as your center can accommodate. Even with a low estimate of 50 kids, that means $500 per night or $2,000 per month.

- *The Little Gym On Wheels.* With a van-based outreach program, you can hold classes in child care centers for 300 to 500 more students per month and earn an additional $6,000 to $15,000 per month. In sum, here are some conservative monthly income projections after your first year in business:

The Little Gym (300 students)	$10,500
Parents Survival Night	2,000
Special programs, camps, etc.	2,000
Little Gym On Wheels (300 students)	9,000
Little Gym Pro Shop	1,000
Birthday parties	3,000
Total	$27,500

These streams could generate $297,000 in annual revenues and gross profits of about 50 to 55 percent, or $148,500 to $163,350. More liberal estimates of a Little Gym with 500 students on site and 300 at child care centers would generate $360,000 in gross revenues and $162,000 in gross profits on a 55 percent gross profit margin.

These constitute exceptional, yet very realizable, returns on an investment of about $60,000. In short, you can and—I believe— you should do well by doing good. The Little Gym gives you an unparalleled opportunity to do both.

DENT DOCTOR, INC.

Dent Doctor, Inc.
7708 Cantrell Road
Little Rock, AR 72207
(501) 224-0500

Dent Doctor is one of those unusual franchises that made me wonder, "How in the world can you make money doing that?" "That" is fixing minor dents and dings *without* damaging the paint on a car. Yet, Dent Doctor's eight company stores grossed more than $1.6 million during 1993, so paintless dent removal clearly has reached an important market of new and used car dealers, rental car fleet owners, auto wholesalers, insurance adjusters, and the general public. President Tom Harris also reported that all the company's franchisees easily exceeded their $78,000 minimum revenue quota by the end of their second year. Furthermore, Dent Doctor has been selected to appear on several "best" franchise lists since 1991.

By the end of 1993, Dent Doctor had eight company stores and 33 franchisees, including six associates, in 13 Sunbelt states. But the company was expanding across the United States, primarily through nonregistration states along the Sunbelt. However, Dent Doctor had terminated nine franchisees, most of them associates, during 1992 and 1993 for failure to comply with quality standards. This occurred during a change in company ownership and what Harris called sorting out the first wave of franchisees who chose not to follow company requirements. By the end of 1993, the situation had stabilized and the company was expanding again.

This concept is so simple and the business so easy to start and manage that Harris's and his franchisees' success convinced me that Dent Doctor has a significant opportunity.

Here's how it works: Using proprietary tools and methods, you "massage away" minor dents and dings, like those caused by hail, in about 45 minutes. But the process takes patience, deft manual dexterity, and extensive specialized training.

Your service, the average cost of which varies from $75 to $80 per dent, saves your customers hundreds of dollars for body and paint shop work and at least one to two weeks' wait getting the car back. With Dent Doctor, a car dealer can call you in for a repair and sell the car the same day: no more cars sitting in paint shops where the dealer cannot sell them.

In addition, the repair does not affect the original finish, does not use chemicals or high temperatures, and applies to late model cars as well as it does to older ones. These benefits convince most prospects that your service more than pays for itself.

You can work from your home with a mobile van or you can open a retail location. Harris maintained that a retail location enables a franchisee to expand his retail business, which helps complement the wholesale business.

Three Franchise Programs

Dent Doctor offers three franchise programs: (1) Primary Franchise, (2) Associate Franchise, and (3) Territorial Commission Agreement (similar to an area representative concept). Briefly, with the territorial agreement, a primary franchisee services and supports one or more associate franchisees. Under the associate franchise, you pay a low franchise fee and commissions to a primary franchisee who allows you to work in his territory, often even in his retail center or from a van. Although an associate cannot open a center within the territory, an associate can relocate his franchise into another territory and convert into a primary franchise.

With a primary franchise, you either operate from a mobile van or open a retail center in a major territory, usually all of a major portion of a metropolitan area. If you do allow associates in your area, you train and service them and receive commissions ranging from 20 to 35 percent of the associates' gross income. This makes a very good deal for primary franchisees who do not have the financial resources to equip more vans in their own territories.

How Much It Costs

Dent Doctor has what appears at first to be a high franchise fee of $29,500 and relatively high start-up costs. But what you receive in return, especially a remarkable eight-week training program, proves the fee's value. The table shows a low to high range of start-up costs for a primary franchise:

Category	Low End	High End
Franchise fee	$29,500	$29,500
Van down payment/lease	1,650	2,500
Opening advertising	2,500	3,000
Training travel (a)	2,000	10,000
Insurance deposits	3,000	5,000
Rent and lease deposit	850	2,000
Leasehold improvements	4,000	10,000
Furniture/fixtures/equipment	1,900	3,000
Signage	2,500	5,000
Start-up supplies (b)	500	800
Prepaid expenses (c)	800	1,500
Working capital (d)	10,000	25,000
Total (e)	$56,950	$97,300

a. Eight-week training program at headquarters means higher than usual costs, especially if you send a manager or employee to take the course in your place.
b. Various uniforms and office supplies.
c. Includes mobile phone installation and service, pager service, utility and business phone deposits, business permits and licenses, local chamber of commerce membership, and so on.
d. Harris insisted that you should have enough money to operate a center and live comfortably for six months or so.
e. Harris said average start-up costs tended toward the lower end with some shops opening at even lower costs.

The estimated start-up costs for an associate franchise range from $21,500 to $27,000; because most of the training program takes place at a primary franchisee's shop, you avoid the expenses to start-up a retail center, and the franchise fee equals only $8,375.

Royalty and Other Fees

You must also pay the franchisor a $2,500 grand opening advertising fee if you open a retail center, but not if you run a van-based primary franchise.

The regular royalty rate is 6 percent of gross sales; although its offering circular provides for an advertising fee, Harris said that the company did not plan to set up an ad fund at this time. But primary franchisees are encouraged to spend 3 percent of their revenues on local advertising.

On the other hand, an associate franchisee must pay to the primary franchisee for his territory a weekly "territorial commission fee" ranging from 20 to 35 percent; Harris said that the company suggests a 25 percent fee. An associate must also pay the company the normal 6 percent royalty.

What You Get

In return for your fee, you receive the following:

- *Exclusive territory.* As a primary franchisee, you receive an exclusive territory based on population, total number of cars, and the number of new car dealerships in the area. It usually follows city or county boundaries.

- *Training.* You receive a very extensive eight-week training program at headquarters, the longest training period in franchising that I have ever encountered. Harris insists that training in the company's proprietary tools and methods requires that much time and effort to ensure high-quality repairs that generate repeat customers.

  An associate franchisee receives much of his training at the local primary center, but also goes to headquarters training.

- *Tool kit.* You lease one proprietary tool kit worth $1,709 as part of the package. Note that you do *not* own these tools; the franchise license and lease only allow you to use them.

- *Vehicle supplies.* You receive a vehicle outfitting and decal package.

- *Grand opening marketing.* You receive a complete ad campaign in return for your additional $2,500 fee to generate interest in your service from your primary markets.

● *Start-up assistance.* A Dent Doctor rep will be on site for three to five days to help you open your center.

Of course, you receive the operations manuals, plans and specifications for center build-out, and other common benefits.

Dent Doctor gives you a thorough program, the most vital of which is its training program and territory to protect your investment. It also provides ongoing refresher training and updates on new technology and methods that the Dent Doctor research staff develops.

How Much Can You Make?

You generate revenue by providing dent removal services, preferably under long-term agreements with major customers, such as fleets, car dealers, and wholesalers. You will not survive if you depend on insurance adjusters and consumer walk-ins.

You charge between $75 and $80 per dent removal, or about 20 percent of the cost of taking the car to a body and paint shop. Harris's figures of about $1.6 million in company store revenues divide into an average of $200,000 gross per store, more than 2,666 jobs per year or more than 53 per week.

But Harris also insisted that the franchisees who followed the proven operating system had no problems exceeding a minimum annual sales quota of $78,000. The demand for this service is real and the benefits of Dent Doctor's service so unusual—and the alternatives so expensive or so hard to find—that the franchise's primary customers quickly accept the concept.

With a center and at least two employees to do the work while you market the business, you can expect to net 20 to 30 percent or a middle five-figure income after the first two years. If you only operate a van, you can earn net incomes in the $30,000 range, but you have limited room to grow your business unless you add more vans and crews. In short, if you start small and grow rapidly into a center, you can attract retail business and build your volume quickly.

PRIORITY MANAGEMENT SYSTEMS, INC.

Priority Management Systems, Inc.
U.S. Address

Suite 1740
Koll Center Bellevue
500 108th Avenue, N.E.
Bellevue, WA 98004
(800) 221-9031
(206) 454-7686

Canadian Headquarters

IBM Tower
701 West Georgia Street
Suite 1700
Vancouver, B.C., Canada V7Y 1C6
(800) 665-5448
(604) 685-0418

Priority Management Systems, Inc. (PMSI), continues as the most dynamic, rapidly growing worldwide management training and personal productivity consulting service with more than 300 franchisees in 17 countries, including 150 in the United States and 44 in Canada. You work as a marketer, trainer, and consultant and receive $400 to $700 per attendee fees and commissions on repeat sales of the process-skills management products and tools that your seminar participants need to practice their new skills effectively. Although the franchisees used to emphasize these after-workshop product sales, many franchisees stated that they now concentrate on building long-term relationships with their client organizations because they want to enhance their professional consulting work and avoid the image of a product salesperson.

More importantly, the company has dramatically expanded the workshops and services its franchisees provide. The basic training system, called The Priority Manager, combines process-skills management methods with materials that include daily, monthly, and yearly planners; a communication planner; a personal financial planner; a project planning guide; a telephone directory; and so forth—all in a complete package for anyone whose most valuable asset is her or his productivity. Next, PMSI continues to offer these variations: The Priority Manager-Administrative Assistant system, its Profile time and sales management process, and The Priority Manager Software—Personal and Network Editions.

However, the most exciting new products launch the company into the booming market for improving white-collar productivity. Called PQI (productivity quality interdependence), this system uses an individual benchmarking measurement tool to identify eight key skill processes that makes a white-collar worker more or less productive. Then, the PMSI franchisee teaches the person how to enhance those eight skills so he or she can become more productive and deliver higher-quality work.

PMSI developed PQ-I to give company executives some way to measure the effectiveness of knowledge workers. During the early 1990s, as the recession hit the training industry hard, executives began to demand measurable results for their training expenditures; PQ-I helps provide that measurement.

Over the long run, perhaps PMSI's most important innovation is an affiliated company called Atheneum Learning Corporation. It provides programs to develop twenty-first-century learning skills for individuals and companies so they can compete in a rapidly changing global marketplace. It encourages them to adopt a lifelong learning philosophy and strategy and express that commitment with ongoing professional development for all their employees. These programs are based on "performance breakthroughs" that occur through a progressive process beginning with the Changemasters workshop, working through on-site individual-team consultation, progressing with the TeamTalk™ workshop, and leading to a continuous effort called The Atheneum LearningLink™.

I suggest that most people with little experience in training or management begin with PMSI and work into Atheneum; that is how PMSI introduced it to its franchisees two years ago.

In any case, I have attended the basic Priority Manager workshop, and I found it very helpful. The franchisee in my area also provided several free follow-up services, including a one-hour visit by an assistant who reviewed progress and made suggestions and a second four-hour seminar that focused on project planning and reviewed and strengthened the process management and productivity skills that the first seminar taught. I found the Priority Manager system somewhat daunting at first, but it has dramatically improved my planning ability and helped me plan my projects and my use of time far more efficiently than before.

What Do You Do?

My experience shows that you must do four activities well to succeed as a PMSI franchisee:

1. Sell your training and its substantial benefits to corporate clients.
2. Lead workshops to train your clients.
3. Provide one-on-one follow-through services; this guaranteed, free service sets you apart from other competing training systems.
4. Maintain relationships with existing clients to generate referrals and repeat sales.

So, a PMSI franchisee must have good presentation skills or have experience as a manager, marketer, or trainer, or all three.

How Much It Costs

PMSI's franchise fee equals $29,500—it has not changed in four years. That makes up most of your start-up costs because you can work from home and minimize your start-up overhead. One of the top six earning franchisees has worked from his basement for almost a decade.

You also pay a 9 percent royalty fee or 9 percent of a minimum monthly quota, whichever is greater:

Month of Agreement	Minimum Monthly Gross/Fee
1–6	$2,000 ($180)
7–12	$3,000 ($270)
13–18	$4,000 ($360)
19–24	$5,000 ($450)
25–60	$6,000 ($540)

You also have to pay a 1 percent advertising fee on gross revenues or the monthly quota ranging from $20 to $60 per month. These ad dollars go into a separate ad fund administered by Priority Management executives and reviewed twice a year by the Independent Associates Council, a 10-member, elected advisory council.

Estimated Start-up Costs

PMSI estimates that your total start-up costs will range from $37,000 to $49,500, but that estimate does *not* include any living expenses for the first three to six months. The company states in its offering circular that its estimates for working capital should include costs for legal and accounting fees, training travel expenses, insurance premiums, business telephone deposits, fax machine, computer, salaries, short-term rentals for workshop sites (usually hotel conference rooms), and so on. However, it does not include any costs for office leases or any significant expenditure for office furniture.

So, you should add $10,000 to $20,000 more for living expenses for a total ranging from $47,000 to $69,500 during your first six months or so.

By the way, on occasion, PMSI will finance up to $20,000 of the fee for 36 months at an interest rate five percentage points above the prime rate. The monthly installment payment equals $25 times the number of workshop participants that you trained during the previous month. For example, if you trained 20 people, your installment would equal $500; thus, the amount of the loan and accrued interest fluctuates according to how much you earn. It should equal about 5 percent of your income.

What You Get

For your fee, you receive the highest-quality, most forward-thinking management training processes in the world and a very sophisticated support network:

- *Territory.* Although PMSI does not grant exclusive territories, it usually grants territories that cover significant portions of major metropolitan areas. For example, the Washington, DC/Baltimore, Maryland, area has two franchisees: One covers Northern Virginia and Washington; the other focuses on suburban Maryland and Baltimore.

  However, your clients may be employees of major organizations with offices around the country, so you may overlap other territories when you travel to other cities. The company has a formal policy that does encourage local franchisees to negotiate with their counterparts in other cities a commission or fee division.

  PMSI's offering circular states more formally that your territory should have at least a population of 250,000 businesspeople and at least 1,000 businesses with at least 20 to 1,000 employees; the territory is usually set by political (city or county) boundaries.

- *Agreement term.* Although the agreement lasts only five years, you can renew for as many terms as you want.

- *Training.* You receive between five and 12 days' training at company headquarters where you are immersed in the company's unique training and marketing methods.

- *Support services.* After you begin, you receive an on-site visit from a PMSI manager within six months to review your progress and other visits at least once a year thereafter. The company also holds an international and regional convention each year. Most important, you receive the benefit of its superior communication, research, and marketing programs, the quality of which is unmatched among training franchises.

- *Low termination rate.* PMSI executives reported only one termination during 1993, and even during the recession, its rate was much lower than average, less than 4 percent per year. A total of 22 franchises were terminated between 1990 and 1992, almost all of which (17) were mutual releases. Only four were terminated for failure to pay royalties and only one for abandonment. As these figures show, the company has a very liberal mutual termination clause in its contract.

How Much Can You Make?

PMSI no longer makes earnings claims nor does it provide pro forma projections, but reports from current franchisees show that you can grow this service to the million-dollar-per-year range after five to seven years. Others noted that you can gross $300,000 to $400,000 with net pretax incomes above $100,000 by the end of your third or fourth year. To achieve a $300,000 gross, you would have to train 600 people at $500 each, or 750 people at $400 each. With an average class size of 10 to 12, you would have to offer seminars once or twice a week to achieve that level.

The secret to building these incomes, however, lies in repeat business and referrals from major organizations that can send dozens of employees to take your courses.

In short, Priority Management Systems, Inc., is a very significant opportunity for any management or marketing professional interested in the dynamic future of enhancing personal and organizational productivity, quality, efficiency, and effectiveness.

MANAGEMENT RECRUITERS INTERNATIONAL, INC.

Management Recruiters International, Inc.
Statler Office Tower, Suite 1400
1127 Euclid Avenue
Cleveland, OH 44115-1638
(216) 696-1122
(800) 875-4000

Although a difficult recession has changed the nature of executive recruiting forever, Management Recruiters has not only weathered this major shift, but also has led the industry to a new focus on human resource services. More importantly, although systemwide revenues were down during the early 1990s, company executives reported that franchisees increased their operating ratios and net profit margins.

With more than 600 offices in its four major divisions, MRI remains the leading management and employment search and recruitment organization, outpacing its nearest franchise competition by many times. About 50 offices are company owned, and 522 (by late 1993) were operating franchisees. The remaining 36 were other types of offices.

MRI concentrates on contingency-fee placement of personnel in permanent jobs through Management Recruiters and Sales Consultants, its two oldest and primary divisions; CompuSearch, for computer systems personnel; and OfficeMates 5, for administrative and clerical support personnel.

MRI has launched several new services that have attracted the strong interest of existing franchisees because they can increase revenues at little or no cost. First, InterExec places middle- and upper-level managers and professionals in corporations on a temporary basis. MRI executives stated that InterExec works like a very-high-level temporary agency for companies that want to hire managers to oversee special projects, replace consultants, replace permanent managers taking family or personal leave, or fill a special, limited role. They added that *Executive Recruiter News* "underestimated" this market at $100 million a year. Rolled out systemwide during September 1993, more than 300 franchised offices now offer InterExec temporary services. This new temporary agency thrust reflects the dramatic change in hiring at the corporate executive level. With the huge downsizing effort that has swept corporate America, many companies find that they need executive expertise for short-term projects or special roles, but they do not want to provide the benefits or salary a full-time executive would require.

Second, ConferView is a video teleconferencing system that offers long-distance interactive candidate interviews. For example, without leaving his office, without rearranging schedules for busy executives, and without the costs of flying recruits from around the country, a corporate executive can interview numerous candidates during a series of video teleconferences at MRI franchise and company-owned offices. In one actual case, an executive interviewed five candidates in one afternoon while he sat in an MRI office in Chicago. He decided to invite only two to travel to the headquarters for more interviews. This service will save MRI clients thousands of dollars in executive time and saved travel dollars, dramatically increase the convenience of interviewing for all involved, and cement the clients' loyalty toward the local MRI office. However, a ConferView facility requires a franchisee to make monthly payments on about $25,000 of equipment, so by late 1993, some 80 offices had installed the system.

Third, Career Pathways is a new service through which MRI offers outplacement seminars and services. MRI executives stated that Career Pathways "teaches outplaced employees how recruiters place people. We teach them that they can be their own recruiters." Attendees also are entered into the national MRI data bank and may become involved with the InterExec service.

Lastly, MRI is affiliated with Sales Staffers International, Inc., which provides temporary sales employees for special events and promotions. Perhaps a company wants to carry out a new product blitz across a region or the nation. It may need hundreds of temporary salespeople or merchandisers to sweep the area for two months. MRI provides the temporary salespeople and seeks to establish a permanent, continuous relationship with the company.

In short, MRI has dramatically changed direction; it wants to become its clients' Human Resources Center for most of their staffing requirements.

Perhaps more important to prospective franchisees, MRI has one of the most highly regarded franchise relations and communications programs. In the late 1980s, it won the International Franchise Association's Franchise Relations of the Year award. Company executives unequivocally state that MRI's success comes from putting their franchisees first. Three out four new franchisees are referrals from existing franchisees. Nine out of 10 franchisees give the company high ratings on questions about service and support. And at corporate headquarters, the top 15 executives average more than 10 years' longevity with the company.

As a franchise opportunity, MRI has been rated—for many years and across all rating services—as the leader in its segment of the employment services industry.

A typical office includes four or five account executives, an owner-manager, and a clerical support person. It is usually located in or near major cities, but more and more, MRI offices specialize in industry niches. Many offices are in rural areas and small cities, for example, Pike's Peak, Colorado, because with telecommunications, telemarketing, and videoconferencing, the niche specialists can work with clients and candidates all over the country. For example, one very successful MRI office operates from the small city of Salisbury, Maryland; it succeeds because it specializes in the poultry industry, and Perdue Chicken's headquarters are in Salisbury. But it does business with poultry industry companies around the country. In fact, MRI considers its franchisees' specialization in more than 50 industries one of the strengths of the system it has developed.

How Much It Costs

This dramatic change in emphasis to industry niches means that since 1990, MRI has changed its franchise fee structure. Instead of a fee based on population, MRI charges a franchise fee of $40,000, so now instead of finding a specific territory with lots of white-collar job openings, you and your account executives need to have specific industry knowledge and experience to maximize your contacts in that field.

Start-up Costs

Under the system, your additional start-up costs are relatively low and averages from $8,500 to $15,000. However, these estimates do not include at least six months' living expenses that you should have in the bank or that a spouse could provide while you build your business during the first year. The table following estimates these costs:

Category	Low End	High End
Franchise fee	$40,000	$40,000
Office lease (a)	1,500	3,000
Office furniture (b)	500	7,000
Telephone system	700	1,500
Licensing/bonding	150	200

Training travel costs	1,800	2,800
Insurance	800	1,100
Legal/professional fees	200	500
Office supplies	200	500
Additional capital (c)	18,200	33,500
Miscellaneous	250	500
Total	$66,100	$90,600

a. This includes estimates for between 750 and 1,200 square feet of office space ranging in cost from $9 to $20 per square foot. Of course, if you can recruit for your industry from a small city or rural area, you can sharply reduce this cost.
b. MRI recommends that you borrow $7,000, more or less, from the bank so you can purchase the furniture and equipment you need, or perhaps, you can use a lease/purchase program.
c. This amount includes three to six months of living expenses and additional capital for salaries and unexpected expenses.

Account Executive Commissions

To sell your services and place candidates, you must hire account executives, but you do not have to pay them a salary. Most franchisees pay only commissions earned on fees received from actual placements. You can expect these commissions to range from as low as 30 percent to as high as 50 percent with a first-year average of 35 percent. Of course, you must pay a salary to any secretarial support you hire. Commissions, payroll taxes, and unemployment compensation costs should equal about 40 to 45 percent of your gross revenues. Commissions also increase for each account executive depending on how much revenue they generate; it increases from 30 percent of the first $5,000 of "net cash-in" to 50 percent of the excess over $20,000 with the increases at the $5,000 increments.

Royalty and Fees

MRI now has a straight 7 percent royalty on your "net cash-in," that is, all cash receipts from your personnel placement business. And you pay a relatively low one-half of 1 percent for national advertising and public relations. The company charges no other fees or royalties, although you have access to a panoply of data banks and support services.

What You Get

- *Franchise structure.* An MRI executive explained that although the company already has more than 500 franchisees, its emphasis on industry niches and available geographic areas mean that the company could easily accommodate 500 more offices. In terms of the available market, millions of people who earn $30,000 to $70,000 per year change jobs. Yet, only 15 percent of those people get new jobs through personnel recruiting firms; therefore, about 85 percent of the market remains untapped. And during 1992, MRI offices made only 25,000 placements worth $172 million in gross revenues—and MRI is the largest company in the industry. Clearly, the market for these and MRI's newest services remains strong.

  The term of the franchise has changed to give you a choice. You can choose an agreement term ranging from five to 20 years, and you may renew, at your option, for additional 10-year terms with new additional franchise fees.

- *Sophisticated training.* MRI's training program is one of the most extensive in the franchising industry. Owners and managers during training are strongly urged to manage their own offices and work at least half time as an account executive to generate their own placements. They must spend three weeks at the Cleveland corporate headquarters going through an intense, multimedia, multilevel training program. It includes classroom work, work with videos, taped and critiqued role-playing sessions, actual interviews with clients and candidates, and telemarketing in a local market. But the training focuses on how to hire and train account executives, because eventually, they will form the foundation of your success. Next, a regional manager comes to your office and works with you for three weeks while you set it up, hire account executives, and start cultivating both clients and candidates. The regional managers make timely visits, and you can ask for additional training both at headquarters and at your office.

  You also receive perhaps the best marketing program in the industry and a superb nationwide public relations and promotion effort. Clearly, MRI offers the most extensive support effort in the industry.

- *Failures and terminations.* The company's offering circular reports that during 1992 (the latest available figures), 41 franchises were terminated for the following reasons:

Mutual consent termination	23
Failure to pay royalties	7
Failure to operate the business	5
Franchisor refused to renew	3
Franchise reacquired	2
Other reasons	22

This represents a realistic attrition rate. The company also added dozens of new franchisees, and it has continued to expand the total number of offices. Further, I believe that the terminations occurred during a severe recession and a dramatic change in how the industry functions. Further, MRI had much less attrition than its franchise competitors.

How Much Can You Make?

With the high level of support and service, you can earn very high returns on your cash investment within three years, especially if you borrow some of the funds. The company's 1993 national awards publication shows that the top MRI offices in the country had these gross incomes during 1992:

More than 14 desks	$2,500,612
11 to 13 desks	1,427,263
8 to 10 desks	1,231,380
5 to 7 desks	1,200,182
2 to 4 desks	647,775

The best new MRI office earned $368,374 during its first year. Of the sales consultants offices, the highest revenues ranged from $1,513,366 for the largest offices to $532,538 for the smaller offices.

Among individual MRI account executives, the "net cash-in" revenues for the top ten ranged from $563,575 to $239,785.

MRI also publishes among the most open and complete financials of any franchisor in the country. Every year for 21 years, it has published an operating ratio study of its franchisees' offices. This study (given shortly) compares the "net cash-in," that is, the actual fees collected, operating expenses, and net profit before royalties and owners' compensations for three categories of offices.

The 1992 results (the latest available) revealed that even in a four-desk office you can quickly recoup your investment. MRI estimates that you reach breakeven during your third or fourth month and start earning a return on your investment thereafter.

After operating expenses of about 55 to 60 percent and royalties of 7.0 percent plus one-half of 1 percent for national ads, you can expect to net before taxes between 33.5 and 37.5 percent of your net cash-in. But to earn substantial six-figure profits, you must continue to grow your business with additional account executives or you must work your desk and generate placements. The combination increases your profits considerably. Today, the average office has four to five account executives and receives a net cash-in hovering in the $500,000 range.

Management Recruiters International, Inc.
1992 Operating Ratio Study of Management Recruiters and Sales Consultants Offices, for the 12 Months Ending December 31, 1992

Offices with 2–4 Desks

Net cash-in	High Quartile		Mid Range	
	$	%	$	%
Net cash-in	$365,200	100.0%	$183,400	100.0%
Operating expenses				
Account executive compensation	$88,800	24.3%	$53,900	29.4%
Office payroll	15,600	4.3	10,400	5.7
Hopitalization and insurance	10,000	2.7	8,100	4.4
Payroll and other taxes	12,900	3.5	8,300	4.5
Advertising	4,000	1.1	2,100	1.1
Dues and subscriptions	1,300	0.4	900	0.5
Equipment: lease, depreciation, etc.	5,400	1.5	4,300	2.3
Office supplies and expenses	6,700	1.8	4,300	2.3
Professional services	4,400	1.2	2,500	1.4
Rent and utilities	18,200	5.0	13,400	7.3
Telephone	20,200	5.5	14,200	7.7
Travel and entertainment	9,700	2.7	4,500	2.5
Miscellaneous and repairs	3,500	1.0	2,400	1.3
Total	$200,800	55.0%	$129,100	70.4%
Net profit before royalties or Owner-manager compensation	$164,400	45.0%	$54,200	29.6%

Management Recruiters International, Inc.
1992 Operating Ratio Study of Management Recruiters and Sales Consultants Offices, for the 12 Months Ending December 31, 1992

Offices with 5–7 Desks

Net cash-in	High Quartile		Mid Range	
	$	%	$	%
Net cash-in	$662,600	100.0%	$463,800	100.0%
Operating expenses				
Account executive				
compensation	$215,100	32.5%	$182,900	39.4%
Office payroll	28,600	4.3	23,300	5.0
Hopitalization and				
insurance	20,000	3.0	22,200	4.8
Payroll and other taxes	28,000	4.2	22,500	4.9
Advertising	8,100	1.2	5,900	1.3
Dues and subscriptions	1,700	0.3	1,600	0.3
Equipment: lease,				
depreciation, etc.	8,100	1.2	9,900	2.1
Office supplies and				
expenses	10,300	1.6	8,900	1.9
Professional services	8,000	1.2	6,400	1.4
Rent and utilities	25,800	3.9	32,400	7.0
Telephone	35,900	5.4	29,300	6.3
Travel and				
entertainment	18,000	2.7	10,400	2.2
Miscellaneous and				
repairs	4,200	0.6	3,900	0.8
Total	$411,800	62.1%	$359,600	77.5%
Net profit before royalties				
or Owner-manager				
compensation	$250,800	37.9%	$104,200	22.5%

Management Recruiters International, Inc.
1992 Operating Ratio Study of Management Recruiters and Sales Consultants Offices, for the 12 Months Ending December 31, 1992

Offices with 8 and up Desks

Net cash-in	High Quartile		Mid Range	
	$	%	$	%
Net cash-in	$1,550,100	100.0%	$852,100	100.0%
Operating expenses				
Account executive compensation	$650,000	41.9%	$381,800	44.8%
Office payroll	47,400	3.1	36,900	4.3
Hopitalization and insurance	46,300	3.0	29,700	3.5
Payroll and other taxes	62,200	4.0	36,600	4.5
Advertising	18,600	1.2	12,300	1.4
Dues and subscriptions	2,500	0.2	3,100	0.4
Equipment: lease, depreciation, etc.	16,800	1.1	13,000	1.5
Office supplies and expenses	21,100	1.4	15,400	1.8
Professional services	11,800	0.8	9,300	1.1
Rent and utilities	54,300	3.5	43,300	5.1
Telephone	73,200	4.7	45,700	5.4
Travel and entertainment	31,000	2.0	17,500	2.1
Miscellaneous and repairs	4,900	0.3	6,000	0.7
Total	$1,040,200	67.1%	$652,600	76.6%
Net profit before royalties or Owner-manager compensation	$509,900	32.9%	$199,700	23.4%

AMERICAN LEAK DETECTION, INC.

American Leak Detection, Inc.
888 Research Drive, Suite 109
Palm Springs, CA 92262
(619) 320-9991

American Leak Detection is one of the most forward-looking and straightforward franchises in the country. I know President Richard B. Rennick, his staff, and many of his franchisees very well, and Rennick and his staff consistently show a serious concern for their franchisees' success and well-being. Rennick is also acknowledged as a courageous innovator in the franchise industry because he is always pushing the franchising elite to be more open and honest with their franchisees, to encourage their franchisees to network with each other, to push forward reforms before the government clamps more regulations on the industry, and to take other steps that help their franchisees. Unfortunately, many in the franchise elite do not agree with Rennick's positions, but fortunately, he practices what he preaches.

As a franchise system, American Leak Detection (ALD) is another of those amazing ideas: using ALD's proprietary and other advanced sonar, radio, and sound technologies, you locate and repair leaks from pipes in swimming pools, spas, water mains, gas lines, sewer systems, and so on, *without* tearing out walls, pavement, floors, yards, grounds, landscaping, and so on. In short, you save home and property owners thousands of dollars in torn-apart floors, walls, pools, and yards and all the messy inconvenience that digging things up creates. You do especially well wherever you find many pools and spas, houses or buildings built on concrete slabs, or buried pipelines. Most home and apartment owners have little or no idea where to find their pipes, so when a leak develops, they can either hire a plumber to rip everything out, or if they're lucky, hire American Leak to find the leak *before* they create a terrible mess.

During 1993, ALD grew very rapidly; by late 1993, ALD had more than 80 individual franchise owners operating in about 190 licensed territories, a 31 percent increase since 1992. The existing franchises also reported significant revenue growth with the largest operations grossing almost $1 million a year. The average franchise that had been operating about three years reported gross revenues in excess of $200,000 with 30 percent net pretax profits. ALD is also very forthcoming about its earnings.

ALD plans to expand throughout the United States with a 1994 goal of being in 40 states and exceeding 200 franchise territories. It also has master franchises in Spain, Australia, Canada, Saudi Arabia, and the six Arab Emirate states and plans to expand in more international countries as well.

Far more important for its future, ALD has a key position in perhaps the most important market in the United States—the water industry. The United States is experiencing a serious crisis securing freshwater supplies for its future growth. At least 10 percent—a very conservative estimate—of all potable water is now lost because of leaks, mostly in homes and residential buildings. ALD's Rennick has realized that the company must become a major "player" in the critical water conservation industry, and he intends to build his company around a simple concept: ALD saves water.

This is a very powerful concept everywhere from California to Connecticut, from Florida to Washington state, and from the United States across the world because pollution, economic growth, and severe restrictions on new water development projects threaten to restrict the available supply. In fact, Rennick stated that in some parts of Spain, the water is shut off from 11 P.M. to 6 A.M. to conserve water and its power-generating capacity.

Rennick also agrees with industry leaders who assert that during the twenty-first century, the major struggle for resources will occur not over oil or minerals, but over water supplies.

As an ALD franchisee, you could help play an important role in resolving this crisis not only by detecting and repairing leaks, but by promoting many forward-looking programs that Rennick has in the planning stages. Again, as I've said often, you can do well by doing good: ALD gives you a marvelous opportunity to do that.

How Much It Costs

ALD has a relatively high franchise fee for a service franchise, $45,000, but that includes a complete equipment, products, and training package valued at $25,000. On rare occasions, where a territory has a relatively small number of swimming pools, the fee may be lowered. However, in a benefit, the total start-up costs vary from only $50,000 to $75,000, depending on how much working capital you need and whether a spouse brings in enough income to pay basic living expenses. The table lists this range:

Category	Low End	High End
Franchise fee	$45,000	$45,000
Hand tools (a)	200	3,000
Work vehicle (b)	500	10,000
Insurance (c)	750	3,000
Telephone deposits	50	400
Business licenses (d)	50	250
Office equipment/supplies (e)	100	750
Sales taxes (f)	0	800
Shipping (g)	0	150
Miscellaneous	2,500	7,500
Working capital (h)	2,500	10,000
Living expenses (i)	2,500	10,000
Total	$53,150	$90,850

a. The more hand tools you already own, the better to reduce this expense.
b. You are required to have a work vehicle, and ALD advises you to lease a used van or truck with cover. You must paint it ALD colors and use ALD's decals. Most often, you pay the lower figure as a lease deposit.
c. For required comprehensive business liability and vehicle policies and any required bonding if you obtain a plumber's license.
d. For any plumber's, occupational, or city business licenses.
e. ALD encourages you to work from home to reduce your start-up and operating costs, but within the next year, ALD will require new franchisees to buy a personal computer system and use company software to manage the franchise's operation. Now, this figure covers the costs of home office equipment and supplies.
f. ALD must collect sales taxes on your equipment package for some states. This may or may not apply to your situation; ask how you can legally avoid them.
g. Covers the cost of shipping ALD equipment to your location.
h. ALD does not include any estimates for working capital to pay your first few months' operating expenses, so I've added this range. It varies according to how

fast you can grow your business and break even.
i. ALD also does not include any estimates for living expenses, but you can minimize this if your spouse brings in a second income.

Financing and Sliding Scale Royalties

In a benefit, ALD may finance the part of your franchise fee that does not pay for the equipment and training package for up to five years at an interest rate between 12 and 15 percent per year. However, it insists that you pay for the equipment.

More importantly, ALD charges a sliding scale royalty that helps you make more money as you grow. The royalty schedule includes

Monthly Gross Volume	Percentage
Up to and including $5,000	10%
From $5,001 to $10,000	9%
More than $10,000	8%

For example, if your monthly gross volume equals $13,000, you would pay $1,190 divided like this: $500 on the first $5,000, $450 on the second $5,000, and $240 on the remaining $3,000.

However, you must pay a very low $100 minimum royalty that may be adjusted each year for the cost of living, but to help new franchisees, they do not have to pay the minimum for the first 90 days they are in business.

Furthermore, ALD does *not* charge an advertising fee, but it does encourage its regions to form advertising cooperatives to which they contribute agreed-upon amounts. At present, the Northern California region manages a very substantial and successful co-op, and Florida and Texas are developing co-ops, but most of the other regions are too small or dispersed to gain much direct benefit.

What You Get

ALD provides superior, comprehensive training, marketing, and support services that truly seek to help its franchisees build their revenues.

- *Exclusive territory.* ALD grants a territory with between 7,500 and 10,000—usually about 9,000—in-ground pools, spas, or fountains. If you can find an area with thousands of pools and spas and thousands of homes or apartment or commercial buildings built on concrete slabs, you should do very well. In fact, many new franchisees have moved from less desirable areas to more desirable ones: for example, from Iowa to South Florida and from Massachusetts to middle Georgia. But franchises in Washington state, Colorado, Kansas, and Pennsylvania have done very well, too. You need to investigate your area for its market opportunities or listen to ALD executives' advice about good locations.

- *Extensive training.* You receive a very thorough three-phase training program. You begin with at-home, evening self-study manuals before you go to its offices in Palm Springs, California (a very pleasant experience, for sure). Second, at headquarters, you spend 30 days or more in classroom and on-the-job training with company crews, or you may do some on-the-job training with the Atlanta franchisee, Bill Dischinger. The corporate trainers and Dischinger are acknowledged as the technical "whizzes" in the system. Third, you receive setup training on management, sales, and marketing during your Palm Springs visit. After you return home, you work through an additional 90-day home-study course that helps you improve your technical expertise.

- *Networks of franchisees.* After your training, you are encouraged to turn to the network of franchisees to help you grow. Rennick also provides superior corporate support, but he believes very strongly that new franchisees should network with each other to foster teamwork. In fact, many franchisees loan equipment to others or even visit different, often distant, territories to help new franchisees complete difficult detecting jobs.

- *Marketing programs.* ALD has very successful public relations programs at both the national and local levels and provides updated marketing programs. The company also encourages its franchisees to share their successful marketing efforts with others.

- *Ten-year term.* ALD grants a 10-year term with a five-year "successor" agreement at low or no cost. The "successor" agreement also gives you the right to keep the royalty schedule you had if it is more favorable than the one that applies to the new agreement.

- *Termination by mutual consent.* The company also allows any franchisee to cancel the agreement by mutual consent at any time, a truly unusual benefit compared to most franchises. In fact, only two franchises had been terminated between 1985 and the end of 1993, a very strong record. And one long-time franchisee had retired and sold his territory for a substantial profit, and another franchisee had sold his territory for at least two to three times what he paid for it.

Furthermore, upon termination and again, unlike most franchises, ALD may choose to pay you fair market value for all your assets, including equipment, vehicles, furniture, signs, and so on, less depreciation.

With these policies, ALD prevents many of the sources of conflict that often arise between franchisors and franchisees.

How Much Can You Make?

As I noted, the most successful franchisees gross close to $1 million a year, and they operate five crews and trucks. Several others operate three or four crews and trucks and gross in the $250,000 to $600,000 range.

Although ALD does not make any formal earnings claims for how much money an individual franchisee will make, it does publish a thorough discussion of gross revenues. A chart published at the end of 1993 shows that average monthly gross sales of actual franchise operations rose from $4,751 after the first six months to as high as $21,913 by the beginning of the fifth year.

Within three years, you should have at least two crews and two vehicles generating gross revenues of at least $10,000 per month per truck or more. If you continue to work from home or an inexpensive office, and keep your overhead low, you should earn net pretax profits in the 30 to 35 percent range, or $60,000 to $70,000. The most successful ones more than double that amount. Remember that this is all labor-intensive costs; you sell a service, not a product, so your net profits depend upon how well you manage your labor.

However, you should realize that during the first year or two, you must not only do the work, but also sell and market your business. Most often, a spouse manages the paperwork and the work schedule at first, but you should plan to hire part-time secretaries and independent contractors or part-time technicians so you can grow more rapidly.

In sum, you would be hard-pressed to find a more congenial and more caring group than Rennick and his ALD staff or a more important franchise that gives you an opportunity to provide an increasingly valuable service with enormous long-term potential.

100 More of the Best Franchises

This list gives you 100 more relatively low-cost, high-profit franchises that you may wish to consider. They form a quality group, the Top 5 Percent, of all franchises. They are listed first by total start-up cost, either below $100,000 or between $100,000 and $150,000 and then by industry category.

START-UP COSTS BELOW $100,000

Athletic and Sporting Goods and Apparel

- Sport It, 4196 Corporate Square, Naples, FL 33942.
- Auto After-Market Distribution Services
- Matco Tools, Inc., 4403 Allen Road, Stow, OH 44224.
- Snap-on Tools Corp., 2801 80th St., Kenosha, WI 53141-1410.

Business Services

- Advantage Payroll Services, Inc., 800 Center St., Auburn, ME 04211.
- Parson-Bishop Services, Inc., 7870 Camargo Road, Cincinnati, OH 45243.

355

- Professional Dynametric Programs, Inc., 400 W. Hwy. 24, #201, Woodland Park, CO 80866.
- ProForma, Inc., 4705 Van Epps Road, Cleveland, OH 44131.
- Sandler Systems, 10411 Stevenson Road, Stevenson, MD 21153.
- Dr. Vinyl & Associates, 13665 E. 42nd Terrace, Independence, MO 64055.

Children's Products and Services

- Friday Nite Live!, 1901 N. Central Expressway, #220, Richardson, TX 75080.
- Kids Kab International, 101 Southfield Rd., Ste. 202, Birmingham, MI 48009.
- Kinderdance Int'l, Inc., 2150 Atlantic St., P.O. Box 510881, Melbourne Beach, FL 32951.
- Primrose School Franchising Co., 5131 Roswell Rd., N.E., Marietta, GA 30062.

Clothing and Shoes

- Cobblestone Quality Shoe Repair, 5944 Luther Lane, Ste. 402, Dallas, TX 75225.

Construction: Building, Services, Remodeling

- ABC Seamless, 3001 Fechtner Dr., S.W., Fargo, ND 58103.
- Archadeck, 2112 W. Laburnum Ave., Suite 109, Richmond, VA 23227.
- Kott Koatings, 27161 Burbank, Foothill Ranch, CA 92610.
- Mr. Build Total Property Services, 3345 N. Arlington Hts. Rd., #C, Arlington Hts., IL 60004

Environmental Products and Services

- Environmental Biotech, Inc., 1390 Main Street, Ste. 510, Sarasota, FL 34236.

Food: Distributorships

- Jerky Hut International, Inc., Hamlet Route 934, Seaside, OR 97138.
- Philly's Famous Soft Pretzel Co., 2000 W. Glades Rd., Ste. 200, Boca Raton, FL 33431.

Food: Health and Nutrition

- General Nutrition Centers, 921 Pennsylvania Ave., Pittsburgh, PA 15222.

Food: Ice Cream and Yogurt

- Ice Cream Churn, Inc., P.O. Box 1569, Byron, GA 31008.

Home Services

- Carpet Network, Inc., 109 Gather Drive, #302, Mt. Laurel, NJ 08054.
- Citizens Against Crime, 1022 S. Greenville Avenue, Allen, TX 75002.
- Housemaster of America, 421 W. Union Avenue, Bound Brook, NJ 08805.
- Mr. Miniblind, Newport Trade Center, 20341 Irvine Ave., Ste. One, Santa Ana, CA 92707.
- Service Center, Inc., 7655 E. Gelding Drive, Ste. A-3, Scottsdale, AZ 85260.

Maintenance, Cleaning, Janitorial and Restoration Services

- CleanNet USA, 9861 Broken Land Parkway, Suite 208,. Columbia, MD 21046.
- Coustic-Glo International, Inc., 7111 Ohms Lane, Minneapolis, MN 55435.
- Coverall North America, 2174 N. Gladstone Court, Suite C, Glendale Heights, IL 60139.

- Jani-King International, Inc., 4950 Keller Springs Road, Ste. 190,. Dallas, TX 75248.
- OMEX International, Inc., 3905 Hartzdale Dr., Suite 506, Camp Hill, PA 17011.
- O.P.E.N. Cleaning Systems, 2398 Camelback, Phoenix, AZ 85016.
- Paul W. Davis Systems, 8933 Western Way, Suite 12, Jacksonville, Fl 32256
- Racs International, Inc., 931 E. 86th St., Indianapolis, IN 46240.
- Sparkle Wash International, Inc., 26851 Richmond Rd., Bedford Hts., OH 44146.
- Steamatic, Incorporated, 1320 University Drive, Ste. 400, Ft. Worth, TX 76107.

Packaging, Mailing, Business Communications

- Pak Mail Centers of America, Inc., 3033 S. Parker Rd., #1200, Aurora, CO 80014.
- Parcel Plus, Inc., 2666 Riva Road, Ste. 120, Annapolis, MD 21401.
- PostalAnnex+, 9050 Friars Road, Ste. 400, San Diego, CA 92108.

Photography and Supplies

- Universal Art Photographic Services, 1525 Hardeman Lane, Cleveland, TN 37311.

Printing Services

- American Wholesale Thermographers, P.O. Box 777, 12715 Telge Rd., Cypress, TX 77429.
- Business Cards Tomorrow, 3000 N.E. 30th Pl., 5th Floor, Ft. Lauderdale, FL 33306.

Publications

- Bingo Bugle, K & O Publishing, Inc., P.O. Box 51189, Seattle, WA 98115-1189.

Real Estate Services

- Century 21 Real Estate Corp., P.O. Box 19564, Irvine, CA 92713.
- Coldwell Banker Residential Affiliates, 27271 Las Ramblas, Mission Viejo, CA 92691.

Retail Stores: Specialty

- Play It Again Sports, 1550 Utica Ave. South, Ste. 775, Minneapolis, MN 554516.
- Wild Birds Unlimited, Inc., 3003 East 96th Street, Ste. 201, Indianapolis, IN 46240.

START-UP COSTS BETWEEN $100,000 AND $150,000

Auto After-Market

- AAMCO Transmissions, 1 Presidential Blvd., Bala Cynwyd, PA 19004.
- The Brake Shop, 44899 Centre Court, Suite 104, Clinton Township, MI 48038.
- MAACO Auto Painting and Bodyworks, 381 Brooks Rd., King of Prussia, PA 19406.
- Meineke Discount Mufflers, 128 S. Tryon St., Suite 900, Charlotte, NC 28209.
- Merlin Muffler & Brake, One N. River Lane, #206, Geneva, IL 60134.
- Midas International Corp., 225 N. Michigan Avenue, Chicago, IL 60601.
- Mr. Transmission, 29200 Vassar Avenue, Suite 501, Livonia, MI 48152.
- Motorworks, 4210 Salem Street, Philadelphia, PA 19124.
- Oil Can Henry's, 1200 NW Front Ave., #690, Portland, OR 97209.

- Precision Tune, Inc., 748 Miller Drive, S.E., Leesburg, VA 22075.
- SpeeDee Oil Change & Tune-Up, 6660 Riverside Drive, Ste. 101, Metairie, LA 70003.
- Valvoline Instant Oil Change Franchising, Inc., P.O. Box 14046, Lexington, KY 40512
- Ziebart/Tidy Car, 1290 East Maple Road, Troy, MI 48007-1290.

Business Services

- American FASTSIGNS, Inc., 4951 Airport Parkway, #530, Dallas, TX 75248.

Children's Products and Services

- Tutor Time Child-Care Systems, Inc., 4517 N.W. 31st Ave., Ft. Lauderdale, FL 33309.

Clothing and Shoes

- T-Shirts Plus, Monograms Plus, 3630 I-35 South, Waco, TX 75706.
- Hakky Instant Shoe Repair, 1739 Sands Place, Ste. F, Marietta, GA 30067.

Educational Products and Services

- Sylvan Learning Systems, 9135 Guilford Rd., Columbia, MD 21046.

Employment Services

- Health Force, 1600 Stewart Avenue, Westbury, NY 11590.
- Staff Builders International, Inc., 1981 Marcus Lane, Lake Success, NY 11042.

Food: Baked Goods

- Auntie Anne's, Pretzels, 5325 Lincoln Hwy., Gap, PA 17527.
- Katie McGuire's Pie and Bake Shoppe, 17682 Sampson Lane,

Huntington Beach, CA 92647.

- Mrs. Field's Cookies, 333 Main St., P.O. Box 4000, Park City, UT 84060-4000.

Food: Coffee and Beverages

- The Coffee Beanery, G3429 Pierson Place, Flushing, MI 48433.
- Gourmet Cup of America, Inc., 11 North Skokie Highway, Lake Bluff, IL 60044.

Food: Fast Food Restaurants

- Cousins Subs, 13400 Leon Road, Menomonee Falls, WI 53051.
- Jerry's Subs and Pizza, 15942 Shady Grove Road, Gaithersburg, MD 20877.
- Magic Wok, 2060 W. Laskey Rd., Toledo, OH 43613.
- Mr. Bain's Deli, Inc., Springfield Mall, 1250 Baltimore Pike, Springfield, PA 19064.
- Philly Connection Franchising, 120 Interstate N. Parkway, E., Suite 112, Atlanta, GA 30339.
- Roli Boli, 15 Engle Street, Suite 202, Englewood, NJ 07631.
- Schlotzsky's Original Deli, 200 West 4th, Austin, TX 78701.
- Seawest Subshops, One Lake Bellevue Drive, Ste. 107, Bellevue, WA 98005.
- Stuff 'n Turkey, 10019 Reistertown Rd., Owings Mills, MD 21117.
- Sub Station II, 425 North Main Street, Sumter, SC 29150.

Food: Ice Cream and Yogurt

- Baskin-Robbins USA, Inc., 31 Baskin Robbins Place, Glendale, CA 91201.
- Ben & Jerry's Homemade, Rt. 100, Box 240, Waterbury, VT 05676.

Food: Retail Stores

- Heavenly Ham, Paradise Foods, Inc., 8800 Roswell Rd., #135, Atlanta, GA 30350.

Hair Salons and Services

- The Barbers and City Looks; Salons Int'l., 300 Industrial Blvd., N.E., Minneapolis, MN 55413.
- Fantastic Sam's, 3180 Old Getwell Rd., Memphis, TN 38181.
- Magicuts, 3780 14th Ave., Suite 106, Markham, ON L3R 9Y5, Canada
- Supercuts, 555 Northgate Drive, San Rafael, CA 94903.
- We Care Hair, 325 Bic Drive, Milford, CT 06460.

Home Services

- California Closet Company, 1700 Montgomery St., #249, San Francisco, CA 94111.
- The Great Frame-Up, 8335 Belmont Avenue, Franklin Park, IL 60131.
- Lawn Doctor, Inc., 142 Highway 34, Matawan, NJ 07747.
- Spring Crest Drapery Centers, 505 W. Lambert Road, Brea, CA 92621.

Printing Services

- The Printhouse Express, 222 Catoctin Circle, S.E., Ste. 201, Leesburg, VA 22075.

Travel Services

- Cruise Holidays International, 9665 Chesapeake Dr., #401, San Diego, CA 92123.
- Travel Agents International, 111 Second Avenue, N.E., 15th Flr., St. Petersburg, FL 33731.
- Travel Network, 560 Sylvan Avenue, Englewood Cliffs, NJ 07632

- Uniglobe Travel (International), Inc., 1199 West Pender St., #900, Vancouver, BC V6E 2R1.

Weight Control

- Inches-A-Weigh Weight Loss Centers, P.O. Box 59436, Birmingham, AL 35246.

Index

N